Strategic Marketing of Higher Education in Africa

Strategic Marketing of Higher Education in Africa explores higher education marketing themes along the lines of understanding higher education markets, university branding and international marketing strategies, digital marketing, and student choice-making.

The Higher Education landscape around the world is changing. There is global competition for students' enrolments, universities are competing within their home market as well as in the international market, and as government funding for public universities is reducing there is pressure on universities to seek additional income by increasing their student enrolment. African universities are not an exception in this competitive market. This book is unique in providing a composite overview of strategic marketing and brand communications of higher education institutions in Africa. It recognises that there is a growing need for universities to understand the stakeholders and develop strategies on how best to engage with them effectively. Highlighting the unique characteristics, nature, and challenges of African universities, this book explores the marketisation strategies of African universities, with focus on the strategic digital marketing and brand management.

The book provides significant theoretical and marketing practice implications for academics, higher-education administrators, and practitioners on how best to market higher education in Africa and reach out to prospective students. International practitioners aiming to market to Africans and start a partnership with an African university will also find this relevant in understanding the dynamics of the African market.

Emmanuel Mogaji holds a PhD in Marketing, and he is a Lecturer in Advertising and Marketing Communications at the University of Greenwich, and a Fellow of the Higher Education Academy (HEA) and a Certified Management & Business Educator (CMBE).

Felix Maringe is a Professor, Head of Wits School of Education Research, and Assistant Dean Internationalisation and Partnerships at the University of the Witwatersrand. He is also a Visiting Fellow within Southampton Education School at the University of Southampton.

Robert Ebo Hinson is an Extraordinary Professor at the School of Business and Governance, North West University, South Africa. He is also Head of the Department of Marketing and Entrepreneurship at the University of Ghana and Acting Director of Institutional Advancement at the same university.

Routledge Studies in Marketing

This series welcomes proposals for original research projects that are either single or multi-authored or an edited collection from both established and emerging scholars working on any aspect of marketing theory and practice and provides an outlet for studies dealing with elements of marketing theory, thought, pedagogy and practice.

It aims to reflect the evolving role of marketing and bring together the most innovative work across all aspects of the marketing 'mix' – from product development, consumer behaviour, marketing analysis, branding, and customer relationships, to sustainability, ethics and the new opportunities and challenges presented by digital and online marketing.

For more information about the series, please visit https://www.routledge.com/Routledge-Studies-in-Marketing/book-series/RMKT

Strategic Marketing of Higher Education in Africa

Edited by
Emmanuel Mogaji, Felix Maringe, and Robert Ebo Hinson

Routledge
Taylor & Francis Group

LONDON AND NEW YORK

First published 2020
by Routledge
2 Park Square, Milton Park, Abingdon, Oxon OX14 4RN

and by Routledge
52 Vanderbilt Avenue, New York, NY 10017

Routledge is an imprint of the Taylor & Francis Group, an informa business

British Library Cataloguing-in-Publication Data
A catalogue record for this book is available from the British Library

Library of Congress Cataloging-in-Publication Data
Names: Mogaji, Emmanuel, editor. | Maringe, Felix, editor. | Hinson, Robert Ebo, editor.
Title: Strategic marketing of higher education in Africa / edited by Emmanuel Mogaji, Felix Maringe, and Robert Ebo Hinson.
Other titles: Routledge studies in marketing ; 9.
Description: Abingdon, Oxon ; New York, NY : Routledge, 2020. | Series: Routledge studies in marketing; 9 |
Includes bibliographical references and index.
Identifiers: LCCN 2019045378 (print) | LCCN 2019045379 (ebook) | ISBN 9780367336356 (hardback) | ISBN 9780429320934 (ebook)
Subjects: LCSH: Universities and colleges--Africa--Marketing. | Education, Higher--Africa--Marketing. | College publicity--Africa. | Branding (Marketing)--Africa.
Classification: LCC LB2342.82 .S77 2020 (print) | LCC LB2342.82 (ebook) | DDC 378.0688--dc23
LC record available at https://lccn.loc.gov/2019045378
LC ebook record available at https://lccn.loc.gov/2019045379

ISBN: 978-0-367-33635-6 (hbk)
ISBN: 978-0-429-32093-4 (ebk)

Typeset in Bembo
by Taylor & Francis Books

Contents

Illustrations

Contributors

Editors

Emmanuel Mogaji holds a PhD in Marketing, and he is a Lecturer in Advertising and Marketing Communications at the University of Greenwich, and a Fellow of the Higher Education Academy (HEA) and a Certified Management & Business Educator (CMBE). Emmanuel's primary area of interest is ABCDE of Marketing Communications – Advertising, Branding, Communications, Digital and Ethics, with a strong focus on higher education and financial services marketing. He recently authored a book on Emotional Appeals in Advertising Banking Services published by Emerald. He has published several peer-reviewed journal articles and book chapters, and presented his work at many national and international conferences. In recognition of his research productivity, he was awarded the 2019 Emerald Literati Highly Commended Paper Award for a co-authored paper published in the *Asia Pacific Journal of Marketing and Logistics*. He has co-edited books on marketing higher education in Africa published by Routledge and Springer Nature.

Felix Maringe is a Professor of Higher Education and Head of the Wits School of Education. Previously he held positions as Assistant Dean for Internationalisation and Partnerships at the University of the Witwatersrand. He received his Doctorate in Education at the University of Southampton. Felix's research interests are in the fields of Globalisation and Internationalisation of Higher Education. With an extensive publication record, he has 6 books to his record and is currently leading research in international higher education in post colonial countries.

Robert Ebo Hinson is an Extraordinary Professor at the School of Business and Governance, North West University, South Africa. He is also Head of the Department of Marketing and Entrepreneurship at the University of Ghana and Acting Director of Institutional Advancement at the same university. He started his professional career in advertising and has since become an academic and taught a diversity of undergraduate and postgraduate courses. Apart from his experience in teaching, Prof. Hinson has a keen interest in research and in recognition of his research productivity, was awarded the 2008 Emerati Highly Commended Paper Award for a co-authored paper published in *Corporate Governance*, the 2009 Journal of African Business Best Paper Award, the 2010 Emerati Outstanding Paper Award for a co-authored paper published in the *Journal of Research in Interactive Marketing*. Professor Hinson is published in or has had papers accepted for publication in rated journals like the *International Journal of Public Sector Management, Internet Research, International Journal of Bank Marketing, Journal of Financial Services Marketing, Journal of Business and Industrial Marketing*, and the *Thunderbird International Business Review*.

Contributors

Babatunde Abina is a Lecturer at the Department of Marketing and Consumer Studies, School of Economics, University of Ibadan, Nigeria, with over six years' experience in teaching marketing and management-related courses. He earned a PhD in Business Administration with specialisation in Marketing at the University of Ilorin, an MSc in Marketing and a BSc in Mass Communication from the University of Lagos. His research interest is in the area of branding, advertising, and marketing communications.

Oluseyi Ajayi is a Lecturer in the Department of Marketing and Consumer Studies, School of Economics, University of Ibadan. He has a first degree in Business Administration, an MBA, an MSc, and a PhD in the same field of study. He specialises in strategic management and marketing. His research papers have been published in recognised national and international journals. He has more than six years' lecturing experience.

Mark Camilleri is an Associate Professor in the Department of Corporate Communication at the University of Malta. He finalised his PhD (Management) in three years at the University of Edinburgh in Scotland, where he was nominated for his 'Excellence in Teaching'. Prof. Camilleri has published 7 books and more than 80 contributions in peer-reviewed, high-impact articles, chapters, and conference proceedings. Currently, he is a member of the editorial board of several journals and is a frequent speaker and reviewer at the Academy of Management (AOM), Academy of Marketing Science (AMS) and in the British Academy of Management's (BAM) annual gatherings.

Otilia Chiramba is a doctoral candidate at Witwatersrand University. She is an emerging academic who has impeccable interest in researching under-privileged groups such as refugee students in higher education and young scientists. She has co-authored and published an article in the *European Education Journal*. She has also written four chapters which are in press. Otilia has worked for a global research project, the Global State of Young Scientists (GloSYS), collecting and analysing qualitative data and has co-authored the narratives yet to be published. She has also been involved with tutoring undergraduates and postgraduate students at the university.

Temitope Farinloye has a first degree from the University of Bedfordshire, Luton, and is presently working towards her master's degree at Kings College London. She presently works at Questbury Research Services as a Research Associate. Her research interests are in the marketing of higher education, social media and qualitative analyses of user-generated contents. She has published her works in reputable journal articles and book chapters and presented her work at conferences.

Tai Kieu received a doctorate from Western Sydney University (Australia). Currently he works as both an academic and a business partner. Tai has previously held senior managerial positions in marketing, advertising, and higher education, including programme directorship of international higher education institutions in Vietnam. He has published research in SSCI and *Scopus* journals and presented papers at international conferences such as AMA, AMS, WMC, and ANZMAC. He also frequently serves as a reviewer for academic journals and international conferences.

Ruth Kiraka is an Associate Professor of Strategy & Entrepreneurship at the Strathmore University, Kenya. She earned her PhD from Victoria University, Melbourne, Australia, her MSc from Wageningen University, the Netherlands, and her BSc from Egerton University, Kenya. She has published two books, two conference proceedings, two research reports, over 25 journal articles and book chapters, and 12 case studies. She has supervised several PhD and Masters' students. Her teaching performance won her a university teaching excellence award. She has served as an external examiner for Erasmus University, the Netherlands and an external peer reviewer for the National Council of Higher Education, Namibia and Kenya's Commission for University Education. Prof. Kiraka is a journal reviewer for *Eastern Africa Social Science Research Review; International Journal of Knowledge, Culture and Change Management; Knowledge and Process Management;* and *International Academy of African Business and Development.*

Josué Kuika Watat is a Digital Advisor at AMBERO Consulting Gesellschaft mbH for the Deutsche Gesellschaft für Internationale Zusammenarbeit (GIZ). Before becoming a digital advisor, he obtained a master's degree in Management and Information Systems from Catholic University of Central Africa. Josué holds two bachelor's degrees, in Computer Science and Management Economics. His early work focused on the influence of social media on academic performance and was published at the Americas Conference on Information Systems (AMCIS). His areas of interest are mainly focused on Social Computing, ICT4D, Big Data, Artificial Intelligence for sustainable development, Machine Learning, IS theories & models, Quantitative Analysis, PLS-SEM.

Azeez Lawal is a Lecturer at the Department of Business Administration, Al-Hikmah University, Ilorin, Nigeria. He is a Fellow of the African Young Leadership Program of Accra Business School, Ghana, and multiple scholars of the Lagos Business School's Sustainability Centre in Nigeria. He is also a member of the National Institute of Marketing of Nigeria, the Chartered Institute of Personnel Management of Nigeria, Teachers Registration Council of Nigeria and the International Society for Development and Sustainability, Japan. He has 13 years cross-industry working experience in telecommunication, banking, academia, and the social sector, and has several pieces of research in print at international and local conferences, peer-reviewed journals and books. His areas of specialisation are marketing, entrepreneurship, and general management.

Christine Mwebesa is a PhD student in Education Leadership and Policy at the University of the Witwatersrand, South Africa. She holds an MBA from Uganda Martyrs University, a PGD in Human Resource Management from Uganda Management Institute (UMI), and a Bachelor of Business Administration (BBA) from Ndejje University, Uganda. She has 12 years as an educator and six years of leadership in a university. Her study is on the Corporatisation of Higher Education. Her research interest is on understanding and harnessing globalisation transformations in African Higher Education. She is one of the founding members of Network for Education and Multidisciplinary Research Africa.

Sunday Olaleye is a Postdoctoral Researcher at the Department of Marketing, Management and International Business of Oulu Business School, University of Oulu. He has an MSc in Information Systems from the Abo Akademi University, Turku, Finland, a Master of Business Administration (MBA), Lapland University of Applied Sciences, Tornio, Finland, an NMS iICT Certificate, Innovation and Entrepreneurship, Nordic Master School of Innovative ICT, Turku Centre for Computer Science (TUCS), Turku, Finland. He has presented papers at conferences and published in academic journals. His research interests are emerging mobile technologies, tablet commerce, mobile commerce, circular economy, and mobile apps.

Omolola Oluwasola is a Lecturer in Applied Communications at Afe Babalola University, Nigeria. She has a research interest in Advertising, Public Relations and Marketing Communications. Omolola has published academic papers in these areas.

Samer Sarofim is an Assistant Professor in the Department of Marketing and Logistics at the California State University, Fresno. Sarofim's research was honoured by the Best Paper Award in Consumer Behavior Track at the American Marketing Association Summer conference (2016). In recognition of his innovative and impactful teaching methodology, Sarofim has been a winner (2016) and a finalist (2015) of the Marketing Management Association Outstanding Teaching-Scholar Doctoral Student annual competition. In his research, Sarofim focuses on consumer financial decision-making and the effects of emotions on consumers' reactions to advertisements. Additionally, he investigates the dynamic branding environment within sports marketing. He has multiple research projects both under advanced stages of review and ready-to-submit to major marketing journals. Sarofim brings to his research projects and classrooms 13 years of professional experience, working in healthcare, pharmaceuticals, consulting, and corporate training.

Hicham Sebti is a Professor of Management at the Euromed University of Fes and is Director of the Euromed Business School. Hicham Sebti holds a PhD in Management Sciences from Paris-Dauphine University. He has been teaching for 15 years in graduate and executive education, within different institutions in France (the University of Paris-Dauphine, The National Conservatory of Arts and Crafts of Paris, HEC-Paris, etc.) and Morocco. Hicham Sebti is the author of several academic and mainstream media articles. He is also the author of several case studies in management.

Sandrine Simon has a background in Ecological Economics. She has worked in various interdisciplinary institutions (Keele University and the Open University in the UK and the Euro Mediterranean University of Fes in Morocco). Her areas of interest include environmental protection, governance and education, sustainable water management, and cultural and societal changes. Her works on education, communication, and raising awareness have been published in the online *Innovation Review*, the *Journal of Gender, Technology and Development*, as well as in the *Journal of Physics Education* and the *International Journal of Disaster Risk reduction*. She is currently researching in Morocco.

Taiwo Soetan obtained his PhD from the University of North Dakota, Grand Forks, USA, two masters' degrees from the University of Manitoba, Winnipeg, Canada, and Strathclyde Business School, University of Strathclyde, Glasgow, and his first degree from the University of Ibadan, Nigeria. He was a past Vice-Chairman of the Canadian Institute of Marketing and he presently lectures in the Business Administration programme at the School of Business & Applied Arts, Red River College, Winnipeg, Canada.

Dandison Ukpabi is currently on the concluding stages of his PhD in Marketing at the University of Jyväskylä in Finland. Dandison's research interest centres on understanding consumers' behavioural use of emerging technologies such as social media, mobile applications and robotics/artificial intelligence. His research context focuses mostly on tourism; however, he makes occasional forays into banking and retail. In line with his educational experiences that cut across countries in Africa, Europe and Australia, he has also gained over ten years of working experience in various roles including academia as a lecturer/researcher in Africa, the United Kingdom, Australia, and Finland.

S Pee Vululleh has several years of educational experience – teaching, developing educational material resources, and administering educational institutions. He holds an M.Ed in Educational Administration & Supervision. S Pee is a member of several educational organisations including the Association for the Study of Higher Education (ASHE), American Educational Research Association (AERA), and the Mathematical Association of America. He serves as the Director of Education, Research and Evaluation at TechPro Initiatives, and is Chair on Education/Scholarship Committee for UNICCO in the United States. He offers peer-review and book-chapter services to academic publishers. S Pee is a person with vision and is a consultant and innovator in the field of education. His main interests include research and developing human resources and causes of learning.

Thomas Wayne is a Research Associate at Questbury Research Services. He has over ten years of industry experience in advertising and marketing communications. He has worked on various brand development and integration projects. His academic research interests are in marketing with a specific focus on higher education, financial services, and sports. He has published works in reputable journals, book chapters, and presented his work at conferences.

1 Introduction

Higher education strategic marketing and brand communications in Africa

Emmanuel Mogaji, Felix Maringe, and Robert Ebo Hinson

Introduction

Strategic marketing of higher education encompasses the efforts made by tertiary or higher education institutions to develop a better understanding of the needs of their prospective customers in order to design products and services to meet and exceed these needs. These marketing activities of tertiary institutions should usually be carried out through the execution of purposeful conversations with all the university brand stakeholders, and this is the function of brand marketing communications (Mogaji, 2016). Brand marketing communications seeks to integrate multiple consumer contact points that occur through the purchase of commercial messages in paid, earned, and owned media to deliver persuasive and impactful statements about higher education brands. Persuasive brand communications is a critical pillar in the successful marketing efforts of universities worldwide, and this new edited book focuses on marketing and brand communication issues from an African perspective.

Africa is the second-largest continent, both in area and population, of the seven continents in the world. The continent is vast as is its education system designed to meet the educational needs of its citizens; however, there is a dearth of insight into this vast education system, especially its higher education institutions despite the fact that higher education is known to support countries' social, economic, and cultural progress (Alcaide-Pulido, Alves, & Gutiérrez-Villar, 2017). While acknowledging the limited theoretical insight into marketing higher education in Africa (Maringe & Foskett, 2002; Ivy, 2008) research abounds on higher education in the developed countries, highlighting a gap in knowledge that needs to be filled.

Universities in Africa are continually advancing towards providing better quality education (Olaleye, Ukpabi, & Mogaji, 2020). While there is a shortage of funds for existing universities, governments are still creating more universities, private institutions are also establishing universities to meet these growing demands, and likewise, universities in the developed countries are opening international branch campuses in Africa (Chee, Butt, Wilkins, & Ong, 2016; Maringe, 2009). The changing demographics of prospective students in Africa is also changing – they are more demanding, mobile, and tech-savvy and take time to search for information (Michael, 2004). These dynamics within the sector is necessitating the need for strategic marketing of higher education as universities are becoming more business-oriented in the competitive higher education market (Ndofirepi, Farinloye, & Mogaji, 2020).

Marketing of higher education is necessitated based on the need to deliver a service to the market to those who can afford it (Mogaji & Yoon, 2019). In other words, some prospective students want to acquire tertiary education, and likewise, some universities need more students in order to remain commercially viable. Universities need to be strategic to portray how different and unique they are as this becomes a competitive advantage (Mackelo & Drūteikienė, 2010) and building this unique brand image as a university means more significant advantages are possible (Hemsley-Brown & Oplatka, 2006). The African context with these marketing dynamics, however, needs to be acknowledged.

A significant challenge that colleges and universities in Africa face apart from the state and standards of the campuses is that they are not deemed to be competitive enough for consumers to perceive them as offering better products and services than their competitors. Besides, there are external challenges, often not in control of the university. There are challenges with the countries in terms of safety, security, and opportunities, as well as the macroeconomic stability living standards, inflation, and unemployment.

The challenges of African universities are multifaceted. They face unique developmental challenges located in narratives of poverty, postcolonialism, coloniality, and more recently, decolonisation (Maringe, 2020). There is a gap in knowledge with regards to the marketing of higher education on the continent as the strategies adopted in the developed countries with a developed educational sector may not necessarily work in Africa (Mogaji, Farinloye, & Aririguzoh, 2017). Even though there are some developed higher education systems in Africa, such as in South Africa and Egypt, there is still a gap in knowledge about the African higher education market. Thus, there is need for better understanding of the higher education market and importantly their marketing challenges which informs the marketing communications strategies to be adopted.

This book fills that gap in knowledge. It addresses one of the many sectors involved in developing the capacity of universities in Africa. While there are challenges with the administration of the universities, funding structure, curriculum, and quality of education (Maringe, 2005; Mogaji, 2019), this book focuses on the strategic marketing communications of the universities as they engage with various stakeholders and enhances managers' decision-making capacity. This book offers empirical insight into the higher education market across the continent. It offers significant theoretical and marketing practice implications for academics, higher education administrators, and practitioners on how best to reach out to prospective students in the competitive higher education market using digital media and creating a brand that stands out. Likewise, international practitioners aiming to market to prospective African students or wishing to start partnerships with existing African universities will also find this relevant in understanding the dynamics of the African higher education market. We hope that this book meaningfully advances our comprehension of marketing higher education in Africa and that it will stimulate further research.

Coverage and content of the book

Following a process of double-blind refereeing, 12 articles were selected that reflect some of the main challenges and themes of higher education marketing in Africa which represent a relevant area of research, both for scholars and practitioners. The chapters are grouped into four different themes. Part I has four chapters with a focus on the *marketisation in African universities*. There are four chapters in Part II that explore digital marketing in African universities. Part III is *branding and reputation management* explored over three chapters. Part IV is *moving from research to practice* explained in one chapter.

This first chapter provides a background to the study and introduced the coverage and contents of the book, highlighting the different themes and chapters.

Felix Maringe and Otilia Chiramba open with the second chapter titled 'Marketisation in African universities in an era of decolonisation: Continuities and discontinuities'. The chapter argues that marketisation in higher education had become a widespread phenomenon across the world. Driven by neo-liberalism, and the strengthening of global capitalism, marketisation has influenced higher education sectors across the world to adopt business and profit-motivated strategies. In the process, the language and practices of business have become endemic in higher education sectors. The chapter calls for marketisation, which seeks to mitigate these effects in higher education sectors of the Global South. With the increasing pace of decolonisation, the chapter notes the potential this has to increase and widen inequalities between higher education sectors of the global North and South and identifies ways in which global imperatives could speak to the imperatives of decolonisation in new marketisation arrangements.

The third chapter, 'An integrative model for marketing higher education in Africa: Branding beyond survival for posterity' by Christine Mwebesa and Felix Maringe, further builds on the marketisation of higher education in Africa. These two chapters set the pace for understanding the sector before developing marketing strategies. The authors recognise the impact of globalisation and commercialisation on the higher education market in Africa. The chapter noted that African universities are failing to engage the appropriate marketing practices to preserve the future and remain viable through enhanced student recruitment strategies. Qualitative interviews with senior executives of universities in Uganda gave insight into the changing higher education value system in Africa. The chapter concludes by developing an integrative model for marketing higher education in Africa.

The fourth chapter presents a more focused idea of exploring the challenges of marketing tools adopted by universities in Africa. The chapter titled 'Digital marketing of higher education marketing in Africa: Challenges, prospects, and opportunities' recognises that while some higher education institutions still report success in some traditional marketing techniques, such as open days, there are still challenges in adopting digital marketing communications in marketing African universities. This chapter identifies and explores the critical challenges of higher education marketing in Africa and provide recommendation for university marketing managers and administrators and policymakers, which addresses the identified challenges.

With a specific focus on Morocco, Sebti Hicham and Sandrine Simon present their research which focuses on student recruitment on a new programme. The chapter titled 'Missing a trick: Challenging the harmful effect of informational dissonance on new programmes students' recruitment: A Moroccan case study' acknowledges that theoretical knowledge about marketing strategies to influence prospective students' choice in Africa remains weak. In this chapter, they attempted to understand students' recruitment in the context of a young North African university. The study explored rational and emotional issues that influence students' choice for a higher education institution, distinguished students' self-centric criteria referring to social and self-esteem motivations, and university centric issues related to the perceived value the university offers. The chapter also identified three 'informational cognitive dissonance' situations where university messages mismatch with prospective students' representations. The chapter concludes with a set of strategic and operational marketing recommendations for managers and practitioners.

Mark Camilleri's chapter titled 'Higher education marketing communications in the digital era' examines the global marketing environment of today's higher education institutions (HEIs). The chapter recognises that universities are increasingly behaving like for-profit organisations as they seek new opportunities and resources to prioritise revenue creation. The chapter further deliberates on contemporary integrated marketing communications that are intended to support HEIs to promote their quality, a student-centred education, as well as their high-impact and meaningful research in global markets. It concludes on the need for universities to keep investing inadequate resources, competences, and capabilities to leverage themselves amid intensifying competition in challenging socio-economic environments.

The seventh chapter provides a holistic view of social media as strategic communication for universities. The chapter titled 'Social media marketing: A strategy to reach university stakeholders' by Temitope Farinloye, Emmanuel Mogaji, and Josué Kuika Watat notes that social media have transformed how consumers interact with brands and how brand-related content is consumed. The advent of readily available social media applications has created opportunities for dialogic, and more interactive engagement between brands and consumers and universities are not excluded from this use of social media to engage with their stakeholders. Unlike most other brands, universities do have a diverse range of stakeholders which inadvertently influence their communication strategies, suggesting the need to recognise and embraces the benefits and opportunities that social media can bring as a tool. This chapter briefly discusses seven social media networks that are often used by universities and also recognises the African context that makes strategic communications on social media unique. The chapter concludes with recommendations on how African universities can adopt social media for strategic communication.

With a specific focus on social media in a specific country, Sunday Olaleye, Dandison Ukpabi, and Emmanuel Mogaji presented how Nigerian universities are using Facebook to communicate with their stakeholders in Chapter 7. The chapter, titled 'Social media for universities' strategic communication: How Nigerian universities uses Facebook', notes that while several studies have examined modes and methods of HEIs communication with stakeholders, there is a shortage of knowledge about how universities in the developing countries are using social media. The study employed stakeholder theory to give new understanding to social media marketing as a strategy to reach university stakeholders in Nigeria. The study utilised an inductive, generic, qualitative approach in a netnography context to achieve the aim of this study. The study adopts a unique methodology to capture the usage of social media by the universities and explored their level of activity and analysed stakeholder responses.

Chapter 9 by Omolola Oluwasola provided insight into digital marketing strategies by private universities. The chapter, titled 'Digital marketing communication strategies for private universities in south western Nigeria', investigates the digital marketing tools private universities in Nigeria deploys to promote their institutions. The study interviews universities' public relations officers who disclose the digital marketing tools they are using and the challenges they are facing in fully adopting and integrating digital marketing in their student recruitment process. The study concludes by recommending the continuous integration of both offline and online channels for integrated marketing communication.

The third part of the book focuses on branding and reputation management strategies of African universities. Chapter 10, 'University reputation management' by Ruth Kiraka, focuses on the Kenyan higher education market. The chapter interviews senior university administrators of both public and private universities to understand reputation management strategies. The chapter further presents strategies for managing reputation, dealing with reputation crisis, and challenges in sustaining university reputation. The chapter concludes that reputation is an asset that must be managed like any other assets of the university. Importantly, all employees in the university have a stake in building and sustaining a good reputation. Where challenges are experienced, or in case of a reputation-damaging event, the university must face them head-on with speed, clarity, and focus.

Universities are making efforts to present themselves as unique brands as they reach out to their stakeholders. Branding in universities has become an increasingly topical issue among practitioners, as universities invest a huge amount of money in repositioning themselves. In Chapter 11, 'Analysis of

African universities' corporate visual identities' by Temitope Farinloye and Emmanuel Mogaji, presents the result of the analysis of the brand identities of the top 200 universities in Africa. The study seeks understand the creative elements adopted in creating visual brand identities for African universities. While there are many forms of visual brand identifies, this chapter focuses primarily on logos. The study finds that overall there appears to be a lack of understanding with regards to creative design of brand identities by African universities, though with some exceptions as illustrated in the top 20 logos selected in the chapter. The chapter concludes with some suggestions to extend the current body of knowledge in the literature on the corporate logo and corporate visual identity, especially with focus on HEI brand and in the African context. This study presents a theoretical framework of universities' brand identities which focuses on the shape, colour, and typeface of the logo.

'Leveraging university's value through branding' by Abina Babatunde, Ajayi, Oluseyi, and Lawal Azeez Tunbosun is presented in Chapter 12. They focus on the need for universities to leverage their values through branding, as the perception of African universities has changed drastically in contemporary times, particularly with the globalised and highly competitive nature of the university environment. This contribution identifies ways universities can adopt and deploy branding strategies to improve the brand image of their institutions. This is because like all other brands in the market, universities should also strive to earn high equity by working towards delivering on their brand promises.

The Chapter 13, 'Marketing higher education in Africa: Moving from research to practice' by Kieu Tai, Emmanuel Mogaji, Christine Mwebesa, Sarofim Samer, Taiwo Soetan and S Pee Vululleh, brings together collective insight from several expert contributors to present critical recommendations for university managers working on marketing communications. The chapter moves away from research to present the practical implications of strategic marketing communications. With the market expansion by international higher education institutions and the emergence of private higher education institutions, African higher education institutions, private or public, are facing and will soon have to adopt a marketing orientation. The chapter briefly discusses the new reality of marketing higher education in Africa, followed by a marketing orientation checklist for a higher education marketing manager to keep to their hearts. A large part of the chapter discusses ideas drawn from emerging research and well-proven practices to build, integrate, and develop the brand for African higher education institutions.

The final chapter, 'Conclusion: Emerging challenges, opportunities and agenda for research, practice, and policy on strategic marketing of higher education in Africa' written by the editors Emmanuel Mogaji, Felix Maringe and Robert Ebo Hinson, provides a summary of the book. It presents the practical implications and critical insights into strategic marketing and brand communications of higher education institutions in Africa. Agendas for future research were also provided. It is anticipated that this will shape further discussion and theoretical advancement which will be relevant for scholars, students, managers, practitioners, and policy-makers in the field of higher education marketing.

Conclusion

This book has been conceptualised to offer empirical insight into the higher education market across Africa. It provides significant theoretical and marketing practice implications for academics, higher education administrators, and practitioners on how best to market higher education in Africa and reach out to prospective students.

The selected chapters provide a wide variety of stimulating insights into knowledge advancements in marketing higher education in Africa. We believe this book represents a significant milestone in the study of marketing higher education in Africa, which has been under-researched. Finally, we thank all the authors who submitted articles for consideration in this edited book; over 24 papers were initially received.

All chapters were subject to a double-blind reviewing process. We are grateful to the reviewers who contributed their valuable time and talent to develop this edited book and ensured the quality of the chapters with their constructive comments and suggestions. We believe this book contains significant work which is profoundly meaningful for the higher education marketing field, and not just for Africa.

This book on higher education marketing and brand communications in Africa that focuses on strategic marketing and communications of higher education institutions in Africa has delivered profound insights into African university marketing and communications from both brick-and-mortar and digital perspectives. The authors have covered different geographies on the continent and employed different methodological approaches to reach their study conclusions. The authors' affiliations are also international in scope. The collection reflects the diversity and breadth of current research within this stimulating and evolving research area.

We hope you will find the chapters in this book both enriching and thought-provoking and that the insights provided in the collection of research materials will enhance the understanding in this area, inspire further interest in marketing higher education in Africa, and provide a basis for sound management decisions and stimulate new ideas for future research.

References

Alcaide-Pulido, P., Alves, H., & Gutiérrez-Villar, B. (2017). Development of a model to analyze HEI image: A case based on a private and a public university. *Journal of Marketing for Higher Education*, 27(2), 162–187.

Chee, C. M., Butt, M. M., Wilkins, S., & Ong, F. S. (2016). Country of origin and country of service delivery effects in transnational higher education: A comparison of international branch campuses from developed and developing nations. *Journal of Marketing for Higher Education*, 26(1), 86–102.

Hayes, T. (2007). Delphi study of the future of marketing of higher education. *Journal of Business Research*, 60(9), 927–931.

Hemsley-Brown, J., & Oplatka, I. (2006). Universities in a competitive global market-place: A systematic review of the literature on higher education marketing. *International Journal of Public Sector Management*, 19(4), 316–338.

Ivy, J. (2008). A new higher education marketing mix: The 7Ps for MBA marketing. *International Journal of Educational Management*, 22(4), 288–299.

Kazoleas, D., Kim, Y., & Moffitt, M. A. (2001). Institutional image: A case study. *Corporate Communications: An International Journal*, 6(4), 205–216.

Luque-Martínez, T., & Del Barrio-García, S. (2009). Modelling university image: The teaching staff viewpoint. *Public Relations Review*, 35(3), 325–327.

Mackelo, O., & Drūteikienė, G. (2010). The image of a higher education institution, its structure and hierarchical level: The case of the Vilnius University Faculty of Economics. *Ekonomika*, 89(3), 105–121.

Maringe, F. (2005). Interrogating the crisis in higher education marketing: The CORD model. *International Journal of Educational Management*, 19(7), 564–578.

Maringe, F. (2009). Strategies and challenges of internationalization in HE: An exploratory study of UK universities. *International Journal of Educational Management*, 23(7), 553–563.

Maringe, F., & Foskett, N. (2002). Marketing university education: The southern African experience. *Higher Education Review*, 34(3), 35–51.

Maringe, F., & Gibbs, P. (2008). *Marketing higher education: Theory and practice*. Maidenhead: McGraw-Hill Education.

Michael, S. O. (2004). In search of universal principles of higher education management and applicability to moldavian higher education system. *International Journal of Educational Management*, 18(2), 118–137.

Mogaji, E. (2016). University website design in international student recruitment: Some reflections. In T. Wu & V. Naidoo (Eds.), *International marketing of higher education* (pp. 99–117). New York: Palgrave Macmillan.

Mogaji, E., Farinloye, T., & Aririguzoh, S. A. (2017). *Marketing higher education in Africa: A research agenda*. London: Kingston University London, Academy of Marketing of Higher Education SIG.

Mogaji, E., & Yoon, C. (2019). Thematic analysis of marketing messages in UK universities' prospectuses. *International Journal of Educational Management*, 33(7), 1561–1581.

Mohd Yasin, N., Nasser Noor, M., & Mohamad, O. (2007). Does image of country-of-origin matter to brand equity? *Journal of Product & Brand Management*, 16(1), 38–48.

Morrish, S. C. & Lee, C. (2011). Country of origin as a source of sustainable competitive advantage: The case for international higher education institutions in New Zealand. *Journal of Strategic Marketing*, 19(6), 517–529.

Ndofirepi, E., Farinloye, T., & Mogaji, E. (2020). Marketing mix in a heterogenous Higher Education Market: A Case of Africa. In E. Mogaji, F. Maringe, & R. E. Hinson (Eds.), *Understanding the higher education market in Africa*. London: Routledge.

Olaleye, S., Ukpabi, D., & Mogaji, E. (2020). Public vs private universities in Nigeria: Market dynamics perspective. In E. Mogaji, F. Maringe, & R. E. Hinson (Eds.), *Understanding the higher education market in Africa*. London: Routledge.

Polat, S. (2011). The relationship between university students' academic achievement and perceived organizational image. *Educational Sciences: Theory and Practice*, 11(1), 257–262.

Rutter, R., Lettice, F., & Nadeau, J. (2017). Brand personality in higher education: Anthropomorphized university marketing communications. *Journal of Marketing for Higher Education*, 27(1), 19–39.

Part I

Marketisation in African universities

2 Marketisation in African universities in an era of decolonisation

Felix Maringe and Otilia Chiramba

Introduction

This chapter is a largely theoretical contribution to the field of marketisation in higher education. However, some of the evidence it utilises comes from doctoral research conducted in Zimbabwe between 2000 and 2003 and from a global survey on globalisation and internationalisation conducted between 2008 and 2012 at the University of Southampton.

The marketisation of higher education in the African university is an idea in flux on four broad levels. First, unlike in universities of the north, marketisation in universities in Africa has not adequately taken root largely because educational markets in Africa existed for exploitation by their erstwhile counterparts in the Global North. Secondly, African universities face unique developmental challenges located in narratives of poverty, post colonialism, coloniality, decoloniality, and more recently decolonisation. These narratives share little in common with the post-modern narratives that shape developmental contexts of universities in the north. Thirdly, like other ideas that shape transformation in higher education in Africa, marketisation originated in the Global North and tended to be applied uncritically in many universities of the Global South including those in Africa. Fourthly, emerging as it did in the early periods of globalisation, marketisation is part of a basket of neo-liberal ideas that were assumed to have universal appeal and application across all geo-spatial spaces worldwide. As such the idea has tended to suffer tissue rejection in the African university. However, to describe Africa and its institutions as homogeneous is to commit the same cardinal mistake often made by colonisers who saw Africa only in terms of opportunities it offered for the exploitation of its resources. There is a tapestry of different developmental contexts across countries on the African continent, which has created opportunities for intra continental exploitative relations that mimic those between Global North and Global South nations and their institutions.

Drawing its evidence from a doctoral study conducted between 2000 and 2003 in Zimbabwe and from data in a global survey of the impact of globalisation and internationalisation in higher education conducted between 2008 and 2012 at the University of Southampton, this chapter asks three critical questions about marketisation in African universities.

1. How has the idea of marketisation been conceptualised and developed in African universities?
2. What global and local imperatives have shaped the marketisation of higher education in African universities?
3. In the context of an emerging narrative of decolonisation, how might the marketisation of higher education be conceptualised and operationalised in the African university?

In attempting to respond to the above questions, the chapter will be developed within the following structure: we begin with a conceptual discussion of the ideas of markets, marketing marketisation, globalisation, and internationalisation of higher education, colonisation, coloniality, decoloniality, and decolonisation. This is followed by a discussion of empirical evidence related to the central questions of the research. Conclusions and implications for the future of marketisation in African universities will constitute the final aspect of the chapter.

Conceptual discussion

Markets

Markets and marketing are essentially business and economic concepts, which define the parameters for the exchange of goods and services between suppliers or service providers on one hand and consumers and customers on the other (Kotler, 2003). Markets encompass the spaces where supply and demand for goods and services are met. Much happens in these spaces, such as, on the demand side first, the quantity and quality of demand, the speed with which this demand can be met, the changing or evolving nature of the demand amongst other. On the supply side, critical considerations might include the capacity of the supplier to meet demand, the speed with which supply can be delivered, the quality of the supply chain, and the extent to which consumers' or customers' needs are being met, the entire gamut of processes defining the value chain in the transaction (ibid.). In the context of higher education, markets could depict groups of people in specified geographical spaces who are targeted by institutions as students (Maringe, 2003). For example, in highly recruiting countries of the Global North, such as the USA, UK, and Australia, the Chinese, Korean, Japanese, and African markets feature prominently in the strategic recruitment documents of these countries. The major challenges associated with recruiting from these countries vary from country to country but tend to include issues of market entry and penetration; programmes to mitigate assumed academic, social, and cultural deficits in the new students; funding for post-graduate study especially; language barriers and strategies for surviving in a highly competitive market-place amongst others.

Marketing

Similarly, marketing as a concept and idea for reforming higher education has grown out of its origins in the business world. Essentially the concept deals with the ideas related to bringing services closer to the people, both in terms of affordability and access, but also in terms of meeting customer needs effectively and profitably more than competitors.

> It is that aspect of the organisation which is concerned with developing and maintaining an organisational focus upon the needs of the market-place and with developing mechanisms for satisfying those needs through long run mutually beneficial exchange relationships. (Smith, Scott, & Lynch, 1995, p. 1)

The adoption of the marketing idea in education and especially in higher education has not been a smooth sailing process. Primarily contestations revolved around the notion of the creation of new identities in the academy wherein students had to assume a new identity as customers or consumers (Scullion, Molesworth, & Nixon, 2011). Traditional educational values could not and continue to resist the idea that students are customers, being more amenable to views of students as co-creators of value in the educational enterprise rather than as purchasers of value created and delivered by universities and other educational institutions (Maringe, 2003). Marketing has also been resisted in the academy because it was seen as an endorsement of the commodification or commoditisation of education, a concept about which critics of the market in higher education such as Gibbs (2008), have written quite extensively. Bassett (2006) has also noted that as marketing became formalised through the World Trade Organisation (WTO) and the General Agreement on Trade and Services (GATS), opinions about its relevance to the central mission of universities grew increasingly polarised. McMillan and Cheney (1996) put forward four propositions regarding the unsuitability of the marketing ideology in higher education. They claim that the metaphor distances students from the educational processes, that the focus on customer satisfaction is a misplaced idea in higher education, that the market data driven processes trivialise the educative intention and that a wholesale adoption and application of business ideas and concepts in education does little to promote the values of higher education. We take these propositions as hypothetical positions through which research in higher education can indeed be driven.

Marketisation

Marketisation denotes both the processes leading to the adoption of marketing and the growth of a business culture in higher education institutions. The major impetus towards both views is located in the discourse of liberalism as a way to strengthen capitalism (Kotler, 2003). Most developed nations, if not all, consider capitalism, especially its arguments around competition, an unyielding focus on profit making as the fundamental engine and stimulus for economic growth. Liberalism fundamentally suggests that markets should be left alone to behave in their own ways as they have a natural tendency towards stabilising around the dyadic relationship between supply and demand. Education and educational markets, however, based as they are on middle-class value systems, if left alone, would show tendencies towards cementing privilege, inequality, and epistemological disjunctures between groups from different socio-economic backgrounds (Apple, 2001). For example, a profit motive understood strictly in terms of financial health and viability of educational institutions would imply that educational institutions would not have to bother about educating poor students as they are unable to pay for the educational services. This would not only entrench inequality in society, but causes the gaps in poverty and opportunity to widen even further (Brown & Carasso, 2013). Marketisation in higher education is also critiqued along arguments of commodification, commoditisation, and the corruption or erosion of the fundamental values and goals of education as a public good for which all have an equal right to engage with and participate in (see for example Scullion, Molesworth, & Nixon, 2011).

Strategic marketing, recruitment, customer service, customer satisfaction, branding, and value chain and delivery have emerged as the key strategies used in educational institutions to strengthen the competitiveness and profitability in the higher education market-place (Maringe, 2003).

Globalisation

The growth of marketing, markets, and marketisation in higher education received a major boost due to the strengthening of globalisation and internationalisation in the early 1980s. Globalisation, a phenomenon depicting an increasing homogenisation of the world in terms of its politics, economy, social, and cultural relations, values among others provides a force through which the ideas of markets and marketing are assumed to be central to the growth and competitiveness of global economies. Statements such as marketing is everyone's business (Kotler, 2003) gained wide acceptance across all sectors of human endeavour including in higher education.

Internationalisation

On the other hand, internationalisation, defined by Knight and De Wit (2018) as the purposeful integration of international dimensions in to the educational objectives and activities of a university has served the purpose of bolstering the discourse of markets and marketing as an international concern and priority and in doing so, strengthening the global significance of educational markets and marketing in higher education. As internationalisation grew, a range of new strategies became visible in universities. These included student exchange, staff exchange, partnerships, and collaborative research and teaching. Essentially, these strategies gave a different impetus and complexion to existing markets, thus contributing of the transformation of markets and marketisation in higher education. Gordon (2011) refers to this as the development of new geographies of knowledge production in the academy.

Colonisation and colonialism

These terms, which we describe together, are strongly connected and ideologically and historically loaded. Largely, they are offshoots of the imperialist project of the late 18th-century industrial revolution in Europe. As industries grew, the demand for products and services also increased. In order to maximise profits, there was a need to ensure the supply of the cheapest resources and labour. Countries outside Europe, especially in Africa, South America and Asia were targeted initially through the so-called 'Voyages of Discovery'. Once the voyagers 'discovered' these 'new found lands', they settled, occupied, and plundered the resources for the benefit of the industries back home. A key strategy used by colonisers was to provide minimalist education to convert the 'pagans' into effective, loyal, and unquestioning servants of the colonisers. As practice had it, the first act of settlement and occupation was to hoist the flag of their home countries in their 'new-found lands'. This scramble for resources in the so-called 'dark continents' resulted in the establishment of colonial states, rules by the overseas governments. In Southern Africa, Britain and to a lesser extent Germany and Portugal were the chief architects of colonialism. The French were prominent in West Africa while the Spanish and Portuguese were mostly active in South America and North Africa. The continent of Africa was divided into countries to suit the agreements of colonial nations in Germany at the Berlin Conference in 1884–1885 in order to regulate colonisation and trade in Africa. It is generally agreed that colonialism had deleterious effects on development in Africa (Rodney, 1973), politically, economically, socially cultural and any other way in which development may be conceptualised.

Decolonisation

The concept of decolonisation is associated with any act of defiance whether successfully accomplished or otherwise, initiated by the local or indigenous populations in colonised nations against the white settler communities and governments. The first wave of decolonisation generally involved armed struggles, which resulted in the transfer of power to local or indigenous administrations following negotiations and international pressure. Although this phase was associated with significant loss of life, some people argue that it was the easier part in the process of decolonisation. The second phase is what countries of the continent are going through now. The tendency of a post-colonial country to return to the colonial condition through persistent and abiding preference of everything Western/colonial and an inward rejection of local identities and culture, in almost all spheres of life. Ndlovu-Gatsheni (2012) and Maldonado-Torres (2007) explain coloniality as an invisible power structure that sustained colonial relations of exploitation and domination long after the end of direct colonialism. It took South Africans almost 30 years following democracy in 1994 for example to realise that the colonial machinery was very noticeable in every sphere of life. Despite efforts to increase and widen participation in education, the majority of students who fail, do not complete or drop out from the system prematurely tend to be the very ones who were previously disadvantaged. Decolonisation of higher education is thus about interrogating the legacies of colonialism in the system and finding ways of turning things around in order to restore some social justice, equality, equity, and human dignity. It is about deliberately providing enabling environments and resources to previously disadvantaged sectors of the academy so they can attain and achieve at the same levels as those young people from more privileged communities.

Decoloniality

Decoloniality is perhaps the highest form of decolonisation (Maldonado-Torres, 2007), where people decide to fight, not colonialism per se, but the causes of the tendency to return to the colonial relationship of dominance, dependency, and living in the shadows of the coloniser. It is the highest form of the struggle for transformation. There is as yet no record in history where countries have won against coloniality.

What we know about marketised higher education

This section deals what we know from empirical research regarding marketisation in higher education.

Drivers of marketing and marketisation in higher education

At a very broad level, the growth of marketing in higher education was steamrolled by three major factors across the globe (see Smith, Scott, & Lynch, 1995)

- The expansion of educational opportunities to more people or the massification of higher education. This massification implied that new markets were being opened up in the quest to widen and broaden participation.
- A second reason which is closely related to the above is the diversification of markets necessitating differentiated forms of attracting and serving students' needs.
- Thirdly markets grew out of a growth of competition and competitiveness. The allocation of resources by governments and funding agencies required the use of data and metrics to determine need in different institutions. Those that recruited more students, or those of a specific type tended to be

favoured in the funding decisions. As a result institutions competed some-times quite fiercely for students and resources and used the tolls and stra-tegies of marketing to give themselves the competitive advantage in the market-place.

Marketing models in higher education

Marketing gradually assumed a higher purpose when its mission became associated with value creation. The Four Ps model was the first and most enduring framework for marketing goods and products in the business sectors. Seen as providing value at the Product, Price, Promotion, and Place, the marketing mix provided a comprehensive framework through which value sought by customers could be, identified, developed, and delivered. How-ever, this was modified in the more service-oriented sectors. Service sector industries differ fundamentally from product supply industries in that the value sought and delivered is often intangible. For example, the receptionist who serves with a smile might just be what the customers are looking for in a relationship with a service provider. Grönroos (1982) model is perhaps the most representative of service marketing models. The provision of services recognises that people, processes of utilisation, and the physical environment need specific focus beyond the Four Ps. Hence, services marketing often recognises 7Ps.

Afro centred models for higher education marketing

Two marketing models have tended to dominate higher education marketing. The one is by Ivy (2002) while the other is by Maringe (2003). Interestingly both models have been developed with data from the African context. Ivy's model was developed in the context of business administration students in South African universities. The research underpinning this model involved the administration of over 1,400 semi-structured questionnaires to newly registered MBA students in 12 state funded business schools in South Africa. The questionnaires sought to determine these students' responses to the vari-ety of marketing strategies and tools they encountered in their enrolment journeys to the degree programmes. Using complex statistical methods, seven factors were identified as significant in the recruitment choices of the stu-dents. First group of significant influencing factors were the **Premium** mix of factors, which include identified value associated with enrolling on an MBA degree programme. Such value was identified in terms of availability of accommodation on campus, the total number of credits for the degree, size of classes and most significantly employment opportunities for graduates. **Pro-minence** factors, which included the reputation of both the university and the academic staff members came second in order of significance. This was followed by the **Promotion** mix of factors, which include the variety of marketing, advertising tools and the impact these have on students' choices.

The university and course **Prospectuses** stood as the fourth strongest influence on students' decisions. **Price** emerged as the fifth strongest factor, through consideration of costs, flexibility in payments, and the opportunity costs related to giving up other things including employment in order to embark on a degree programme. **Programme** factors including the mix of courses and the mix of electives were the sixth most important factors. The **People** factor was the seventh most significant which included variables such as qualifications of tutors and the opportunities tutors provided for face-to-face contact and tutorials. On one hand, Ivy's work has had significant impact on the development of targeted marketing approaches in African universities and elsewhere and indeed in the development of strategic marketing options required for successful recruitment in higher education.

On the other hand, Maringe (2003) drew data for a doctoral study from seven universities in Zimbabwe to determine how the marketing concept was understood, implemented, and problematised. The universities included a mix of traditional, technological, vocational, and ODL institutions in which senior academics and staff in marketing related departments were interviewed. Data also was drawn from pre-university students in six high schools totalling just under 450 to determine the factors they would consider in enrolling in university. To a large extent, the results confirmed IVY's findings although in the context of Zimbabwe, students placed Prominence factors ahead of Premium. More significantly, the findings from this study show that four factors appear important in developing effective marketing strategies in universities in this country. These include, **Context factors**, which recognise the specific factors associated with individual universities and their missions. **Organisational factors** which include how the curricula are organised, the structures and systems developed. The third element is the **research value** and status of the university and how this drives institutional strategies. The final element is the **four dominant ideas**, which lead to successful marketing strategies. This model is widely known as the CORD model and has substantial influence in some universities in Africa and Europe and has been used as a framework for developing courses in educational marketing in some universities both on the continent and abroad. Taken together, the two models provide a sound basis for developing effective marketing tools and also for conceptualising the contextual, organisational, research, and developmental issues related to creating maximum value for students in higher education.

Dominant discourses of marketing and marketisation in African higher education sectors

The research briefly described above and that of others on the continent provide a range of interesting ideas about the marketing of higher education in African universities. Four dominant ideas are briefly discussed below.

Marketing as an alien concept

There is a widespread view among academics and administrators in African universities that the idea of marketing is alien to the values of higher education. This view is nevertheless not homogeneously spread across different types of people in the universities. It seems to be most widely spread among academics and less thinly visible in the senior university administrators. Research by Beneke and Human (2010), Maringe and Foskett (2002), Ivy (2002) all allude to that fact. It is often described as an intrusion in to the traditional values of education. However, there is also an increasing recognition that despite it being seen as an alien concept, it is an idea, which is here to stay and that universities and administrators can no longer do without it. Its value is mostly associated with recruitment, branding, and positioning activities and is seen as driving value to universities in an increasingly competitive higher education environment.

Marketing as an endorsement of the commodification of higher education

The traditional understanding of education as a non-profit undertaking continues to prevail in the higher education sectors on the African continent. This is, however, being challenged by the increasing privatisation of higher education seen on the continent. Private education in African countries is rapidly increasing to cater first to the needs of a fast growing middle class amongst indigenous populations (Tamrat, 2017). In addition, the underfunding of higher education in many African countries is seen as an important stimulus for the growth of marketing. The traditional funding of universities from donors and sponsors can no longer sustain the significantly expanded higher education sectors in Africa. Competition for prominence and reputation has also driven universities in Africa to embrace the marketing idea (Teferra, 2013).

Marketing as an idea delivered in unsuitable models

Research by Maringe (2003) clearly shows that while the attraction of large student numbers in order to remain profitable is important, marketing as a value creation process is largely ignored. The use of business focused and product driven models generally is considered to miss the significance of context and curriculum and service. Beneke and Human (2010) for example found that relationship marketing models widely used in universities in Africa bring little value to the experiences and profitability of universities. Instead, they suggest that marketing models need to be developed along the lines of the value chains describing the experience of teaching and learning in the African university. The value of imported wisdom in marketing should be tested for its applicability and utility to local contexts before wholesale adoption.

Marketing as a value creation process

The underlying rationale for value creation is the centrality of innovation, seen here primarily as a continuous process of improvement in delivering on the needs of customers. Srivastava (2016) argues that value creation utilises the idea of innovation as its key weapon. Education institutions on the other hand are fundamentally traditional and conservative. The notion that we have always done things this way seems quite pervasive in our institutions. However, customers or consumers are always looking for improved services and goods. Apple, the highly successful mobile manufacturer produces a new phone every 12 months, a lesson which Nokia, the early trendsetter in the business learnt the hard way. Nokia thought that as they were the first in the business, and as their mobile phone literally took the world by storm, they did not have to do anything to improve their product. Until recently when they started working on newer mobiles, Nokia has since trailed other mobile manufacturers in profits, reach, and sales. The major difference between them and the competitors is that other manufacturers have seen the value of innovation, reform, reinvention, and continuous improvement. Customers place a premium on products and services that undergo continuous improvement. In universities, though, we see courses whose content has not changed in the past many years. We see courses taught using the same methodologies and we know how assessment strategies continue to be based on tests and individual assignments. There is not much value added that happens in our universities. We remain stuck in the traditions of repositories and conservatories. We seek to preserve more than we try to innovate.

It is important, nevertheless, to acknowledge a variety of approaches through which the essence of value creation has been developed in the context of higher education. Adopting a quality perspective, Akareem and Hossain (2016) explored how different student characteristics influenced quality perceptions in higher education. They found that quality perceptions in higher education varied along lines of study levels, parental occupation, age and immediate past performance. This suggests that value creation cannot be assumed to be a homogeneous process but rather that its creation should be sensitive to different students groups and demographics. Nthiiri, Gachambi and Kathuni (2014) looked at value creation from a student recruitment and staff retention perspective. They identified that successful strategies for student recruitment could more readily be developed through creating value around profiling staff and key university competences, providing university accommodation, and highlighting university graduation records and graduate employment records. Melewar and Karaosmanoglu (2006) work is especially valuable as it identifies seven dimensions which universities need to invest in order to create value through identity development. The seven dimensions include communication, design, culture, strategy, behaviour, and identity. Finally, Kimandu, Njogu and Sakwa (2012) explored success indicators among private universities in Kenya and found that funding, convenience, and flexibility, blended learning opportunities and employability were the key areas which drive success amongst private universities in Kenya. The significance of these developments is that value creation should be seen as a multifaceted concept, whose effectiveness and impact depends on an equally wide range of factors. This leads us to the final part of this chapter, which speaks to the question of marketing higher education in turbulent times.

Marketing higher education in the decolonial turn

Post-colonial societies, many of which are on the African continent are in a moment of the decolonial turn. Maldonado-Torres and Saldivar (2015) and Mignolo (2003) have dealt quite succinctly with the notion of the decolonial turn. The decolonial turn marks a period in the history of nations, especially post-colonial nations, when there is all consuming passion to deconstruct colonialism, and especially reinvent themselves through processes that focus on equality, equity, social justice, and human dignity. These are values, or rather goals which, without doubt, colonialism did not seek to promote through either policy or education.

In truth, decolonisation started the moment colonisers set foot on the continent. History tells of numerous quashed uprisings and min revolutions. But in most African countries, of which South Africa is the most prominent example, the decolonisation of higher education began in earnest in 2015 when students at University of Cape Town brought down the statue of Cecil John Rhodes, the architect of colonisation in Southern Africa, from the university campus. This was swiftly followed by student protests which began at the University of the Witwatersrand in 2016 and which engulfed the entire university sector in the country in a storm of protests based on three basic demands of transformation. Students demanded higher education to be decolonised; they wanted university education to be free and they demanded high-quality education. Although there was no shared understanding of what these demands meant amongst the student body politic, the coherence of the demand, never mind what it meant was universally accepted. The following examines what appear to be emerging as rationales for decolonisation.

Rationales for the decolonisation of higher education

Despite the absence of a shared understanding and coherent narrative about decolonisation, five key and overlapping rationales can be proposed.

The first is an economic rationale; a key dimension in any economy is the development of its human capital. There is a realisation in arguments of decolonisation for the need of new knowledge, skills, and attitudes, which are in keeping with new developmental challenges. A decolonised education is envisaged to transmit and develop knowledge that enables society to grapple with the issues of poverty, inequality, unemployment, and the restoration of people's identities (Maringe & Sing, 2019). These areas define a new economic development focus based on a vision of restoring lost legacies and repairing the damage underwritten by colonialism.

The second is a social justice rationale; in relation to the above, decolonised education seeks to create the foundations of a more socially just society, one which seeks to erase all forms of discrimination from society. The creation of equal opportunities for all in terms of access, success, retention, and progression are assumed to be the building blocks of the new African university. New methodologies are created which underpin the principles of socially just pedagogies (Osman & Hornsby, 2018).

The third is an equalitarian rationale; this rationale provides a confluence of the ideas of equity and equality motives behind the decolonisation project. In terms of equity, the purpose of decolonised education is to develop an education that is fair in its distribution of benefits and opportunities to the learners. For example, opportunities should not be determined by socio-economic background factors. Abolishing fees is thus seen as way to ensure access to higher education by even the poorest of students. Equality motives on the other hand speak to creating opportunities for all students to experience the high-quality curricula and education, and being exposed to resources that enable effective learning and enhance epistemological access (Morrow, 2009).

The fourth is an Identity and human dignity rationale; colonial education systems are described as intellectually harmful, culturally dispossessing, identity dislocating (Fanon, 2007) while attempts at decolonising education suggests attempts to correct these shortcomings.

The fifth is the expanding the geographies of reason rationale; colonisation has literally displaced the African continent as a follower and dependent of the rest of the world. Despite its rich resource reserves, it remains the poorest continent in the world. The development of new knowledge systems, which seek to harness and process the continent's resources, would propel Africa to levels of competitiveness. New geographies of reason (Gordon, 2011) imply that African universities need to establish diverse partnerships and collaborations, which are not limited to Western universities only.

Essentially then, if the above rationales are accepted, a new marketing rationale for higher education in decolonising universities of the Global South would have to be reimagined. The value anticipated from this reimagined marketing rationale would have to encompass a range of key ideas. First, is the need for a new economic imperative, which seeks to drive university profits, not just in terms of financial gain but also along the direction of equalising opportunities for varying groups of students. Second, is marketing which seeks to create greater epistemological access especially for students from poor socio-economic backgrounds. Third, would be marketing models which draw on a need to recreate new identities of the decolonial scholarship, both in terms of the purposes and content of education. Fourthly, the new marketing imperative would have to integrate new geographies of collaboration in order to reimagine new ways of knowledge creation and generation. The current focus on Western models to inspire what we know and do in Africa needs to be infused with knowledge from other spaces especially in the post-colonial world to break the hegemony of the west on the African continent.

Conclusions

Going back to the three research questions set out in the introduction to this chapter, we can conclude, first with reference to the conceptualisation of marketing in African universities that:

- Staff in African universities are a little conflicted about the importance of marketing in the academy. There appears to be some ambivalence about its significance.

- Some see it as an unnecessary intrusion into the values of education, and point to the issues of commodification and commercialisation of education as polluting the traditional values of education.

- Others however, see it as an inevitable and logical development in a world, which has decidedly become neo-liberal and capitalist in outlook. Those who hold such views also associate marketing with value creation especially with respect to attending more closely to customer or consumer needs.

Secondly, that the key drivers of marketisation in African universities are similar to those that have driven the same phenomenon in the higher education sectors of the Global North. These include the massification of higher education, the diversification of student bodies in universities, the emerging ideology of neo-liberalism and the significance of the idea of markets as the key determinants of business products, quality, and success.

Finally, in relation to the question of creating value in a decolonising context, we conclude this chapter by identifying three crucial aspects for a new marketing strategy in higher education institutions in Africa and with a few cautionary observations.

Creating value in the post-colonial era will thus entail the following:

- Deconstructing the idea of decolonisation, including how institutions can create strategies around the new and shared meanings. Clearly, the notion of decolonisation has a wide range of interpretations and meanings. Specific institutions have to develop shared understanding about what they want to mean by the term.

- The curriculum, broadly understood to be the vehicle through which university teachers teach and train students, research and manage their programmes has four central components which can be used as determinants for value creation in higher education. The four elements are the **Purposes** of higher education, the **Content** of higher education, the **Methodologies** we use to educate and research and the means by which we carry out **Assessment and Evaluation** of the curriculum (Tyler, 1947).

- It is these four critical elements which can constitute programmes of renewal and reinvention, innovation, and continuous improvement which students are calling for.

Marketing which fails to achieve this will be an antithesis of the value our students on the African continent, and I believe in the rest of the post-colonial world are seeking.

In this chapter, we have argued that marketing in the African university is in a state of flux, occupying spaces dictated by the need to respond to global and international imperatives, which emphasise competitiveness in market driven environments, but also in increasingly contested spaces dictated by the need to decolonise higher education. Decolonisation calls not so much for market driven global competitiveness but for a local refocusing of the missions and strategic repositioning of universities. This decolonisation has to elevate concerns for equality, equity, quality, and social justice in ways, which respond to the key demands for a free higher education. Universities that will continue in the traditional mode of storage and conservation will be superseded by the competition. Value created according to the dictates of decolonisation will, in the moment of this decolonial turn hold sway. Through their curricula, universities will need to realign their marketing strategies around new purposes of higher education, new content, new methods, and new assessment measures.

References

Akareem, S. H., & Hossain, S. S. (2016). Determinants of educational quality: What makes students perception different? *Open Review of Educational Research*, 4(4), 435–447.

Apple, M. W. (2001). Comparing neo-liberal projects and inequality in education. *Comparative Education*, 37(4), 409–423.

Bassett, C. (2006). Cultural studies and new media. In G. Hall & C. Birchall (Eds.), *New cultural studies: Adventures in theory* (pp. 220–237). Edinburgh: Edinburgh University Press.

Beneke, J., & Human, G. (2010).Student recruitment marketing in South Africa: An exploratory study into the adoption of the relationship orientation. *African Journal of Business Management*, 4(4), 435–447.

Brown, R., & Carasso, H. (2013). *Everything for sale? The marketisation of UK higher education*. London: Routledge.

Fanon, F. (2007). *The wretched of the earth*. New York: Grove Press.

Gibbs, P. (2008). *Marketers and educationalists: Two communities divided by Time?* London: MCB Press.

Gordon, L. (2011). Shifting the boundaries of reason in an age of disciplinary decadence. *Transmodernty*, 1(2), 95–103.

Grönroos, C. (1982). An applied service marketing theory. *European Journal of Marketing*, 16(7), 30–41.

Ivy, J. (2002). University image: the role of marketing in MBA student recruitment in state subsidised universities in the Republic of South Africa. (Unpublished PhD thesis). University of Leicester.

Kimandu, L. N., Njogu, G. W., & Sakwa, M. (2012). An analysis of the competitive strategies employed by private Universities in Kenya: A case study of private universities in Nairobi. *Management Science and Engineering*, 6 (2), 55–70.

Knight, J., & De Wit, H. (2018). Internationalization of higher education: Past and future. *International Higher Education*, 95, 2–4.

Kotler, P. (2003). *Marketing Management*. International Edition (11th ed.). New Jersey: Pearson.

Maldonado-Torres, N., & Saldivar, J. (2015). *Latinas in the world system: Decolonisation struggle in the 21st Century*. New York: Routledge.

Maringe, F. (2003). Marketing university education: An investigation into the perceptions, practice and prospects of university marketing in Zimbabwe. (Unpublished PhD thesis). University of Southampton.

Maringe, F., & Foskett, N. H. (2002). Marketing university education: The South African experience. *Higher Education Review* 34(3), 35–51.

Maringe, F., & Sing, N. (2019). School leadership in developing countries: The case of South Africa. In T. Bush, L. Bell, & D. Middlewood (Eds.), *Principles of educational leadership* (pp. 350–370). London: Sage.

McMillan, J., & Cheney, G. (1996). The student as consumer: The implications and limitations of a metaphor. *Communication Education*, 45, 1–15.

Maldonado-Torres, N., & Saldivar, J. (2015). *Latinas in the world system: Decolonisation struggle in the 21st century*. New York: Routledge.

Melewar, T. C., & Karaosmanoglu, E. (2006). Seven dimensions of corporate identity: A categorization from practitioners' perspectives. *European Journal of Marketing*, 40 (7/8), 846–869.

Mignolo, W. (2003). *The darker side of the Renaissance: Literacy, territoriality, and colonization*. Ann Arbor: University of Michigan Press.

Morrow, W. (2009). *Bounds of democracy: Epistemological access in higher education*. Cape Town: HSRC.

Ndlovu-Gatsheni, S. J. (2012). Global coloniality and the challenges of creating African futures. *Strategic Review for Southern Africa*, 36(2), 181–202.

Nthiiri, C. M. Gachambi, P., & Kathuni, I. (2014). Effectiveness of competitive strategies for student enrolment, staff attraction and retention in Kenyan universities: A case of universities in Thataka Nithi and Meru Counties in Kenya. *European Journal of Business and Social Sciences*, 3(9), 160–180.

Osman, R., & Hornsby, D. (2018). Possibilities towards a socially just pedagogy: New tasks and challenges. *Journal of Human Behavior in the Social Environment*, 28(4), 397–405.

Rodney, W. (1973). *How Europe underdeveloped Africa*. London: Bogle-L'Ouverture Publishers.

Scullion, R., Molesworth, M., & Nixon, E. (2011). *The marketisation of higher education and the student as consumer*. London; New York: Routledge.

Smith, D., Scott, P., & Lynch, J. (1995). *The role of marketing in the university and college sector*. Leeds: Heist Publications.

Srivastava, R. (2016). Marketing as value creation: 12 lessons for Global growth. Retrieved from www.marketingjournal.org/marketing.

Tamrat, W. (2017, 2 December 2017). The scourge of unscrupulous private higher education institutions. *World University News*, 210.

Teferra, D. (2013). *Funding higher education in sub-Saharan Africa*. Dordrecht: Springer.

Tyler, L. E. (1947). *The psychology of human differences*. New York: Appleton-Century-Crofts.

3 An integrative model for marketing higher education in Africa

Branding beyond survival for posterity

Christine Mwebesa and Felix Maringe

> Today, the world is one market. The rapid advance of globalization means that every country, every city and every region must compete with every other for its share of the world's consumers, tourists, investors, students, entrepreneurs, international sporting and cultural events, and for the attention and respect of the international media, of other governments, and the people of other countries.
>
> (Anholt, 2007, p. 1)

Introduction

Marketing higher education (HE) has significant advantages as a means of global scholarly positioning (Maringe & Gibbs, 2009). Through literature, however, marketing practices, are portrayed as new invaders of higher education's (HE) space. These practices are blamed for many violations of academic values because of focusing on market forces (Bostock, 1998; Reading, 1996; Rolfe, 2013; Tuchman, 2009; Yahaya & Abdullah, 2004) other than the core values of HE (Sanderson & Watters, 2006). Secondly, such practices are new to the academic environment, and hence, the marketing idea in the academic space is always resisted (Maringe, 2005). What many opponents of this concept forget is that, in the changing global landscape, higher education institutions (HEIs) are utilising these practices in their space regardless of whether they support them or not. For instance, use of words like; customer care, student as a client, teacher as service providers, all allude to marketing lingual (Furedi, 2012; Hemsley-Brown & Oplatka, 2006; Maringe & Foskett, 2012; Molesworth, Scullion, & Nixon, 2010). The intention is to achieve academic competitiveness both nationally, regionally, and internationally, what Anholt (2007) refers to as competitive identity. Challenges, however, facing HEIs is that even those aware and in support of this notion, fall short of engaging the marketing practices appropriate for HE (Gibbs, 2002; Gibbs, 2012). In this chapter we argue that while Africa grapples with the necessity to redeem the image, redefine the identity, and provide direction for the future of higher education, there is need to develop models that will promote and preserve the future African universities. The models must, however, address and transcend three challenges facing African HE; reduced public funding and poverty of the society, inadequate support to manage change and the conflicting role of government in regulating the operations of the university. Set in debates on the commercialisation of HE, this chapter makes a theoretical and empirical contribution towards marketing HE beyond the 21st century. With emphasis on branding for posterity, this chapter seeks to answer the vital question: *How can African universities build long-term brands beyond mere survival?*

The chapter will start by defining and examining the vital concepts for marketing HE; then drawing from the ongoing doctoral study at a university in Uganda and existing literature, we will review the extent of challenges facing marketing African HE. Finally, we will present an emerging integrative model for marketing HE in Africa through branding for posterity.

Engaging with vital concepts of this study

With globalisation and the changing HE environment, there are some concepts which need to be explained to understand the scope of this change and the justification of the adoption for the idea of long-term branding for HE. For this chapter, concepts which include; Market, Marketing, Marketisation, Survival branding, posterity branding, and key players in the successful marketing of HE in Africa, will be evaluated.

Market and marketing

First, it is vital to define what precisely a market is, before discussing marketing and branding. As Gibbs (2002, p. 326) argues, a 'market narrative in the context of marketing where consumptive models hold sway'. A market has two dimensions: the first is the economic definition 'a market as a place where buying and selling of goods or services take place'. This could be a geographical/physical place (Elzinga, 1981) or virtual market space (Weiber & Kollmann, 1998). The second definition is based on existing and potential buyers who must have the capacity and ability to purchase the product (Grönroos, 1989).

On the other hand, marketing happens when a transaction takes place between two or more parties to achieve the maximum benefit for all those involved (Maringe, 2005). Grönroos definition, on the other hand, describes marketing as a concept which derives its identity and authenticity from a marketing philosophy which states:

> the firm should base all its activities on the needs and wants of customers in selected targeted markets. At the same time, restrictions due to the surrounding society (laws, industry, agreements, norms, etc.) must be recognised. If the firm considers this underlying philosophy, its operations should be successful and profitable (1989, p. 52).

Grönroos' definition is more of a statement of what marketing tries to achieve other than what it is. Moreover, both definitions – market and marketing, are not applicable when it comes to HE because of what Maringe calls the failure to identify its core business and so failing to tailor the whole practice to the area of HE (Maringe, 2005; Maringe & Gibbs, 2009). The two concepts come under the wings of marketisation, which is viewed as an accomplice of neoliberalism and globalisation agendas (Hemsley-Brown, & Oplatka, 2006; Ogachi, 2009). We use the term accomplice deliberately because neoliberalism and globalisation have long been condemned in the HE spaces. Thus, promoting these practices advances the same game plan.

Marketisation and branding

As referred to in the paragraph above, marketisation is believed to be so much part of the globalisation and neoliberalisation agenda. Whereas globalisation enables nations to collaborate facilitate trade and other forms of relations (Maringe & Foskett, 2012), marketisation is the arm which drives and entrenches market traditions in the different public institutions within the global market place. The marketisation of HE is thus identified through use of commercial practices which transform education into a commodity to be consumed (Furedi, 2012; Gibbs, 2012; Hemsley-Brown & Oplatka, 2006; Maringe & Foskett, 2012; Molesworth, Scullion, & Nixon, 2010; Sehoole, 2004). While the entrenchment of this practice is driven by the need to seek out alternative means of sustainability in the face of decreased government funding towards HEIs (Bolsmann & Uys, 2001; Brownlee, 2014; Cox, 2013; Maringe & Gibbs, 2009), many universities have been forced into *firefighting* mode for survival (short-term branding).

Owing to this immediate desire for intervention, therefore, universities have been driven to define their identities uniquely in order to position themselves in the market place (Marginson & Van der Wende, 2007). Ivy (2001) supported this view '... as competition for students increases and funding decreases, universities and technikons need to create and maintain a distinctive image in the market place' (p. 276). According to Chapleo (2010), the image is identity built over some time through a combination of elements. This is what many scholars have defined as a brand. Brakus, Schmitt, and Zarantonello (2009) define a brand as that part of a good or service that must be easily recognised by the consumer through the senses or mind. In other words, for a brand to be acknowledged and appreciated above other brands, it should have been experienced by the consumer in comparison to others through how it satisfied the need. Another definition looks at a brand as an image created through a combination of many elements to form a unique identity of the institution or its products to compete favourably in the market (see Chapleo, 2010; Wæraas & Solbakk, 2009). Finally, a brand is an *indelible impression* in the mind of the consumer (Blackett, 2004, p. 17). Branding, on the other hand, is the process of creating a brand. The process according to Blackett (2004, p. 81) follows several steps which include:

- the need to understand your stakeholders in the broadest sense, both internally and externally,
- the generation of information, insights, ideas and possibilities,
- an active definition of your 'position' or your brand platform, and the expression of that position through visual and verbal identity, products, services and behaviours,
- the disciplined application of a brand architecture system to optimise the value of the positioning,
- the continuous development, management, and evaluation of the positioning over time.

The process is cyclic because each step builds onto the other with the final stage dependent on the first one and vice versa. It is against this backdrop that posterity branding of HE beyond the 21st century should be positively embraced.

Survival branding

Survival branding occurs when there is either higher demand than the supply of the good/service or sudden stiff competition in the industry. Stiff competition forces HEIs to define their position in the highly competitive market (Hemsley-Brown & Goonawardana, 2007). Unfortunately, most institutions during such times, get panicky and engage the 'survival gear'. Consequently, HEIs end up building short-term brands – firefighting. While this practice might bring in many customers it is always for the short term.

Posterity branding

It takes a lot of determination and deliberate planning to build a long-lasting brand. While branding for generations might not be new in European and North American universities (commonly referred to as the Global North), it is still slippery ground in African HE because of various constraints. African HE owes its challenges to political, economic, social, historical, cultural, and global factors (Teferra & Altbach, 2004). Therefore, HE as a brand and branding HE requires deliberate effort to transcend those barriers for a successful brand (Toma, 2003). Chapleo (2010) posits that '*successful brands show a greater degree of congruence between the values firms develop for their brands and the rational and emotional needs of the consumer*' (p. 171). A long-term brand, therefore, should go beyond firefighting and aim at attracting all categories of clientele both locally and across the borders; national borders, demographic borders-and cultural borders. This is what Keller (2002, p. 152) refers to as a strong brand which demonstrates (micro (consumer familiarity, knowledge, preferences) and macro (market leadership or market share position) considerations).

Important players and their roles in marketing HE in Africa

This section presents important players in the successful branding of HE in Africa – it identifies the triple relationship between government, industry, and university. Also, it shows how this triple relationship interplays with selected HE functional and marketing models. Understanding this three-way link is very important for long-term branding of HE or managing any new university intervention.

Government, university, and industry – the tripartite relationship

The three elements in this relationship cannot be separated, as demonstrated in Figure 3.1. Secondly, their members are interlinked and overlap. For example, students can be 'customers' seeking entry into the university, process as a continuing student and a product on graduation. The same student on graduation can be input into the industrial system and government as a new employee. Much as this might be contested by those who are against market terminologies in HE spaces, Clayson and Haley argue that a student is neither a customer nor a product, but a partner. They further posit that treating the student as a customer, 'ignores the multiple stakeholders (parents, alumni, government and

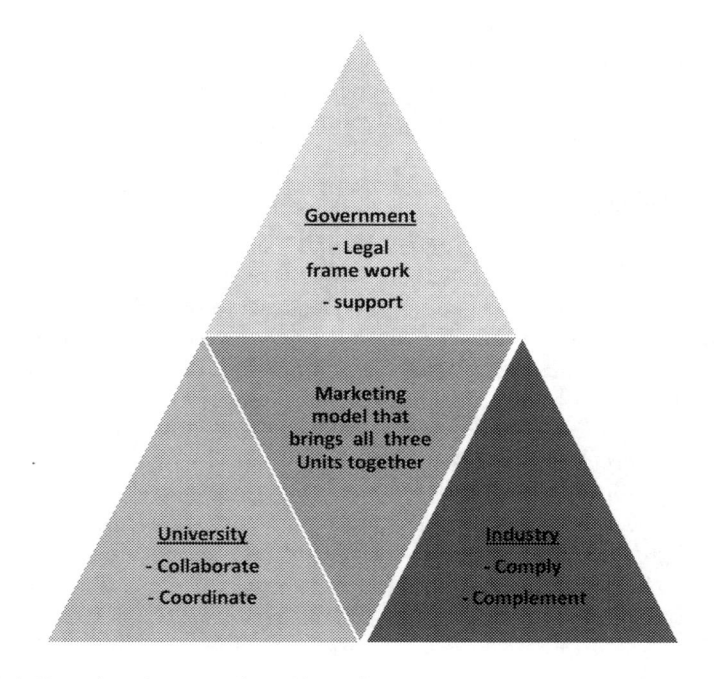

Figure 3.1 How the tripartite relationship of government, university, and industry relates to the marketing models in HE
Source: Developed by authors, 2019

business) of HE' (2005, p. 1). Sharrock in Maringe argues that to call student customers is limiting – according to him students have four identities they align within their day-to-day lives: *customer, clients, citizens and subjects* (see Maringe, 2005, p. 567). This also means that while students are central to the functions of the university, not only do they take on different personas depending on their needs but also they are not the only *stakeholders*.

This is an important dimension to understand for the successful marketing of HE in Africa, where marketing practices and procedures are still treated with suspicion and scepticism. Terms like the *customer is the king* will raise questions: who is the king? Guardians, students, employers – different categories demand different/differential treatments. Then what is the service or product being offered and to whom? What is the role of faculty and management in the whole process of product production? Providing appropriate answers to these questions will guide in identifying and developing the relevant model(s) for branding and marketing African HE for many generations.

Marketing models in higher education

Several marketing models have been developed in the context of HE. The majority of these appear to promote business imperatives more than they focus of educational values. Gibbs (2002) lists some of them and argues that con-sumption models cannot be appropriate for a HE's paradigm which advances 'humanitarian principles of a general well-being' (p. 326). Similarly, Ivy (2008) confirmed Gibbs' argument that indeed the traditional marketing mix does not fit into the marketing of the educational sector. Therefore, for the success and survival of the universities in Africa, there is need to identify marketing models which recognise and reinforce the core values of HE. It is to this end that Ivy's model of 7Ps and Maringe's CORD framework are considered. These models have been selected because of the scope of their dimensions concerning the functions of HE and specifically curriculum-related aspects (see Ivy, 2008, p. 297; Maringe, 2005, p. 570).

Marketing HE falls in a different genre from traditional marketing. HE, therefore, requires a different marketing mix. The initial marketing mix of 4Ps (product, promotion, price, and place) developed by Kotler (1982) was for profit-making organisations and especially consumer goods. Later three more Ps (people, physical evidence, and processes) were added to cater for services (Ivy, 2008). Ivy, however, contends that marketing; HE is different and hence proposes 7Ps for marketing HE which include:

a) Premiums – those things that add special value to an offering.
b) Prominence – university image including the reputation of academic staff and university ranking.
c) Promotion (traditional one split into two – i) maintaining old elements and i.e.) becoming prospectus).
d) Prospectus – print outs and direct mail from university.

e)   Price – tuition.
f)   Programme – the range of courses and room for choice.
g)   People – face-to-face (Ivy, 2008, pp. 292–295).

These 7Ps make a distinction between marketing HE and marketing services. While it maintains the three traditional 3Ps, the other 4Ps are unique to HE, and even the traditional three are tailored explicitly to HE aspects. Owing to this specificity, this model is selected for this chapter to be part of posterity branding for African HE.

The role of universities is to generate, preserve, and share knowledge as a public good. This role is achieved through research, teaching, and enterprise (Altbach, 2009; Chen, Wang, & Yang, 2009). This identity, however, puts universities in a vulnerable position which demands frameworks or interventions that specifically distinguish and address the uniqueness of HE as different *from business as usual*. Maringe proposes CORD framework (an acronym for *Contextualisation, Organisation and co-ordination, Research and Development*) as one of marketing strategies which can address HE's specificity (2005).

Posterity branding ought to identify and address what constitutes a successful brand. Chapleo identifies a successful university brand as one that has a sustainable competitive advantage (2010, p. 171). Doyle in Chapleo (2010) recognises three aspects that a successful brand should possess: *an effective product, distinctive identity, and added values*. A brand, therefore, is not a noun or just a marketing term but a package of attributes (Chapleo, 2005).

As universities across the globe scramble for endorsement from present and prospective customers – different stakeholders, there is a grave tendency to lose focus of their mandate. As Andrews (2006) posits:

> If, in a market economy, a profession does not renew the social contract through continuing education, money and economic efficiency will eventually sweep the field to define all professional relationships as simply economic transactions between consumers and service providers for profit. (p. 17)

Andrews' emphasis is on public institutions preserving their own identity amid many market demands. Much as he is not against adoption of market practices, he has a grave concern that this will cause these public institutions to abandon their values. It is against this background that those who oppose business practices entering HE, base their case. However, considering the proposed Doyle's aspects of a successful brand, the fears of turning universities into commercial entities would be allayed. They are identifying what an effective university product and its distinctive features, would, therefore, guide on the kind of values to be adopted or reinforced. In that way the contentions existing between marketing HE and academic values (Bok, 2009; Bostock, 1998;

Brownlee, 2014) would not only be assuaged but also a successful (long-term) HE brand would be achieved.

Branding the African university through and beyond the 21st century requires revisiting its core functions. Through the model of scholarship, Boyer (1990) proposes four types of scholarship (full range of academic functions as he calls it) through which universities can reward faculty; a) scholarship of discovery – where research falls, b) scholarship integration – aligning or relating one's research into the bigger existing research body/debates, c) scholarship of application – translating one's research into solving real-life problems, and d) scholarship of teaching and learning – promoting epistemological access and productive pedagogy. Productive pedagogy consists of four dimensions: 1) intellectual quality, 2) connectedness, 3) supportive classroom environment, and 4) recognition of difference (Ahmad, Jamil, & Razak, 2012, pp. 149–150; Lingard, 2007). Boyer's concern is how some universities will consider some types superior over others. Thus, the scholarship of teaching and learning (which is foundational for the existence of the others) is compromised (Fongwa & Wangenge-Ouma, 2016). Similarly, Boyer posits that '… The scholarship is not an esoteric appendage; it is at the heart of what the profession is all about … moreover, "to weaken faculty commitment for scholarship" … is to undermine the undergraduate experience, regardless of the academic setting' (1990, p. 1). Therefore, for posterity branding, such concerns must be addressed.

In this globalised environment, African HE must identify and reinforce its areas of competitive advantage – core academic values. Porter's model of competitiveness is hinged on five forces at play in industry and how they shape the survival or demise of any player within that industry. This model is relevant to HE especially in the 21st century where national boundaries are dissolving into the global village. According to Mathooko and Ogutu (2014) '… the model can help universities as they define the parameters within which new rules, participants and markets continue to emerge' (p. 334). It is not enough now for universities to hide in their ivory towers but to step out into the world where there are real issues and problems. Incidentally stepping out requires an understanding of what that world holds and how to take it on. It is against this background that elements of Porter's model of competitive advantage are adopted. Drawing from Porter's model of five forces, Barney (1991) discusses 'Four empirical indicators of the potential of firm resources to generate sustained competitive advantage–*value, rareness, imitability, and substitutability*' (p. 99). For posterity branding of HE in Africa, we can borrow these indicators and brand the universities.

Methodology

The empirical evidence to support this chapter was drawn from an ongoing doctoral study on how 14 purposely selected deans understood and responded to corporatisation of HE at a university in Uganda. The study used the university website to see the deans' profiles and contact information. Emails were sent to request for appointment for the interviews, but only two responded to the emails. The researcher walked into their offices and managed to get only five. So, the ones who had accepted to be interviewed were requested to assist with connecting with those who have not responded. This university was one of the first World Bank market models in East Africa (Mamdani, 2008). The study used a qualitative research approach springing from an interpretivist paradigm and narrative design (Merriam, 1998; Patton, 2002). All interviews were conducted within the deans' respective offices. The interviews lasted between 35 and 70 minutes.

A modified biographical narrative interpretive method (BNIM) was used to collect data from 14 deans resulting in 17 interviews. The first interview (1st & 2nd steps), 10 deans were interviewed. In the last interview (3rd step), semi-structured interviews were administered to three of ten deans that participated in the first interview and additional four deans who never participated in the first interview. The first four deans, BNIM was used (1&2 step interview) following Wengraf and Chamberlayne three-step interview (2006), but the same information was being arrived at, especially in the first step interview. Therefore, for the next six deans, The first step format was maintained but changed the second step by probing more on the unique points arising from the first one to understand one's orientation and conceptualisation of the phenomenon. In the 3rd step, first three of the ten were selected, probing both for the unique points as well as elements of the research questions that needed further answers. Later four more deans were selected, different from the first ten and followed 1st step, skipped 2nd step, addressed 3rd step by asking only those areas of the research questions that were not yet addressed by the previous interviewees. The data collection was stopped at four after achieving saturation. University policy documents were also used as complementary data. The analysis was both descriptive and interpretive following Kelchtermans' two-phased process (1999). I used manual coding – pencil and pen (Saldaña, 2015), first by analysing each story and secondly by comparing the emerging themes across the stories.

Key findings from the study

The participants were 14 deans purposely selected from a university in Uganda with at least a dean from each of the nine colleges and one transiting school. Out of 14 deans, only two were females. All the 14 deans interviewed were alumni having done at least their first degree from this university, some serving their final term of Deanship, others about to finish their first term and while others were just new in the post. Six experienced all the privileges of being in a public university whereby there was no paying of fees, and instead they were paid allowances (called boom). The other eight; three joined the year all allowances were scrapped, and cost-sharing was being introduced, and five came in when the university introduced privately sponsored students. The preliminary findings show that each dean's story was informed by the time he or she joined the university and how they saw the change take place or heard from those who were present before change was introduced: each perspective presented two images either comparing the before and after or the present and the anticipated future.

The dichotomy showed the existing gap between the initial and desired end. The stories showed three categories of people: 1) those stuck in the past and not ready to change; 2) others were ready for change but disappointed at inadequate or inappropriate support from government, unpreparedness on the side of the university and lack of a proper framework to facilitate university/industry collaboration; 3) those that received harnessed and embraced the change.

Discussion and research implication

Understanding all the three categories is critical to building a successful brand, and until the gap is bridged, posterity branding would remain a dream. Chapleo (2005) proposes some factors that promote successful branding in universities, and among them three relate with the case under study; *working with the public, building a reputation,* and *consistent, clear, appropriate visual identity and communication* (p. 62). In all the three categories discussed in the previous paragraph, these factors stood out. First was the need for a proper legal framework to define the acceptable collaboration between the university and industry (different publics). Secondly, building reputation through internal customers (faculty and administration) before attracting the external ones (industry, guardians, present, and future students–publics).

Inadequate funding and poverty

African universities, like all other HEIs across the globe, have been affected by reduced public funding. In Africa, the impact is far more significant because of the poverty level of the people. Whereas the economic crisis of 2008 brought the Global North to its knees, Africa had experienced its own almost 30 years back. This ushered in the intervention of the World Bank and International Monetary Funds (Olukoju, 2004). The reforms not only paralysed the functions (research, teaching, and community) of the African universities but also severely impaired the public universities of their values and identity as knowledge powerhouses (see Kajubi, 1992; Mamdani, 2007; Mamdani, 2008; Olukoju, 2004). The after-effect of the reforms introduced practices which promoted commercially driven innovations contrary to the educational values. Moreover, these creations favoured some courses/programmes over others, resulting in neglect of '*non-selling courses*' (refer to Mamdani, 2007). Posterity branding would be one that reverses such discourse and rewrites a better one that promotes knowledge creation and dissemination regardless of the discipline.

Inadequate funding was defined as the government's failure to finance university operations appropriately. Chapleo (2005; 2007, p. 29) identified limited budgets to HE as the most significant barrier to successful branding and successful image since they lead to compromised quality of teaching and learning.

Inadequate support to manage change

The study showed that there was less support to manage the change that had come into the university and in the end, the change process was never completed affecting the image as well as the future of the institution as argued by one of the deans:

> If we had gone full commercialisation but again we did not reach. I would not say we went full corporatisation, in my understanding we did not. We moved to midway where the state could still give a little funding which is still inadequate … (Dean 7)

To gain from change, it must be supported from beginning to the end because failure to do so would lead to disorganisation and impact on the image of the institution and hence the brand (Chapleo, 2005).

The role of government in regulating and harmonising the universities internal operations and external relationships

The study showed that the government had a significant role to play in managing the transformation and preserving the image of the University. It was, however, evident that government was blamed for two things:

1. failing to manage/regulate the vital relationship between university and industry;
2. playing a double role of convenience and conflict of interest by either interfering or intervening in the university interactions with the public.

From the study and what Chapleo (2005, 2007, and 2010) classifies as factors/barriers to successful branding, indicate that there are key-related elements (players) that must be recognised. How this relationship works out along with relevant HE marketing models, will determine the success or failure of the African HE brand (as demonstrated in Figure 3.1). While there are many short cuts to achieving survival branding, posterity branding demands vigilant, committed, and focused the effort of all these players working together in harmony.

As one of the Deans put it,

> First, I would want to look at the stakeholders that are relevant in our operations. Here we have students, their sponsors who are parents and guardians then we have Industry. The industry is a significant stakeholder encompassing these; government and private sector. (Dean 2)

Thus every intervention or marketing strategy for the successful branding of the university should put into consideration all the other stakeholders. The role of each element in the tripartite relationship is shown in Figure 3.2. The figure shows that the role of the government runs through university to industry and vice versa, as shown by the double-pointed arrow. This means that the government sets the rules and provides support (moral, financial, physical, conducive environment) between the university and industry. The university then collaborates and coordinates the information between its stakeholders (students, alumni, parents, sponsors, faculty, top management, and administrative staff) and industry. Hence, industry receives the information, complies with it, and complements the roles of both government and university. Finally, all the three arms must have a feedback loop on what is acceptable/what should be amended or room for negotiation for all the parties in the relationship.

Accordingly, while it is evident that research promotes scholarship; it is teaching and learning, which provide the 'raw materials' to proceed. Most universities are shifting from undergraduate led to postgraduate led programs. One of the deans asked where postgraduates would come from if there were no undergraduates. Branding the university, therefore, begins from within where the faculty and all aspects of what Boyer (1990) advances, are given equal consideration and recognition. In trying to embrace global interventions like the World Bank market model without deliberate checks or proper planning, many values get mixed up. This was identified at a university in Uganda when the World Bank model was introduced, many faculties tried to create programmes that were 'marketable', and *the result was a dramatic decline in quality of teaching and research* (Mamdani, 2008, p. 9). Many deans also echoed this during the interview. For instance, one dean stated, '… that is a serious problem being market or demand-driven. It means whatever courses offered depend on the demand of the person/client not what is

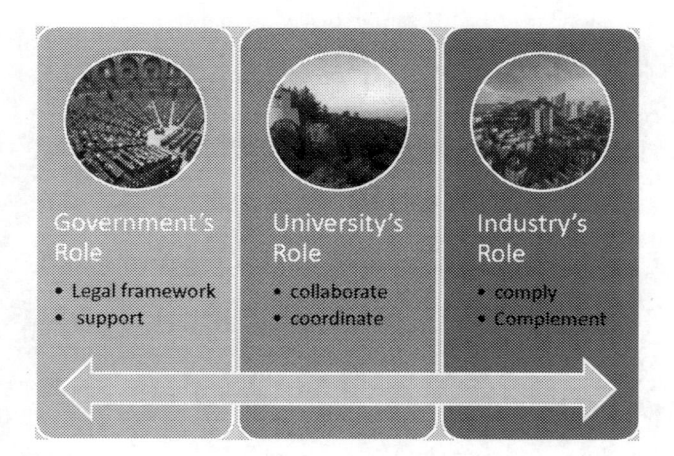

Figure 3.2 Showing the roles of each entity and how they relate
Source: Developed by the authors, 2019

necessarily good to the so-called client' (Dean 7). The challenge with this kind of branding, the brand loses value immediately the clientele base (market) is saturated or once the core values of the brand are compromised for survival. That is why Herman (2000) argues:

> that brands are built for the long term, and the value of the brand to the marketer (Brand Equity) stems, both directly and indirectly, mainly from consumer loyalty. However, it seems that consumer loyalty (even loyalty to a consistent repertoire of brands) is a disappearing phenomenon. (p. 330)

What this means is that a brand benefits the marketer as long as the consumer continues to appreciate and seek after the excellent service. Survival branding in case of HEIs therefore, tends to address short-term needs, targeting local clientele and taking marketing practices without considering organisational/product values. That is why this chapter echoes (Chapleo, 2010; Mampaey, Huisman, & Seeber, 2015, p. 1179) position that there should be a balance between competitive pressures and traditional institutional pressures.

An integrative model for marketing HE in Africa

This section presents an integrative model which identifies the triple link between government, industry, and university. It also illustrates how the relationship interplays with Porter's model of competitiveness, Boyer's model of scholarship, educational marketing model of 7Ps and CORD model for posterity branding of HEIs in Africa.

The model identifies five vital questions that ought to be answered while addressing the issues of marketing HE in Africa:

1. What does HE mean to Africans?
2. What is not being done, right?
3. How can it be made right?
4. How possible is it to brand HE in Africa without falling prey to the business ethos?
5. How can marketing African HE transcend survival branding to posterity branding?

Figure 3.3 gives a diagrammatic representation of the different elements and how they relate hence the integrative name model of marketing HE in Africa.

The funnel and its contents

The funnel in the model represents Boyer's model of scholarship as a sieve. The rest of the elements are to be vetted (sieved through) the funnel. What this implies is that there are five assumptions:

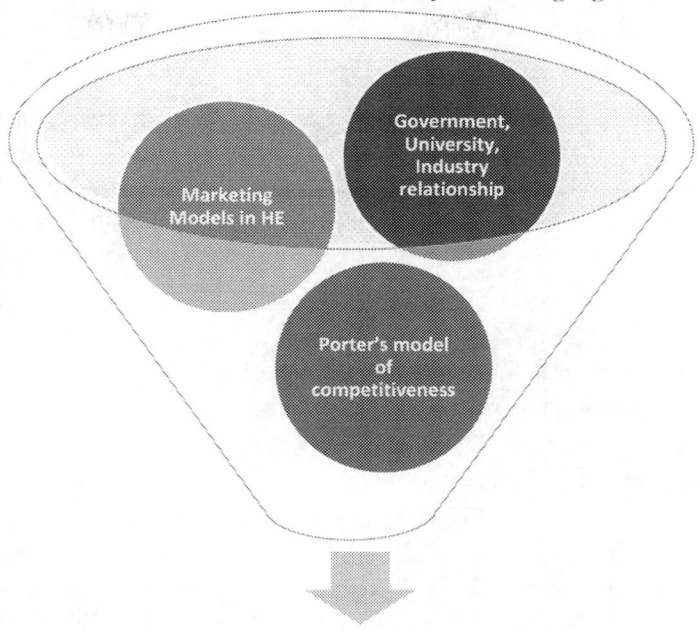

Boyer's model of scholarship: the Sieve

Figure 3.3 An integrative model for marketing HE in Africa
Source: Developed by authors, 2019

1. The relationship between government, university, and industry is critical for the successful marketing of HE in Africa.
2. The government, university, and industry relationship is not enough to drive the successful branding of HE in Africa; other models (marketing and strategic management) need to be integrated as well.
3. For the long-term African HE brand, all interventions must be drawn against the background of three core functions of the university and industry (societal) requirements for relevancy and continuity in the global environment.
4. However good the interventions might seem they must first be checked against the functions of university (research, teaching, and enterprise) as advanced through Boyer's model of scholarship.
5. Whatever marketing model, the core values of the university must be preserved.

The integrative model of marketing HE in Africa is timely because, with the wave of globalisation sweeping across nations, there is demand on all institutions to prove their worth through what they offer and how they differ from the rest. The best way to achieve this is by drawing on market practices and tailoring them to the values of their institution. Marketing HE is necessary, it is no longer optional as observed by Anholt (2007):

> Today, the world is one market. The rapid advance of globalization means that every country, every city, and every region must compete with every other for its share of the world's consumers, tourists, investors, students, entrepreneurs, international sporting and cultural events, and for the attention and respect of the international media, of other governments, and the people of other countries. (p. 1)

Anholt's argument shows that failure to understand the global dynamics in this era leads to the failure of developing appropriate operational tools which tantamount to the loss of image and relevancy.

Summary and conclusion

Marketing HE in Africa is still a new phenomenon, and worse, the changing HE global landscape puts a strain on many HEIs to define their relevancy. What is evident, both in the study conducted and literature reviewed, is that survival branding is practised more than posterity branding for African HEIs. Despite the many challenges facing HE in Africa, the concept of branding is not well understood and hence not given enough attention. African HE, therefore, has three options: 1)either to live in its comfort zone and be alienated from the rest of the world, or 2) leave its academic values to be swallowed up by business ethos, or 3) adopt the market practices but tailor them to own academic values for a long-term brand that can be preserved for centuries.

The integrative model of marketing HE in Africa is therefore proposed in this chapter as the solution to addressing the gaps in branding HE in Africa: 1) the model identifies and integrates the triple relationship between government, university and industry as key players for the successful branding of the university; 2) the triple relationship as a moderator of the university functions and key HE marketing models in HE; and 3) the importance of developing this model is well justified.

It is essential to say that while this model might not address the marketing of all HEIs in Africa, we confidently state that failure to identify a model or framework which can uniquely and successfully brand African HEIs, is more disastrous. The integrative model for marketing HE in Africa therefore, gives us a good starting point to brand our universities for posterity.

References

Ahmad Ansari, M. Z., Jamil, H., & Razak, N. A. (2012). Exploring the classroom practice of productive pedagogies of the Malaysian secondary school geography teacher. *Review of International Geographical Education Online (RIGEO)*, 2(2), 146.

Altbach, P. G. (2008). The complex roles of universities in the period of globalization. In GUNI (Ed.), *Higher education at a time of transformation* (pp. 30–35). Basingstoke: Palgrave Macmillan.

Andrews, J. G. (2006). How we can resist corporatisation. *Academe*, 92(3), 16–19.

Anholt, S. (2007). What is competitive identity? In *Competitive identity* (pp. 1–23). London: Palgrave Macmillan.

Barney, J. (1991). Firm resources and sustained competitive advantage. *Journal of Management*, 17(1), 99–120.

Blackett, T. (2004). 1 What is a brand? Brands and branding. Retrieved from www.culturaldiplomacy.org/academy/pdf/research/books/nation_branding/Brands_And_Branding_-Rita_Clifton_And_John_Simmons.pdf#page=30.

Bok, D. (2009). *Universities in the marketplace: The commercialization of higher education.* Princeton, NJ: Princeton University Press.

Bolsmann, C., & Uys, T. (2001). Pre-empting the challenges of transformation and marketisation of higher education: A case study of the Rand Afrikaans University. *Society in Transition*, 32(2), 173–185.

Bostock, S. J. (1998). Constructivism in mass higher education: A case study. *British Journal of Educational Technology*, 29(3), 225–240.

Boyer, E. L. (1990). *Scholarship reconsidered: Priorities of the professoriate.* Princeton, NJ: Princeton University Press.

Brakus, J. J., Schmitt, B. H., & Zarantonello, L. (2009). Brand experience: What is it? How is it measured? Does it affect loyalty?*Journal of Marketing*, 73(3), 52–68.

Brownlee, M. (2014). Irreconcilable differences: The corporatisation of Canadian universities. (PhD thesis). Retrieved from https://curve.carleton.ca/system/files/etd/b945d1f1-64d4-40eb-92d2-1a29effe0f76/etd_pdf/2fbce6a2de5f5de090062ca7af0a4b1e/brownlee-irreconcilabledifferencesthecorporatization.pdf.

Chapleo, C. (2005). Do universities have "successful" brands? *International Journal of Educational Advancement*, 6(1), 54–64.

Chapleo, C. (2007). Barriers to brand building in UK universities. *International Journal of Nonprofit and Voluntary Sector Marketing*, 12(1), 23–32.

Chapleo, C. (2010). What defines 'successful' university brands? *International Journal of Public Sector Management*, 23(2), 169–183.

Chen, S. H., Wang, H. H., & Yang, K. J. (2009). Establishment and application of performance measure indicators for universities. *The TQM Journal*, 21(3), 220–235.

Clayson, D. E., & Haley, D. A. (2005). Marketing models in education: Students as customers, products, or partners. *Marketing Education Review*, 15(1), 1–10.

Cox, R. W. (2013). The corporatisation of higher education. *Class, Race and Corporate power*, 1(1). Retrieved from: http://digitalcommons.fiu.edu/classracecorporatepower/vol1/iss1/8.

Elzinga, Kenneth G. (1981). Defining geographic market boundaries. *Antitrust Bull*, 26(1981), 739.

Fongwa, N. N., & Wangenge-Ouma S. N. G. (2016). The scholarship of university-community engagement: Interrogating Boyer's model. *International Journal of Educational Development*, 49, 126–133.

Furedi, F. (2012). Introduction to the marketisation of higher education and the student as consumer. In M. Molesworth, R. Scullion, & E. Nixon (Eds.), *The marketisation of higher education and the student as consumer*. London: Routledge.

Gibbs, P. (2002). From the invisible hand to the invisible handshake: Marketing higher education. *Research in Post-Compulsory Education*, 7(3), 325–338.

Gibbs, P. (2012). Adopting consumer time and the marketing of higher education. In M. Molesworth, R. Scullion, & E. Nixon (Eds.), *The marketisation of higher education and the student as consumer*. London: Routledge.

Gibbs, P., & Murphy, P. (2009). Ethical marketing of higher education. *Higher Education Management and Policy*, 21(3), 75–90.

Grönroos, C. (1989). Defining marketing: A market-oriented approach. *European Journal of Marketing*, 23(1), 52–60.

Hemsley-Brown, J., & Goonawardana, S. (2007). Brand harmonization in the international higher education market. *Journal of Business Research*, 60(9), 942–948.

Hemsley-Brown, J., & Oplatka, I. (2006). Universities in a competitive global marketplace: A systematic review of the literature on higher education marketing. *International Journal of Public Sector Management*, 19(4), 316–338.

Herman, D. (2000). Introducing short-term brands: A new branding tool for a new consumer reality. *Journal of Brand Management*, 7(5), 330–340.

Ivy, J. (2001). Higher education institution image: A correspondence analysis approach. *International Journal of Educational Management*, 15(6), 276–282.

Ivy, J. (2008). A new higher education marketing mix: The 7Ps for MBA marketing. *International Journal of Educational Management*, 22(4), 288–299. doi:10.1108/09513540810875635.

Kajubi, S. (1992). Financing of higher education in Uganda. *Higher Education*, 23(4), 433–441.

Kelchtermans, G. (1999). Narrative-biographical research on teachers' professional development: Exemplifying a methodological research procedure. Retrieved from https://files.eric.ed.gov/fulltext/ED432582.pdf.

Keller, K. L. (2002). Branding and brand equity. In B. Weitz & R. Wensley (Eds.), *Handbook of marketing* (pp. 151–178). London: Sage.

Knight, J., & Woldegiorgis, E. T. (Eds.). (2017). *Regionalization of African higher education: Progress and prospects*. Dordrecht: Springer.

Kotler, P., & Kotler, P. (1982). *Marketing for nonprofit organizations* (Vol. 2). Englewood Cliffs, NJ: Prentice-Hall.

Lingard, B. (2007). Pedagogies of indifference. *International Journal of Inclusive Education*, 11(3), 245–266.

Mamdani, M. (2007). *Scholars in the marketplace: The dilemma of neo-liberal reform at Makerere University, 1989–2005*. Dakar: Codesria.

Mamdani, M. (2008). Higher Education, the state, and the marketplace. *Journal of Higher Education in Africa*, 6(1), 1–10.

Mampaey, J., Huisman, J., & Seeber, M. (2015). Branding of Flemish higher education institutions: A strategic balance perspective. *Higher Education Research & Development*, 34(6), 1178–1191.

Marginson, S., & Van der Wende, M. (2007). Globalisation and Higher Education. OECD education working papers, no. 8. OECD Publishing (NJ1). Retrieved from doi:10.1787/173831738240.

Maringe, F. (2005). Interrogating the crisis in higher education marketing: The CORD model. *International Journal of Educational Management*, 19(7), 564–578.

Maringe, F., & Foskett, N. (2012). Introduction: Globalisation and universities. In *Globalisation and internationalisation of higher education: Theoretical, strategic and management perspectives*. London: Continuum.

Maringe, F., & Gibbs, P. (2009). *Marketing higher education: Theory and practice*. London: McGraw-Hill Education.

Mathooko, F. M., & Ogutu, M. (2014). The extent to which public universities in Kenya experience managerial and environmental challenges. *European Journal of Business and Management*, 6(5).

Merriam, S. B. (1998). *Qualitative research and case study applications in education* (Revised and expanded from *Case study research in education*). San Francisco, CA: Jossey-Bass.

Mogaji, E. (2019). Branding private universities in Africa: An unexplored territory. Research Agenda Working Papers, 2019(9), pp. 120–148.

Molesworth, M., Scullion, R., & Nixon, E. (2010). *The marketisation of higher education and the student as consumer*. London: Routledge.

Ndofirepi, E., Farinloye, T., & Mogaji, E. (2020). Marketing mix in a heterogenous higher education market: A case of Africa. In E. Mogaji, F. Maringe, & R. E. Hinson (Eds.), *Understanding the higher education market in Africa*. London: Routledge.

Ogachi, O. (2009).Internationalization vs regionalization of higher education in East Africa and the challenges of quality assurance and knowledge production. *Higher Education Policy*, 22(3), 331–347.

Olukoju, A. (2004). The crisis of research and academic publishing in Nigerian universities. In *African universities in the twenty-first century, Vol. 2, Knowledge and society*. Dakar: Codesria.

Patton, M. Q. (2002). Two decades of developments in qualitative inquiry: A personal, experiential perspective. *Qualitative Social Work*, 1(3), 261–283.

Porter, M. E. (1985). *Competitive advantage: Creating and sustaining superior performance*. New York: Free Press.

Readings, B. (1996). *The university in ruins*. Cambridge, MA: Harvard University Press.

Rolfe, G. (2013). *The university in dissent: Scholarship in the corporate university*. London: Routledge.

Saldaña, J. (2015). *The coding manual for qualitative researchers*. Thousand Oaks, CA: Sage.

Sanderson, D. M., & Watters, J. J. (2006). The corporatisation of higher education: A question of balance. In S. Debowski (Ed.), *Higher education research and development society of Australia annual conference*, 10–12 July 2006, Perth, Western Australia. Retrieved from http://eprints.qut.edu.au/.

Sehoole, C. T. (2004). Trade-in educational services: Reflection on the African and South African higher education system. *Journal of Studies in International Education*, 8(3), 297–316.

Teferra, D., & Altbach, P. G. (2004) *African higher education: Challenges for the 21st century*. *Higher Education*, 47(1), 21–50.

Toma, J. D. (2003). *Football U.: Spectator sports in the life of the American university*. Ann Arbor: University of Michigan Press.

Tuchman, G. (2009). *Wannabe U: Inside the corporate university*. Chicago: University of Chicago Press.

Wæraas, A., & Solbakk, M. N. (2009). Defining the essence of a university: Lessons from higher education branding. *Higher Education*, 57(4), 449.

Weiber, R., & Kollmann, T. (1998). Competitive advantages in virtual markets-perspectives of 'information-based marketing' in cyberspace. *European Journal of Marketing, 32*(7/8), 603–615.

Yahaya, M., & Abdullah, I. H. (2004). Challenges of corporatisation and globalisation: Educational reform in tertiary education. HERDSA 2004 Conference, Transforming knowledge into wisdom: Holistic approaches to teaching and learning, Sarawak, Malaysia, July. Retrieved from https://s3.amazonaws.com/academia.edu.documents/

5427018/a069-jt.pdf?response-content-disposition=inline%3B%20filename%3DChall
enges_of_corporatisation_and_global.pdf&X-Amz-Algorithm=AWS4-HMAC-SHA2
56&X-Amz-Credential=AKIAIWOWYYGZ2Y53UL3A%2F20191103%2Fus-east-1
%2Fs3%2Faws4_request&X-Amz-Date=20191103T135808Z&X-Amz-Expires=360
0&X-Amz-SignedHeaders=host&X-Amz-Signature=4aae6ded5a62a1da771c37a2b10
ca70123369a3bd4d5d26793832d859661d6bc.

4 Digital marketing of higher education marketing in Africa

Challenges, prospects, and opportunities

S Pee Vululleh

Introduction

Higher education marketing has been on the increase in the past few decades, giving the increasing need to use effective marketing communication and strategies, which is an ideal way of maximising the potential of a university (Newman & Jahdi, 2009). Further and higher education marketing have witnessed a paradigm shift in recent years as universities move beyond traditional marketing strategies towards digital and personalised marketing. According to Lopes (2014), the higher education sector has been more affected in recent years by technological revolution with the most significant changes occurring, particularly in their online campaign or communication method.

Using technology in a marketing campaign for higher education institution is growing (Badwan et al., 2017). Over the past decades, marketing of higher education has taken new trends with online space, using a variety of new platforms for engaging and communicating with external partners and prospective students. Literature has shown that there is a growing need to use practical marketing tools, communications, and strategies in higher education to engage with students (Neier & Zayer, 2015; Mogaji & Yoon, 2019); however, there is still a lack of insight and empirical evidence about how African universities are adopting digital communications for their marketing strategies.

While some higher education institutions still report success in some traditional marketing techniques, such as open days, there are still challenges in adopting digital marketing communications in marketing African universities. Even though challenges with technology adoption in Africa are recognised (Farinloye, Mogaji, & Kuika Watat, 2020), there are still opportunities to develop and implement digital communication strategies. A digital strategy is now one of the essential platforms used in higher education marketing and recruitment process around the world, African universities should not be left behind as they offer to recruit talented prospective students from around the world. (Mufutumarl, Greljn, Aarts, & Oyewole, 2010; Sheikh, 2017).

Recognising the increasingly important role that digital marketing is playing in student recruitment and the challenges of African universities, this chapter aims explicitly to identify and explore the critical challenges of higher education marketing in Africa and provide recommendations for university marketing managers and administrators and policymakers which address the identified challenges. This study offers both theoretical and managerial implications for academic researchers and university managers, which address effective planning, customer relationship management, and widening participation for students.

The subsequent section of this chapter offers a more in-depth insight into the challenges of higher education marketing in Africa. The following section offers a broad recommendation to address these challenges, which include effective planning, customer relationship management, and an integrated marketing approach. The last section offers a conclusion and highlights the contribution of the chapter.

Challenges of higher education marketing in Africa

As African universities aim to connect with prospective students and send messages that tend to promote their plates and tailor to their policy for admission procedures, the prospects to enrol and be successful are a huge hurdle to overcome (Manning, 2015; Wilson, 2018). Various challenges are militating against the successful integration of most social media for strategic communications in Africa (Farinloye et al., 2020).

Inadequate computer literacy and primary language (i.e. English or French) barrier among the population also poses a significant challenge to the implementation of higher education marketing campaign. The student inability to perform technology-related tasks is another barrier in the marketing process – the more confidence in skills and knowledge the students are in using computer and the Internet, the more they might accept and explore more about the brand for their purposes (Sarker, Davis, & Tiropanis, n. d.; Vululleh, 2019). The linguistic mismatch is another challenge towards the process of strategic communications with stakeholders in Africa. (Farinloye et al., 2020). In some regions of Tunisia and Algeria students are taught in Arabic while some books are written in French instead of English which is a universal language (Ndofirepi, Farinloye, & Mogaji, 2020). In the South of Africa, especially South Africa, where the constitution recognises 11 official languages, the adopted language of communication can pose a challenge as they try to engage with stakeholders.

Furthermore, additional challenges in using social media are the strict policy restriction on what can be communicated and who should communicate the information. It is important to keep promises and maintain consistency in messaging because campaign easily can be damaged than it can be successfully built. Delivering on the university's promise is one of the most important aspects of branding, which can actualise the brand messages communicated to prospective students and donor agencies. There is a need to ensure that the institution experience is consistent with the promise. Inconsistency can stand out if the institution does not deliver on its promises (Mater, 2007).

On the flip side, generating a comprehensive marketing plan might be different from the successful implementation of the plan. In particular, there is a need for information technology and human resources; these can seem as significant challenges in the implementation of marketing plan in colleges and universities in Africa where there is limited funding for the institutions (Ndofirepi, Farinloye, & Mogaji, 2020). Challenges of investment, financial difficulty, and the rise in tuitions and fees are also paramount in higher education operations, which authorities need to work around not to scare prospective students away amicably. This increased need for investment and finances in higher education marketing regarding tuitions and fees might continue to be an upsurge in future years, as competition for students intensifies locally and internationally, with the number of students reducing because of high annual fees. It is estimated that higher education institutions spend at least 0.75% of their revenue on marketing, to include staff costs, which might even increase over the next few years. The more staff and students are recruited, the more budget is allocated to marketing promotional activities (Mater, 2007).

Farinloye, Wayne, Mogaji, and Kuika Watat (2020) identified a lack of motivation by African universities to engage on social media. There are challenges with the content to be updated, the frequency and relevance of the content. Marketing to reach prospective students is often limited because the universities are oversubscribed. If universities, especially the public universities, do not market, they are still guaranteed to recruit their students. Olaleye, Sanusi, Ukpabi, and Okunoye (2018) also reiterated this lack of interest and effort in their exploration of Nigerian universities' websites which they identified challenges with ease of use, processing speed, aesthetic design, and interactive responsiveness of the websites.

Internet bandwidth still poses a challenge in developing and integrating effective online and digital marketing communication in Africa. Africa is still considered an emerging market, with the rate of Internet penetration still quite low as compared to its Western counterparts (Wawira, 2017). As of June 2019, Internet World Stats estimates a 39.8% Internet penetration rate in Africa, contributing to only 11.9% of the world users (IWS, 2019). This challenge means that most people are still offline, while the university is willing to engage, the challenges of Internet bandwidth inhibits the stakeholders, especially the prospective students who have limited access to the Internet (Farinloye, Mogaji, & Kuika Watat, 2020).

Effective planning and marketing management

Effective marketing planning and management is an important work higher education institution needs to enable them to manage a unified marketing message, which helps to achieve an advantage in recruiting and building loyalty amongst students, staff, and donors. Presenting the brand successfully to potential applicants requires strategic planning and using practical tools. Higher education institutions in Africa should set challenging targets and marketing needs for promoting their brands to maintain a high level of recruitment drive with a focus on the 'inside out', which creates the need to understand the school marketplace and its future direction that can impact the institutions. Diversity in employment is crucial to marketing strategy. While it might be true that it is advisable in most instances to hire many marketing staff in higher education institutions from homegrown sector whose experiences are much more from within the sector, it is equally important to extend employment to other marketing-orientated organisations to access different skills from other markets (Annandale, 2011).

Researchers have found that as higher education institutions forge for increases in investing in marketing activity, they need to focus more attention on outcomes and how greater effectiveness can be achieved, and where resources can be best deployed to consider first in the universities marketing plans (Annandale, 2011; Noaman, 2012). To achieve this goal, there is a need for effective marketing plans and implementation strategies that will provide a drastic overhaul of the higher education institutions current operations with a positive expectation of student preferences being addressed. In addition to the drastic overhaul of the current operations at the universities in Africa, other options are crucially helpful to use in reaching the target audience. Higher education institutions in Africa should learn to use a system of technology to send personalised communications to individuals with inquiries, making web analytics available to determine the needs of prospective students before they attempt to fill out inquiry forms. Furthermore, they should align marketing communication with their target students' expectations before exploring the website, customising their experiences to the extent that adjusts to their needs (Bram, 2009).

Additionally, the old way of periodic reviews of campaign results should be examined in a new way to determine marketing resource allocation by employing the necessary mechanisms and expertise to harness the data captured and current activities based on constant and dependable data analysis. This requires that marketing departments must have the needed sophisticated expertise put in place, with collaboration between systems and reporting as prospective students research the institutions – expanding their analytical know-how and aligning them with outreach and admissions activities. Marketing departments at higher education institutions in Africa need to plan their campaign communications to influence a variety of mobile devices, which can interpret interactive and clear understanding of the institutions throughout enrolment experiences. In another perspective, reflecting on data gathered during pre-enrolment communication might help drive relevant communication and services to students as they work to completion of their educational journey.

Students' information is one of the potential instruments to guide and manage marketing decisions in a variety of ways, including staff ability and availability to produce information that can be utilised throughout the student educational process – from enrolment to graduation. Applying data to ongoing decision-making might help the marketing department to listen to future and current students and respond to their needs. As it is one of their responsibilities to manage enrolment process at the university, they must maintain marketing effort to elevate the prominence of the institutions in representing the voice of potential students in strategic decisions about the institutions. The marketing department needs to communicate the institutions' promises, which ensure that the actual messages and experiences of the universities are being sent out and delivered more tangibly.

The role of marketing at the higher education setting should, in most cases centre around answering concerns or questions such as: What courses should the universities offer? How should the courses be priced? Where (i.e. place, environment) should the courses be offered (including online and on-ground extended campuses)? What message or story should be sent out to prospective students and staff (Maue, 2015; Morrison, 2013)? Marketing departments are also concerned about how higher education institutions can expand their programmes offerings to attract new students, and how many students should be enrolled at a given period. Also, what are the strategies for tuition pricing for different undergraduate and graduate programmes? Should the tuition be the same for all programmes or offer tiered pricing? Also, one of their primary concerns is the concern for where and when the programmes should be offered, which is paramount in the marketing decision-making – whether offer online courses and if so, which programmes best translate to online. An attempt to answer these complicated questions and concerns requires much discussion and many perspectives. Decisions about those concerns might positively or negatively affect all aspects of the higher education institutions one way or the other, which colleges and universities in Africa are of no exception. Higher education institutions in Africa marketing role should typically focus on determining when, where, and how their institutions tell their compelling stories, so they can attract the best students and achieve their fundraising goals (Maue, 2015). The goal of marketing should also be to understand the behaviours of the students and deliver on the promise.

With the rapid growth of educational needs in Africa, higher education institutions must focus on marketing more than has been in the past decades to invest significant time and money to make reliable institutional contacts and create positions to direct the universities in focusing on marketing campaigns. For example, Northwestern University in the US creates chief marketing officer (CMO) positions and make the marketing campaign a core function of the institution (USAID, 2014). Similarly, Purdue University decided to spend and make a significant financial investment in the past years to promote a marketing campaign. They also need to rely on and use research results to determine who, how, and where they should reach their audiences. Higher education institutions in Africa should also use some form of social media such as establishing Facebook or Twitter accounts in their marketing campaign in an attempt to appeal personally to prospective students – posting photos and videos to share campus events and upgrading housing and financial aid opportunities to attract students.

Customer relationship management (CRM) approach

A customer relationship management (CRM) approach might be adopted to allow higher education institutions in Africa to manage their relationships with prospective students, current students, and alumni. Universities in Africa need to adopt and practise robust CRM strategies and then fit the campaign messages to the strategies. In the context of higher education institutions marketing operations, CRM describes the tools, methodologies, and strategies that are used in managing the universities relationships with applicants, which encompasses tools such as databases, software, and Internet capabilities that can help the institutions to manage their relationships in an organised manner. Authors like Bram (2009) and Noaman (2012) refer to higher education CRM system as a tool that can be used for contacting prospective student information management, tuition and fees management, and graduate's information management, and more, merely aiming at improving the institutions' relationships with others to boost the marketing agenda.

According to Bram (2009), these customer relationship management tools can simplify and automate contacting applicants and potential staff members for the universities and provide the institutions with a clear record of what the past communication methods have included, as well as ensuring that everyone on the team is working in collaboration and on the same page. Some of that software would allow the universities in Africa even to send out automatic emails or newsletters, and at the same time manage relationships and interactions with potential applicants – staying connected to students and parents and improve profitability. The CRM system can be set up in three perspectives in the following organised forms: as a technology, as a strategy, and as a process, where marketing staff can use the technological approach to record, report, and analyse interactions between the higher education institutions and the outside users. On the other hand, CRM as a strategy can be used to manage the relationships with the applicants and potential partners in education; and the process perspective, the universities can adopt to nurture and manage those relationships in the campaign process. That software will help the institutions to record applicants contact information such as website social media profile, email, and telephone. This can also help in pulling in other information, such as current and recent news about the universities' activities – storing and organising relevant information about potential applicants' personal preferences to present a complete record of individuals and the universities, providing a better understanding of the relationships over time. Exploring those sorts of contacts can provide an enabling environment for higher education institutions to deepen their relationships and promote their brands with prospective students. A sound CRM system might help to manage relationships fully and keeps track of prospects and what to improve on, considering crucial issues such as acquisition and retention.

Using an internal social network to support marketing platform

There is a wise saying that 'Fire burns the spot it starts from before spreading.' To successfully win prospective students and partners to the university, administrators running higher education institutions in Africa must have a cordial and collaborative internal communication systems amongst the university families, where the students, professors, executives, directors, and employees are working together internally – sharing ideas possibly about their marketing campaign process. When the university is organised in such a collaborative form and manner, they are bound to succeed in their marketing campaign. Hanover Research (2014) consents that higher education institutions that communicate via social networks should also involve their divisions (faculties) in the implementation of their marketing strategies.

Using internal social networks to promote marketing campaign could probably be one of the best options for universities in Africa and perhaps elsewhere, compared to other public access social networks like Facebook. The networks will be visible only to the internal public, which ensures that the information is more focused and can be better controlled by universities marketing department before it goes out to the public ((Lopes, 2014). Each university might use these options in trusting and building relationships with their in-house family which fosters collaborative and cooperative efforts in speaking with one voice to the outside world in their campaign activities about the programmes and services offered at the university.

Furthermore, given the heterogeneous nature of the target audience of higher education institutions which includes students, instructional faculty, support staff, executives, and prospective students, they must invest in efforts to improve their internal communication system. This might help to narrow the gaps in communication and information flows. Using internal social networks as a vehicle for sharing and encouraging the exchange of views can promote collaboration among the heterogeneous population in support of their marketing campaign. Similarly, higher education institutions in Africa should adopt some tools, for example, EdTechReview (ETR) (http://edtechreview.in), which is a community of education technology that involves every participant to connect online to utilise and share knowledge about the best ways technology can provide and improve information sharing to prospective students. This tool can be used to add images and information sharing room where individuals can chat online and bookmarks essential dates regarding the institution's upcoming activities (EdTechReview, 2013).

In another perspective, higher education institutions in Africa can choose to use Twiducate as part of their communication means, which is a social networking tool that their universities might use to learn outside the campuses. This social platform helps universities to create their workspace where they can connect with desired members and send messages to potential students about their institutions. In another study, Lopes (2014) identifies Ning as another social network tool which can offer the appropriate context for creating a tailored experience for communication for the members of the university community and prospective students. For example, Dartmouth University chose to use Ning to improve the connection between different departments of the university, prospective students, and to address issues that may arise from internal communication.

As a result of technological revolution and the complexity in connecting and attracting more students from outside, higher education institutions in Africa should also consider integrating other digital tools such as Linkedin, YouTube, Twitter, newsletters and webinars as supporting arms in the process (Mogaji, 2018, Gökerik et al., 2018). In order to successfully use social networks as tools to support marketing effort, the universities should consider the following: (i) trust for users' privacy, security, personal and professional information; (ii) the practice of ethical behaviour; (iii) and involving their faculties and current students in the implementation of the marketing strategies. There should be an increasing effort towards using and developing digital platforms at universities nowadays to improve communication system to support their marketing campaigns – encouraging the involvement of the staff; sharing and promoting information amongst departments, and coordinating programmes and events.

The university homepage is one of the critical components in the students' experience, which they can use to make intelligent decisions about whether to attend or not (Mogaji, 2016). The higher education institutions homepage must be able to present and appeal to a diverse range of visitors, maintaining the challenge of consistency in the marketing approach. Website navigation should be encouraging, and an integral component where the universities can ensure their homepages are a laid out portal to all of the contents that students are looking for, featuring elements such as navigation bars, slideshows, and multimedia contents. It must also ensure 'calls to action' for instance 'Apply Now' buttons to prompt the navigators to action.

Integrated marketing approach

Higher education institutions in Africa should not only rely on social media for engaging with stakeholders; effort should be towards an integrated marketing strategy which includes social media and other traditional media to reach the stakeholders. In an effort to succeed in marketing campaigns, higher education institutions marketing teams must be consistent across all departments and platforms and integrate current and effective way to monitor digital channels and to quickly respond to negative comments that are tantamount to distracting prospective students looking for college or university to attend (Mushemeza, 2016; Wilson, 2018). They further need to identify the prospects and possibly use CRM to collect, manage, and use student data to personalise communications.

As a result of marketing challenges, higher education institutions should increasingly develop meaningful promotion strategies, where colleges and universities can justify a reputation of excellence and attract the most suitable students. This reputation will create significant value for subject areas, methods of delivery and length of courses. There is a need for an outside-in approach, a situation where the institution takes prospective students' values as its starting and end, focusing on creating and nurturing them by providing high calibre customership and putting themselves in the position of the students. On the other hand, the inside-out perspective, which focuses on the institution's strengths and taking account of resources first, might be limiting and induce slowness in adopting changes. Universities and colleges in Africa should leverage multiple angles to maximise growth, encouraging and using alumni networks and current students as ambassadors to attract more considerable public attention.

Marketing of higher education has changed in recent years with the use of online space, using a variety of different platforms for external communication (Grossma, 2013). In particular, the use of social media and digital marketing such as Twitter, Facebook, and YouTube have enabled institutions to make a more significant improvement in their engagements. Besides, several critical platforms for prospective students need to be organised to identify various campus programmes including but not limited to campus visit for high school students by admission representatives; off-campus meetings for potential students and their parents; encouraging prospective students to apply on the admissions website; and routine contacts by admission's office to assess student reactions to financial aid awards and housing. Although higher education institutions might rely on social media and digital presence nowadays to engage students, it is still recognised that traditional forms of outreach are still effective and popular combination for recruitment tools to increase enrolments. Also, other practical tools and tactics institutions need to use for engagement are radio and running television ads, asking current students and alumni for applicant referrals and online college fairs.

Furthermore, some institutions have elected to attract international students by hiring companies such as Pearson to engage in the direct targeting of international students. The company's effort, along with the institution website, gives student's information to the universities that partner with Pearson. For example, literature indicates that the United States has been successful in recruiting international students, particularly Chinese students, which has increased the number of international student enrolments in the US in recent years, with considerable number of students coming from Saudi Arabia, Kuwait, Iran, China, and Brazil (Hanover Research, 2014). The US achieves these numbers because they maintain their presence at conferences and job fairs overseas, offering financial aid packages to international students, as well as improving social media outreach efforts. Engaging in similar efforts by the higher education institutions in Africa would help to improve their enrolments.

Higher education institutions need to make their programmes more attractive to prospective students by improving the quality of the methods and tools selected. Some of the most common practices should take into consideration designing highly flexible programmes that will meet the needs of students, including expansion in offerings for financial aid and increasing the number of options for online courses. There is a need also to provide flexibility for transfer credits for students. Some higher education institutions might choose to relax standards in the area such as required language proficiency, in favour of admitting those students that exhibit strong academic backgrounds to boost their international enrolments. For example, the US institutions have been in recent years admitting international students with weak language skills (but strong academic skills) on conditional bases who can strengthen their language abilities once they are admitted. Position the university towards widening participation might increasingly help to boost enrolment, but universities must seek to pursue a detailed understanding of incoming student credentials to avoid problems of falsified credentials. University admission officesr should rely on education agents and consultants (based on location) that verify international students' credentials before admission.

Using online education programmes have become an emerging market as one of the popular higher education efforts to conduct classes. It widens participation for students who may otherwise not have attended a university (Mufutumarl, Greljn, Aarts, & Oyewole, 2010). With the development of electronic learning (E-learning), universities in Africa can reach out to more prospective students as classes are conducted, or learning can take place using the Internet – allowing live lectures, video conferencing, and emails possible anywhere and anytime accessible to every student at the same time (Vululleh, 2019). As a result of this technological development, higher education institutions can use this method to support their marketing campaign to tell their stories of opportunities for everyone irrespective of their location (Mogaji, 2019). This innovation brings utterly new development and ways into the field of education, explicitly teaching and learning the process and the innovation associated with technology.

Conclusion

There is no doubt that higher education institutions are in more competition nowadays than ever. They are running a competition to be the first to win and connect with prospective students. It is not only the for-profits but also many non-profit institutions must beef up their advertising budgets and marketing departments to actively hold onto their corners of the market. This chapter identifies the challenges of marketing higher education in Africa and offers critical strategic, practical implications to address these challenges.

As noted by Morrison (2013) that while some universities are still reporting that traditional marketing techniques are still thriving in the methods of recruiting students because of limited technology in some parts of the world, especially in African countries and universities, most universities are using digital marketing strategies as the most effective means of connecting with prospective students. Having these combined marketing agendas for recruitment is significant to successful African university brands.

The chapter recognises that higher education institutions are in the business of looking for new ways to change the trends they use to recruit new students to maintain the enrolment numbers they need to allow them to benefit, operate, and control efficiently, which colleges and universities in Africa are of no exception. It is no doubt that most schools and private homes in Africa have little or no access to the necessary technology, including the Internet and electricity. Because the use of technology is still limited in some parts of African countries, traditional marketing strategies such as newspaper advertisements and campus visit are can still be used by university authorities and marketing departments to engage potential students.

Higher education institutions in Africa must commit to maintaining and improving quality communications in their campaign messages. Effective planning and customer relationship management are essentials. Universities should be presenting facts derived from applicant data evidence, accounting for recruitment of professors and agreements with prestigious partners, which demonstrates the quality of excellence of the institution and strengthens its brand (Mater, 2007). While it might be essential to ensure consistency in strategies and stated goals in campaign messages, it is also essential to carefully monitor the consistency not only of the messages expressed but also those of the professors and students, all communicating the brand image with the same voice. There are opportunities for collecting data, and student learning analytics to shape student experiences and enhance, marketing communication, perhaps article intelligence can play a crucial role (Dwivedi et al., 2019).

From an academic standpoint, this chapter has relevant contributions to the literature, including several research domains involved, for example, online communication, social networks, internal communication, and higher education. In another perspective, it is geared toward strengthening colleges and universities in Africa to identify some of the main challenges they face in promoting their universities. Furthermore, it helps to overcome the shortcoming in marketing communications and to encourage prospective student satisfaction. Although it might be true that the primary purpose of marketing communication is to improve the universities' relationships and contacts with prospective students, plans should be developed and aligned with the cultural dimensions of each university (i.e. public university, private university, non-profit university, and for-profit university), with the priorities and needs of their institutions.

Marketing departments must be concerned about how higher education institutions can expand their programmes offerings to attract new students and how many students should be enrolled at a given period (Maue, 2015). Besides, the strategies for tuition pricing for different undergraduate and graduate programmes should be included in the plan indicating if tuition should be the same for all programmes or offer tiered pricing. In selling the brand, the institution needs to determine where and when the programs should be offered, which is paramount in marketing decision-making. Higher education institutions in Africa marketing role should typically focus on determining when, where, and how their institutions tell their compelling stories, so they can attract the best students, deliver on the promise and achieve their fundraising goals. As universities seek the need for diverse and inclusive student base, successful marketing efforts should become one of the essential activities for the higher education institutions, which tends to foster increasing enrolment and expand fundraising plans.

References

Annandale, W. (2013). Higher education marketing: What a difference a year makes – or does it?*The Guardian*. Retrieved from www.theguardian.com/higher-education-network/blog/2013/feb/04/higher-education-marketing-predications-2013.

Annandale, W. (2011). Five predictions for the future of higher education marketing. *The Guardian*. Retrieved from www.theguardian.com/higher-education-network/2011/nov/28/five-predictions-higher-education-marketing.

Badwan, J. J., Al Shobaki, M. J., Naser, S. S. A., & Amuna, Y. M. A. (2017). Adopting technology for customer relationship management in higher educational institutions. *International Journal of Engineering and Information Systems*, 1(1), 20–28.

Bee, F. K. (2011). Cooperative education in Africa: Opportunities and challenges. ICA Global Research Conference, International Cooperative Alliance. Retrieved from www.helsinki.fi/ruralia/materiaalit/ICA2011/Bee.pdf.

Bram, T. (2009). The 10 best customer relationship management (CRM) tools. *Smartlife*. Retrieved from http://smartlifeblog.com/the-10-best-customer-relationship-management-crm-tools/.

Dwivedi, Y. K., Hughes, L., Ismagilova, E., Aarts, G., Coombs, C., Crick, T., ... & Galanos, V. (2019). Artificial Intelligence (AI): Multidisciplinary perspectives on emerging challenges, opportunities, and agenda for research, practice and policy. *International Journal of Information Management*. doi:10.1016/j.ijinfomgt.2019.08.002.

EdTechReview (2013). Twiducate-social network for schools. EdTechReview. Retrieved from http://edtechreview.in/reviews/234-twiducate-social-network-for-schools.

Farinloye, T., Wayne, T., Mogaji, E., & Kuika Watat, J. (2020). Social media for universities' strategic communication. In E. Mogaji, F. Maringe, & R. E. Hinson (Eds.), *Strategic marketing of higher education in Africa*. London: Routledge.

Gökerik, M., Gürbüz, A., Erkan, I., Mogaji, E., & Sap, S. (2018). Surprise me with your ads! The impacts of guerrilla marketing in social media on brand image. *Asia Pacific Journal of Marketing and Logistics*, 30(5), 1222–1238.

Grossma, D. (2013). Marketing higher education: A historical perspective. The Evolution, A Destiny Solutions Illumination. Retrieved from https://evolllution.com/opinions/marketing-higher-education-historical-perspective/.

Hanover Research. (2014). Trends in higher education marketing, recruitment, and technology. Academy Administration Practice. Retrieved from www.hanoverresearch.com/media/Trends-in-Higher-Education-Marketing-Recruitment-and-Technology-2.pdf.

IWS. (2019). Internet in Africa. Internet World Stats. Retrieved from https://www.internetworldstats.com/africa.htm.

Keystone Academic Solutions. (2017). Higher education marketing. Retrieved from www.keystoneacademic.com/higher-ed-marketing.

Lopes, T. A. (2014). How can a corporate brand (of higher education) benefit from social networks in its internal communication strategy? The case of Catholic University of

Portugal-Porto. Academia. Retrieved from www.academia.edu/7169201/How_can_a_corporate_brand_of_higher_education_benefit_from_social_networks_in_its_internal_communication_strategy_The_case_of_Catholic_University_of_Portugal_-Porto.

Manning, K. (2015). Contemporary challenges facing American higher education. *HuffPost*. Retrieved from www.huffingtonpost.com/dr-kevin-manning/contemporary-challenges-facing-american-higher-educaiton_b_6879416.html.

Maslowsky, C. (2013). Five ways higher education marketing will change in 10 years. The Evolution, A Destiny Solutions Illumination. Retrieved from https://evolllution.com/opinions/ways-higher-education-marketing-change-10-years/.

Mater, P. (2007). Higher education quality assurance in Sub-Saharan Africa status, challenges, opportunities, and promising practices. World Bank Working Papers. Retrieved from http://siteresources.worldbank.org/EDUCATION/Resources/278200-1099079877269/547664-1099079956815/WP124_QA_Higher_Edu_Africa.pdf.

Maue, D. (2015). Marketing in higher education: The 4 P's model. Inside Higher Ed. Retrieved from www.insidehighered.com/blogs/call-action-marketing-and-comm unications-higher-education/marketing-higher-education-4-p's.

Mogaji, E. (2016). University website design in international student recruitment: Some reflections. In T. Wu & V. Naidoo (Eds.), *International marketing of higher education* (pp. 99–117). New York: Palgrave Macmillan.

Mogaji, E. (2018). With the integration of learning apps, what are Moodle's prospects? *Compass: Journal of Learning and Teaching*, 11(2). doi:10.21100/compass.v11i2.826.

Mogaji, E. (2019). Student Engagement with LinkedIn to enhance employability. In A. Diver (Ed.), *Employability via higher education: Sustainability as scholarship*. Cham: Springer. doi:10.1007/978-3-030-26342-3_21.

Mogaji, E., & Yoon, C. (2019). Thematic analysis of marketing messages in UK universities' prospectuses. *International Journal of Educational Management*, 33(7). doi:10.1108/IJEM-05-2018-0149.

Morrison, M. (2013). Why higher education needs marketing more than ever. AdAge. Retrieved from https://adage.com/article/cmo-strategy/higher-education-marketing/244820/.

Mufutumarl, N., Greljn, H., Aarts, H., & Oyewole, O. (2010). Higher education and globalisation: Challenges, threats and opportunities for Africa. ResearchGate. Retrieved from www.researchgate.net/publication/305688677_Higher_Education_a nd_globalisation_Challenges_threats_and_opportunities_for_Africa.

Mushemeza, E. D. (2016).Opportunities and challenges of academic staff in higher education in Africa. *International Journal of Higher Education*, 5(3). doi:10.5430/ijhe.v5n3p236.

Ndofirepi, E., Farinloye, T., & Mogaji, E. (2020). Marketing mix in a heterogenous higher education market: A case of Africa. In E. Mogaji, F. Maringe, & R. E. Hinson (Eds.), *Understanding the higher education market in Africa*. London: Routledge.

Neier, S., & Zayer, L. T. (2015). Students' perceptions and experiences of social media in higher education. *Journal of Marketing Education*, 37(3), 133–143.

Newman, S., & Jahdi, K. (2009). Marketisation of education: Marketing, rhetoric and reality. *Journal of Further and Higher Education*, 33(1), 1–11.

Noaman, A. (2012). Higher education marketing trends for 2012–2013: Ideas, Musings and Inspirations. Retrieved from https://aha.elliance.com/2012/08/09/higher-educa tion-marketing-trends-2012-2013/.

Olaleye, S. A., Sanusi, I. T., Ukpabi, D. C., & Okunoye, A. (2018). Evaluation of Nigeria universities websites quality: A comparative analysis. *Library Philosophy and*

Practice (e-journal), 1717. Retrieved from https://digitalcommons.unl.edu/libphilpra
c/1717.

Sarker, F., Davis, H., & Tiropanis, T. (n. d.). A review of higher education challenges
and data infrastructure responses. Retrieved from https://eprints.soton.ac.uk/271695/
1/A_Review_of_HE_challenges_and_data_infrastructure_responses.pdf.

Sheikh, Y. A. (2017). Higher education in India: Challenges and opportunities. *Journal of
Education and Practice*, 8(1), 2222–1735.

USAID. (2014). African higher education: Opportunities for transformative change for
sustainable development. Association for Public and Land-grant Universities,
Knowledge Center on Higher Education for African Development. Retrieved from
www.aplu.org/library/african-higher-education-opportunities-for-transformative-cha
nge-for-sustainable-development/file.

Vululleh, P. (2019). Review article: Challenges in implementing e-learning in underdeveloped countries. *International Journal of Recent Advances in Multidisciplinary Research*,
6(3), 4739–4741.

Wawira, J. (2017). Hospitality and tourism's relevance to African markets. Retrieved
from https://www.bizcommunity.africa/Article/410/373/164763.html.

Wilson, B. (2018). Higher education marketing challenges: Do you have the solution
for Gen Z? Sterling, Payment Technologies. Retrieved from www.devprojournal.
com/industry/education/higher-education-marketing-challenges-do-you-have-the-
solution-for-gen-z/.

5 Exploring the harmful effect of informational dissonance on students' recruitment

A Moroccan case study

Hicham Sebti and Sandrine Simon

Introduction

Like in the rest of Africa, the higher education sector in Morocco has undergone some significant change in the last ten years with a trend towards a certain *massification* and the rise of private universities. The expansion of these universities can be attributed to several factors such as changes to government educational policy in a context of declining government funding, unmet student demand in public universities and investments of the private sector in higher education. These new private universities attempt to provide what cannot be provided by the public sector.

Contrary to public universities, private universities are well aware of the importance of business issues to stay viable and competitive (Mustafa et al., 2018). Student enrolment serves as 'the lifeblood of colleges and universities' (Kinzie et al., 2004, p. 4). Consequently, 'the need to understand how prospective students decide which higher education institution to attend is becoming of paramount importance as the policy context for higher education moves towards market-based systems in many countries' (McManus et al., 2017, p. 2). Although the level of market orientation remains low within higher education institutions in Morocco, over the last few years, there has been a growing awareness of the need for a marketing strategy. Progressively, marketing has become a central issue and a critical function to the survival of a university. From a consumer behaviour perspective (Craig-Lees et al., 1995), higher education institution making a choice is a complex decision (Angulo et al., 2010). So far, this choice-making process has been poorly explored in the Moroccan, North African and the Arab world context (Mustafa et al., 2018). This chapter, therefore, attempts to tackle this problem.

Marketing studies have shown that psychological discomfort regarding specific products or services can have a negative impact on consumers' purchasing behaviour (Hunt, 1970; Krishna, 2012). Such psychological state can be related to the notion of cognitive dissonance (Festinger, 1957), defined as a feeling of psychological discomfort of an individual when facing a cognitive inconsistency regarding own knowledge, opinions, values, and feelings. In this chapter, we argue that students, in their choice-making process, do experience informational dissonance and therefore can be confused when matching their mental representations with information on universities (Wiese, 1994).

Our contribution aims to provide a better understanding of student recruitment enrolment by tackling the issues of student choice-making process, when facing a situation of cognitive dissonance. The knowledge and insights emerging from this study will enable African marketers of institutions to have a greater understanding of what is likely to influence the behaviour of their prospective students. We suggest a few marketing practices that could help reduce the psychological inconsistency faced by students.

This chapter is structured into four parts. The first part presents the theoretical framework, linking cognitive dissonance and marketing in higher education. The second part focuses on the methodological approach. The third part presents our main findings: first, we explore the rational and emotional issues that influence students' choice-making, second, some dissonance situations where information delivered mismatch with prospective students' representations. We thus describe three types of dissonance. First, space and time dissonance that reflects the inconsistency between the university and the students' prospective visions of the future of the job market. Second, programme content and teaching methodology dissonance that highlights the differences in visions regarding the learning process. Third, a programme purpose dissonance that reflects the search for assurance on the ROI of their studies. In the last part, we then submit a set of strategic and operational marketing recommendations aimed at reducing the three types of dissonance listed above.

Theoretical framework: marketing in higher education and the student choice-making process

Marketing in higher education primarily focuses on the service and product offered to the student, whereby the student is acquiring the knowledge and developing his or her skills in order to gain the qualification and enhance his/her career (Moogan, 2011). According to Levitt's (1980) description of marketing strategies, universities offerings can be classified into three levels. Firstly, the *core offer*: students are buying the benefits that a degree can provide in terms of employment, status, and lifestyle. Secondly, the *tangible attributes of the offer*: they include the physical layout of the campus, the library, laboratories, and sporting facilities. Finally, the *augmented product*: it is made of intangible attributes such as student loans, employment, or placement service.

Kotler and Keller (2015) presented a holistic marketing framework to show how the interaction between relevant actors (customers, company, and collaborators) and value-based activities (value exploration, value creation, and value delivery) helps to create, maintain, and renew customer value (Pinar et al., 2011). Thus, understanding students' needs and offering programs believed to be desired by the students (Maringe, 2005) are critical activities for a successful marketing mix in higher education.

Several empirical works have tackled the issue of student choice-making process, describing it as a key and high-involvement decision in the life of every individual, and as 'a complex process that involves different perspectives and a myriad of factors' (Mustafa et al., 2018, p. 2). Literature in higher education marketing identifies two dominant models of student choice. First, the economic-based model, which stipulates that students would choose a university according to their perceived costs and benefits. Second, the socio-logical based model, which highlights social and cultural issues as the prime factors of choice. In their review of empirical works on higher education institution choice, Mustafa et al. (2018) report social factors of choice that fell into three broad types of influence. First, the student characteristics such as socio-economic variables, academic abilities, parents' occupations and incomes. Second, the institutional variables that include the institution's image and academic reputation, especially regarding the quality of courses and teaching and the quality of facilities. Finally, the cultural background and the significant others influence that impact students decisions. Thus, the final choice is influenced by a complex combination of social pressure and personal expectations, sets of motivation and aspiration, which relate to both rational and emotional perspectives of decision-making (Angulo et al., 2010).

In the literature, there is also a consensus on a three-stage process for student decision-making and choice of higher education institution (Cabrera & La Nasa, 2000). The first stage, called the predisposition stage, helps students to decide whether to go to university or not. The second stage, called information search, focuses on which universities' offerings to explore further. In this stage, both the medium of information transmission as well as the type of information are relevant to understand the university marketing strategy and the student choice. The third stage, called choice stage, relates to the actual selection of – and registration in – a preferred university. In our contribution, we chose to focus on the second and third stages, since we primarily focus on students who do want to attend university.

Cognitive dissonance in the higher education institution choice

Cognitive dissonance (Festinger, 1957) refers to a feeling of psychological discomfort of an individual when facing a cognitive inconsistency regarding their own knowledge, opinions, values, and feelings. This concept, also described as a process-based phenomenon (Harmon-Jones et al., 2009) has been extensively studied area of social psychology and marketing.

Empirical research in marketing and social psychology distinguish two phases of cognitive dissonance (Krishna, 2012) that allow every individual to define the congruence of the message with his/her cognition. First, a phase of conscious and objective sensory experience, through which the individual receives the message (informational or sensory). Second, a subjective phase of awareness, understanding, evaluation, and categorisation of this message. It is also recognised, through empirical works, that the importance given to the decision and the degree of commitment of the actor increases the sensitivity to the message and the perception of cognitive dissonance (George & Manoj, 2009). In that sense, higher education institution choice is highly exposed to the risk of inconsistency perception, as it is a complex and highly demanding decision-making process that involves self-esteem and social recognition issues.

In marketing, cognitive dissonance has mainly been used to study the consequences of an act of purchase (Hunt, 1970), a type of post-decision cognitive dissonance. However, studies have shown that cognitive dissonance has a negative impact on the intention to purchase when a consumer is exposed to inconsistent information with cognition already anchored (Pantin-Sohier et al., 2011). Regarding prospective students, studies argue that, as consumers, they are highly motivated and involved when seeking information (Schmidt & Spreng, 1996, Mogaji, 2016). This can be explained first by the importance and implication of the decision on the students' lives and, second, by their lack of experience in higher education services. Exploring the existing 'informational' dissonance (Vaidis, 2011), which describes the situation when the student receives information about the university that is inconsistent with their knowledge, opinions, values, feelings, and existing cognition, could be useful. This cognitive decision-making dissonance remains scarcely studied while it could help to understand why prospective students could be confused when matching their mental representations with information on universities and courses. It thus clarifies the student-institution fit (Bowman & Denson, 2014).

According to Festinger (1957), the negative state of mind resulting from an informational dissonance acts as a motivational force aimed at reducing the dissonance and re-balancing the understanding of a purchasing environment. The author defines three generic strategies to reduce cognitive dissonance. The first and most studied one is the change of attitude towards the problematic cognition. The second strategy is the addition of new consistent cognition. The third strategy is to reduce the importance of the inconsistent elements. In that sense, marketing practices of higher education institutions should help to avoid the negative impact of the cognitive dissonance on student choice-making by reducing the inconsistency of the delivered.

Research methodology

We used a qualitative approach to investigate student decision-making and the emergence of cognitive inconsistency during that process. The qualitative approach is particularly relevant when attempting to contextualise studies and grasp the complexity of a process such as a choice-making one. Besides, we consider that qualitative data can help make new unexpected situations emerge and thus enrich the understanding of reality by researchers (Miles & Huberman, 2003). We carried out case studies on the summer's 2018 recruitment campaign of a few newly launched academic programmes (in Social Sciences and

Business Studies) in a young Moroccan private university in Fez, The Euromed University of Fez (UEMF).

Context

The UEMF, created in 2015, is organised into six specialised schools of Architecture, Political Science, Business, Social Sciences, Engineering and Applied Sciences. The UEMF defines its offer around seven 'pillars': the wish to promote multi-lingualism, multiculturalism, entrepreneurship, eco-citizenship, international mobility, multimedia & IT and social responsibility. The university is also developing an affirmative action towards young people from underprivileged family by providing grants, hence ensuring that they can move forward professionally in their lives. In our study, we focus on social sciences programmes at undergraduate or master level in Political Sciences, Business Communication, and Tourism.

Data collection

For each programme, we collected data related to programmes curriculum, pedagogical specialities, marketing and communication strategies that characterised the offer, including data emerging from informal interviews with course programmes managers. We also collect data related to students and prospects discourse to capture their cognitive representations and evaluation of the offer. For that purpose, we conducted interviews with students through two focus groups of six students each. We used some guiding questions (such as: academic and social background, the role of the reference groups – friends, family – in the decision-making process; the steps taken in the decision-making process; the type of information gathered by the students; unsettling, ambiguous, unexpected information about the course programmes and the university). These were aimed at grasping common patterns in individual experiences in the choice-making process in order to understand the set of conscious and subconscious means of selection of higher education institutions used by students. We also collected written data from mail and social media interactions between the course program managers and prospect students. We finally used the '*Dossiers d'accreditation*' that describe the entire set of teaching modules, learning objectives and pedagogical plans, teachers and *syllabii* of each course programme.

Data analysis

The collected data were analysed through a content analysis according to the method recommended by Miles and Huberman (2003). Following this method, we derived some 'meaningful subsets' from the data collected by following an inductive multi-thematic coding approach to generate critical themes linked to the research objectives outlined above. This enabled us to lay down intra-programme (i.e. between students talking about the same programme) and inter-programmes (i.e. analysis between different programmes) matrices to draw out patterns of analysis. Table 5.1 presents a list of items used to analyse the data.

Results

Our contribution aims to provide a better understanding of students' recruitment by tackling the issues of student choice-making process when facing a situation of cognitive dissonance.

First, we identified some critical decision criteria used by students to join a programme. This first part of the analysis was aimed at helping us understand better the cognitive realm of prospective students by making explicit the representations that students have of themselves, the student-life they wish

Table 5.1 Codification of items

Concepts	Items	Sub-items	Sub-items of level 2
University offering	core offer		
	tangible attributes of the offer		
	augmented product		
Choice-making	Model of choice	Economic-based	Cost
			Benefit
		Social based	Student socio-economic characteristics
			institutional variables
			cultural background
	Logics in the decision-making	Rational perspective	
		Emotional perspective	
	Choice process	Information collection	Type of information
			Amount of information
		Choice-making	
	Actors of the choice	The student	
		The significant others	Family
			Friends
			Professors
Cognitive dissonance	Consistency of information	objective sensory experience	
		Subjective evaluation	

to experience, and by pointing out what characterises the type of university they wish to join. Students use these criteria to evaluate the consistency of universities' messages and offer and determine the perceived value of each of them. Second, we highlighted informational dissonance situations where information delivered about the university and the programmes mismatched prospects' representations. We described a space and time dissonance, programme content and teaching methodology dissonance, and a programme purpose dissonance.

Students' decision-making criteria: between self-representation and expectations

An in-depth analysis of discourses delivered by students and of the feedback of course coordinators has helped us to distinguish the criteria selected by the students into two categories. On the one hand, some criteria reflect students' self-esteem during their reflexion concerning their studying itinerary and the phase during which they were looking for a university course. We qualify these as 'self-centric criteria'. These criteria include socio-economic and cultural factors of choice. On the other hand, some other criteria refer to the institutional factors that make a university offer valuable. We call them 'university centric criteria'.

Self-centric criteria: building a positive image of oneself

Choosing a university course and an academic itinerary emerges as a committing decision, a critical stage in the life of the young men and women at stake. The importance attached to this decision-making process is a source of high anxiety and stress, for the students as well as for their friends and family. One of the main concerns put forward by the students is the wish that their personal learning experience can correspond faithfully to their aspiration and the image they are building of themselves, and that it can contribute to boosting their self-esteem. This corresponds to a sort of personal desirability. This preoccupation often emerges in the discourse coming from students in social sciences.

> I did not exactly know what I wanted to study … I am still not sure. However, I knew that I wanted to do something that would help me understand society and the world better. I felt the urge to do something that would help me explain and analyse what is happening around me.
>
> I took the national exam from various schools. However, each time, there were many people, and I concluded that this was not for me. I wanted to find something that would feel more exclusive. I was looking for something that is not for everybody.

This self-esteem dimension is even more critical in students whose results are good, therefore allowing them to choose their academic itinerary genuinely.

> I could have easily joined an outstanding engineering school. However, the closest the registration day was getting, the further from an engineering career I could see myself. It did not seem to fit my personality. I had other aspirations. I felt like doing something where I would read, reflect, think, debate. It would not have been the case in an engineering school.

The second dimension related to self-esteem criteria relates to the need to choose a 'socially desirable option'. This social desirability gravitates around the questions concerning the reputation of the chosen university as well as of the jobs the academic itinerary would lead to. The issue concerning the reputation is described in numerous articles on marketing in higher education. Prospective students are particularly concerned about university reputation inside their social environment. Studies need to look serious.

> I have compared various private universities in Morocco. What I liked most about the UEMF was that it is not a "business university" There is something more institutional about it. It feels serious. In other universities, one hears that studies are easy-going, that qualifications are easily obtained. I did not want to have this image associated with my academic efforts.

The other side of the social desirability refers to the more or less prestigious jobs that the academic itinerary leads to. The representations and ethos around what makes a prestigious job change from one social background to another. However, more often than not, students tend to agree on the fact that jobs derived from scientific training (engineers, doctors, pharmacists, architects, etc.) are much better regarded by society than jobs related to social sciences.

> In all honesty, we live in a country where social promotion happens thanks to scientific jobs. In the beginning, my parents objected to the idea of me doing anything else than becoming an engineer or a doctor. It was not only my parents, and it was everybody! This is because these are the jobs that everybody value and admire.

This highlights the significant role that 'the others' play in the decision-making. Even when the student takes its own decision, he is still strongly dependent on the surrounding social pressure when choosing his field of study and work. Choice-making criteria of students are therefore filtered with motivational factors related to the cultural background and the social environment of the student.

University centric criteria

Following Levitt's (1980) description, the university offerings can be classified into three categories: the core offer, tangible attributes, and augmented product.

The core offering: get a diploma and recognition

In the context of Moroccan-North African culture, whether or not the state recognises a specific qualification remains of crucial importance. This point is highlighted in most students' discourse.

> I did not investigate what 'non-recognised' schools had to offer. I limited my research to public universities or recognised private ones because the nature of the qualification is what matters to me. You cannot do anything if your qualification is not recognised. For instance, you cannot carry on doing a PhD, nor can you work in a well-regarded company.

In Morocco, the importance given to the 'national diploma' is considerably reinforced by the attraction that most people have for civil servant positions. The career path in the '*Fonction Publique*' are automatically associated to security and stability in an economical context where unemployment is high and perceived as a high social risk, as the following exchange with student reveals:

> Working for the biggest companies and becoming a civil servant: these are the only stable options in this country. Small firms are fragile. From one day to another, they can close. My parents frankly prefer seeing me becoming a civil servant. That would considerably reassure them

This phenomenon is further accentuated in lower-class students, whose economic and social capital is fragile and who consider their qualification as their unique and valuable capital.

> My father neither has big commerce nor is a civil servant. The only solution for me is to get a good qualification to find a job.

The tangible attributes: looking for a beautiful campus

In addition to the importance given to the qualification, students also take into account some tangible attributes such as the quality of the university campus, its modernity, the hall of residence, the cafeteria on campus, in other words all of the university facilities.

> The campus here has nothing to do with some public universities campuses. The classrooms are beautiful and modern; the video projectors work; It has all equipped and pleasant to work in. It makes me feel more valued as student. I said to myself very pragmatically that choosing this university will allow me to be a better student
> I grew up in Fez and honestly it is such a huge project for this city. When I entered the campus for the first time, I was like 'waaaaaw'. I'm a little embarrassed to say that (laugh), but I posted a picture on Instagram to

say 'hey look at me, I am in the new campus of Fez.' That makes me proud to study here.

Prospective students evaluate the campus and university facilities both from the rational perspective of working conditions and the emotional perspective.

The augmented product: a promise of internationalisation

Other attributes can be described as intangible. First of all, the opportunities to study abroad and to benefit from international academic exchanges seem to be particularly valued by students. It is perceived as an 'opening opportunity', the chance to develop new skills but also, a stepping-stone to pursuing studies abroad and, potentially, to settle there.

> Having a double-diploma with a great French university was what convinced me to register for this course. I know that with this diploma I can envisage leaving and working abroad if I want to. It is a real plus.

Second of all, the fact that pedagogical teams are international, with French, Italian, Spanish (to only list a few nationalities) lecturers were taking part in the delivery of teaching modules, is essential. This is perceived as a sign of prestige and quality.

> There is something different about foreign lecturers. There are good reasons why they come here to teach.
> Researcher: What do you mean?
> Well, you know: they do not go to public universities, do they? They come here. They know it is a good university. Maybe they find the same working conditions, or even better, than in their countries.
> They teach us things that we have not heard before. It is different, and its new. They share their experience from developed countries with us.

The presence of foreign lecturers is thus described as a sign of international standing of the university and students derive from it a form of prestige for themselves.

We described above a set of motivational criteria and influences at stake in the prospective students choice. Those related to the acquisition of status and belonging to a group is of paramount importance in a North African context. We also highlight that students weigh rational and emotional sources of value in the university offers.

Cognitive dissonance: emergence and treatment

In this first analytical part, we have identified some issues that shape prospective students' representations of their interests, needs, and preferences in terms of studies and higher education institutions attributes. The misfit between these representations and the university marketing messages can lead to inconsistency. In the following, we present three situations of information inconsistency, relative to time and space, programme content and teaching methodology and programme purpose dissonance.

Space and time dissonance: the fear of a forward-looking perspective

One of the significant inconsistencies in the provision of information described by the students refers to the link between the academic offer and the students' perception of the job market. In particular, the academic courses that lead to jobs that are not yet well known or are not socially valued and source of prestige generate a certain psychological discomfort in students and amongst their family and friends. This was the case for a student who was keen to study a degree in 'political sciences', for instance.

> My parents cannot see me as a woman who could be politically active. They say that it is not a job for me and that politics is, anyway, only a source of trouble in Morocco. They would prefer me to do a well-regarded job, to stay away from the corruption of politicians.

Other courses, considered as innovative, lead to similar psychological discomfort and uncertainty. In the cognitive representations of prospective students, this form of dissonance represents the biggest reason for not registering to a course. The anxiety to find oneself qualified but unemployed is rather high, as we can notice in the following exchange of Facebook messenger between a prospective student and a professor/programme manager.

> Prospective student: The content of your program in a circular economy is exciting but I do not know anybody working in that field. Are companies recruiting?
> Professor: You are right; this is a new issue in Morocco. However, in the coming years, almost all organisations will have to include sustainability in their strategy.
> Prospective student: Yes, for sure. However, I talked to many people about this, and they all say that it will take many years before Moroccan companies change their mindset and start working sustainably. So what about the two coming years when I finish my master's degree? I find this unsettling, and my parents feel worried about this choice.

Prospective students find refuge in jobs that they are familiar with. Thus, it is a significant challenge for universities to better inform the public about these new jobs, industries, and areas of work.

Programme content and teaching methodology dissonance: the false but tenacious opposition between skills and knowledge?

The second element of information dissonance that is often encountered by prospective students is related to programme content and teaching methods put forward by universities. This type of dissonance seems to reveal a profound mismatch between, on the one hand, the university's wish to innovate pedagogically and, on the other hand, a particular form of conformism in the students and parents' expectations and representation of the learning process.

> I find all you are describing very interesting, but we have not been used to working in this way in secondary school. Seminars, workshops, teamwork, inversed classes, frequent oral presentations … We have always worked with a lesson delivered by the teacher. We learn we take exams. I am anxious I have not managed to adapt to these new ways of learning and working.

This dissonance is further reinforced when the university emphasises the use of 'structuring pillars', fundamental principles underlying the learning philosophy of the institution and requiring for students to develop a new approach of working as a student. This is the case of the entrepreneurial pillar in the Euromed University.

> I have noticed that, in your university, entrepreneurship is very much valued. The problem is that I do not have innovative views. I am not from a wealthy family, and I cannot envisage creating my own business. I do not like taking risks, and I am not prepared to take this kind of initiatives … Well, in short, I am not this kind of person. I want a classical but right quality course that will give me a job.

Myths about visionary and risk-takers entrepreneurs can be intimidating to young people who tend to have a slightly less heroic vision of themselves. More generally, prospective students that lack cultural and economic capital do not see soft skills as an opportunity of personal development but rather as a rather harmful add-on in their academic journey.

Programme purpose dissonance: looking for the ROI

The last form of informational inconsistency refers to the attitude of prospective students towards the purpose of academia. Prospective students are much more preoccupied with the acquisition of qualification than that of knowledge and skills. This representation gap manifests itself very clearly in various instances. Students seem to attach much less importance to the content of the courses than to the forms of recognition of the qualification.

I do not know which course my parents want me to follow. I know that the university is good and that the state recognises the qualifications. This is what matters most. After that, business studies or anything else … It does not matter.

This preference for the qualification rather than for the development of knowledge and skills appears even more clearly when talking about continuous professional training courses.

I like the content of this executive Masters. The problem is that it does not deliver a national qualification at the end. It feels like it is not helping me in any way because, in my company, it will not help me to be promoted. If it was a national Masters, then I could be promoted.

Some prospective students see their higher education choice as an expense than should provide a short-term return on investment through professional opportunities rather than a means of personal development. Thus, any message focused on knowledge and skills, not directly linking to a job, or a promotion opportunity is perceived as inconsistent.

Conclusion and recommendations

In this chapter, we have attempted to provide a better understanding of students' recruitment in the context of a young North African university. We explored the rational and emotional issues that influence the students' choice for a higher education institution. We distinguished, on the one hand, student's self-centric criteria wish to refer to social and self-esteem motivations, and on the other hand, university centric issues that refer to university offer components that are valued by prospective students. Then, we relied on the concept of *cognitive dissonance* to understand the misfit between university messages to define its offer and prospective student's mental representations and cognition. We thus describe three types of dissonance. First, space and time dissonance that reflects the inconsistency of prospective vision of the future of the job market between the university and the students. Second, programme content and teaching methodology dissonance that highlights the gap of vision on the learning process. Third, a programme purpose dissonance that reflects the search for assurance on the ROI of their studies.

Drawing on these conclusions, we make a set of strategic and operational marketing recommendations that could help to change the attitude of prospective students towards the problematic cognition (Festinger, 1957) explored in this chapter. Universities should work in two perspectives that may look paradoxical but are somewhat well connected and complementary. On the one hand, universities should increase the universality of their strategic discourse to society and prospective students. In that perspective, universities should disconnect their strategic vision from local and temporary constraints to be forward-looking and globally oriented. In other words, universities should not be preparing for today's and local jobs but, instead, for future and global careers. On the other hand, operational marketing actions should be more oriented explicitly towards answering local prospective students' expectations and ability to understand innovative messages and methods.

A strategic vision: the universal orientation of the university

As for NGOs, public administrations, or international institutions, higher education marketing strategies should be aimed at promoting a 'cause' (Kotler & Keller, 2015, p. 753) and the 'raison d'être' of the university through its strategic vision. The university needs to build and communicate a vision around what we could call 'jobs of the future' – some of them we may not even know yet – as well as around the new needed skills such as team working, negotiating, resilience and adaptability, open-mindedness, critical thinking, etc. This may sometimes be confusing for students who mostly want to know which profession the diploma is preparing for, or are uncomfortable with new methods of learning.

In that perspective, the content of the university's communication material should not only focus on the description of the programmes. It should instead promote a vision of the future and how the university intends to contribute to making it happens through carefully designed courses. To strengthen and legitimate that vision, universities and programmes managers should work more closely with the socio-professionals when designing and delivering courses. This collaboration would help to identify the knowledge and skills needed for the next years and help students apprehend better what is coming.

Furthermore, MENA and African universities, in general, should invest more time and energy to increase their integration in the global higher education system to strengthen the universality of their positioning. Southern students and scholars should be helped in progressively perceiving themselves as part of a global – or at least regional – community of learners and knowledge producers. Building strong and strategic partnerships between universities – that facilitate the mobility of students and researchers and progressively align pedagogical methods and learning approaches – is a powerful tool to achieve that goal. However, networks of interpersonal links and collaboration between scholars or students associations should also be fostered.

We strongly believe that both efforts for a global and future-oriented strategic vision of the university and the promotion of the universal goals could help to reduce the geographical, temporal, and cultural sources of dissonance that we identified in our contribution. Prospective students should progressively feel comfortable and increase their ability to embrace the representation promoted by the university as it relates to a universal projection into the future.

Operational actions to tackle local contingencies and sources of inconsistency

In parallel to the promotion of a strategic vision, African universities must act at the operational level to eliminate the sources of inconsistency and psychological discomfort carried by their communication messages. To do so, universities should, in the first step, develop tools to better-know prospective students they are targeting, and, in a second step, choose the right communication approach to reach them.

One of the significant difficulties of African universities is the lack of knowledge of the social background and expectations of their prospective students (Ndofirepi et al., 2020). This lack of knowledge leads them to develop messages that are meaningless to young people. Thus, like companies, universities need to improve their understanding of the expectations and motivational levers of students and prospective students. They must rely on marketing studies that help to segment student populations and identify the traits, motivations, and fears of each. This knowledge will make it possible to adapt contents of communication messages to the different profiles of students in such a way as to reduce inconsistency and informational cognitive dissonance for each segment of students. To amplify the impact of this message, universities should use the right communication channels that specifically target their prospective students. In particular, universities should rely on digital marketing to collect and analyse data and use social media platforms and social media influencer to target specific groups of future students.

In a similar vein, universities must rely more heavily on alumni and current students to disseminate their communication messages. Alumni students are significant people with whom prospect students can identify. When the university message is explained by students themselves, it appears less inconsistent, first, because of the language proximity between young people that use the same words, second, because students describe a truly lived and shared consumer experience. More generally, students and prospects share generational codes that reduce the risk of misunderstanding or inconsistency of the message received, as it is very often the case with professors and programme managers.

Higher education institutions in Arab and African countries have historically taken a passive approach to market issues, as it was seen with suspicion and doubt, and marketing activities were believed to be synonymous with sales and promotion that is contrary to the values of the academic community. However, considering the critical challenges new private universities are now facing, they have no choice to incorporate marketing into their culture so they can deliver well consistent communication messages and reach their target students.

References

Angulo, F., Pergelova, A., & Rialp, J. (2010). A market segmentation approach for higher education based on rational and emotional factors. *Journal of Marketing for Higher Education*, 20(1), 1–17.

Benabdallah, M. Z. (2010). L'université maghrébine face aux défis de l'intégration euro-Méditerranéenne. *La Cuestion universitaria*, 6, 117–124.

Bowman, N. A., & Denson, N. (2014). A missing piece of the departure puzzle: Student–institution fit and intent to persist. *Research in Higher Education*, 55(2), 123–142.

Cabrera, A. F., & La Nasa, S. M. (2000). Understanding the college-choice process. *New Directions for Institutional Research*, 107, 5–22.

Cappeleare, G. (2019). MENA's growing young population is a huge opportunity – if we get it right. World Economic Forum. Retrieved from www.weforum.org/agenda/2019/04/menas-growing-young-population-is-a-huge-opportunity-if-we-get-it-right/.

Craig-Lees, M., Joy, S., & Browne, B. (1995). *Consumer Behaviour*. Milton, QLD: John Wiley & Sons.

Festinger, L. (1957). *A cognitive dissonance theory*. Stanford: Stanford University Press.

George, B. P., & Manoj, E. (2009). Cognitive dissonance and purchase involvement in the consumer behaviour context. *The IUP Journal of Marketing Management*, 8(3), 7–24.

Harmon-Jones, E., Amodio, D. M., & Harmon-Jones, C. (2009). Action-based model of dissonance: A review, integration and expansion of conceptions of cognitive conflict. *Advances in Experimental Psychology*, 41, 119–166.

Hemsley-Brown, J., & Oplatka, I. (2006). Universities in a competitive global marketplace: A systematic review of the literature on higher education marketing. *International Journal of Public Sector Management*, 19(4), 316–338.

Hunt, S. D. (1970). Post-transaction communications and dissonance reduction. *Journal of Marketing*, 34(3), 46–51.

Ivy, J. (2001). Higher education institution image: A correspondence analysis approach. *International Journal of Educational Management*, 15(6), 276–282.

Kassarjian, H. H. & Cohen, J. B. (1965). Cognitive dissonance and consumer behaviour. *California Management Review*, 8(1), 55–64.

Kinzie, J., Palmer, M., Hayek, J., Hossler, D., Jacob, S. A., & Cummings, H. (2004). Fifty years of college choice: Social, political and institutional influences on the decision-making process. *New Agenda Series*, 5(3).

Kotler, P., & Keller, K. L. (2015). *Marketing management* (15th ed.). Tours: Nouveaux Horizons.

Krishna, A. (2012). An integrative review of sensory marking: Engaging the senses to affect perception, judgment and behavior. *Journal of Consumer Psychology*, 22(3), 332–351.

Le matin.ma (2016, Nov.). Le marché du travail change … les compétences aussi. Retrieved from https://lematin.ma/journal/2016/le-marche-du-travail-change-les-competences-aussi/257486.html.

Levitt, T. (1980). *Marketing success through differentiation-of anything*. Boston: Graduate School of Business Administration, Harvard University.

Maringe, F. (2005). Interrogating the crisis in higher education marketing: The CORD model. *International Journal of Educational Management*, 19(7), 564–578.

McManus, R., Haddock-Fraser, J., & Rands, P. (2017). A methodology to understand student choice of higher education institutions: The case of the United Kingdom. *Journal of Higher Education Policy and Management*, 39(4), 390–405.

Miles, M., & Huberman, A. M. (2003). *Analyse des donnees qualitatives*. Bruxelles: De Boeck Universite.

Mogaji, E. (2016). Marketing strategies of United Kingdom universities during clearing and adjustment. *International Journal of Educational Management*, 30(4), 493–504.

Moogan, J. (2011). Can a higher education institution's marketing strategy improve the student-institution match? *International Journal of Educational Management*, 25(6), 570–589.

Mount, J., & Belanger, C. (2004). Entrepreneurship and image management in higher education: Pillars of massification. *The Canadian Journal of Higher Education*, 34(2), 125–140.

Mustafa, S. A. A., Sellami, A. L., Elmaghraby, E. A. A., & Al-Qassass, H. B. (2018). Determinants of college and university choice for high-school students in Qatar. *International Journal of Higher Education*, 7(3), 3–15.

Ndofirepi, E., Farinloye, T., & Mogaji, E. (2020). Marketing mix in a heterogenous higher education market: A case of Africa. In E. Mogaji, F. Maringe, & R. E. Hinson (Eds.), *Understanding the higher education Market in Africa*. London: Routledge.

Pantin-Sohie,r G., Gauzente C., & Gallen, C. (2011). Bleue comme une orange ou l'intrusion du design dans nos assiettes. 27ème congrès International de l'Association Française du Marketing, Brussels, Belgique.

Pinar, M., Trapp, P., Girard, T., & Boyt, T. E. (2011). Utilizing the brand ecosystem framework in designing branding strategies for higher education. *International Journal of Educational Management*, 25(7)724–739.

Schmidt, J. B., & Spreng, R. A. (1996). A proposed model of external consumer information search. *Journal of the Academy of Marketing Science*, 24(3), 246–256.

Soffel, J. (2016). What are the 21st century skills every student needs? World Economic Forum. www.weforum.org/agenda/2016/03/21st-century-skills-future-jobs-students/.

Vaidis, D. (2011). *La dissonance cognitive*. Paris: Dunod.

Wiese, M. D. (1994). College choice cognitive dissonance: Managing student/institution fit. *Journal of Marketing for Higher Education*, 5(1), 35–48.

Part II

Digital marketing strategies

6 Higher education marketing communications in the digital era

Mark Camilleri

Introduction

Higher education institutions (HEIs) are influenced by political and socio-economic changes in their marketing environment (Beine, Noël, & Ragot, 2014; Constantinides & Zinck Stagno, 2011; Maringe & Gibbs, 2008; Hemsley-Brown & Oplatka, 2006; Mazzarol & Soutar, 2002; Mazzarol, 1998). Currently, HEIs hailing from the advanced economies are affected by adverse demographic trends. Many developing countries have an ageing population and are experiencing lower birth rates. The annual growth in outbound student numbers is expected to decline from 6% to 1.7% per year till 2027 (British Council, 2018). At the same time, Universities and other educational institutions are facing intensifying competition, as they operate in a global marketing environment (Schofield, Cotton, Gresty, Kneale, & Winter, 2013). Therefore, HEIs and business schools hailing from developed and developing countries have to formulate policies and strategic objectives that will allow them to evolve (Pucciarelli & Kaplan, 2016; Ivy, 2008; Kotler & Fox, 1995). HEIs may have to diversify their student populations by expanding the recruitment of international students in their home campuses (Lee, 2014), and/or by serving new markets, with satellite campuses (Pucciarelli & Kaplan, 2016; Friga, Bettis, & Sullivan, 2003). Thus, internationalisation has become an institutional imperative, for many HEIs (Schofield et al., 2013), as they are increasing offering courses in different settings.

(Semi) Autonomous HEIs are behaving like for-profit organisations as they often seek new opportunities and resources from developing countries in the Middle East, Africa, and South East Asia, among other regions to prioritise revenue creation (Pucciarelli & Kaplan, 2016; Budde-Sung, 2011; Altbach, Reisberg, & Rumbley, 2009). Hence, they internationalise; in terms of faculty, students, and curriculum. Institutions target international students because they pay higher tuition fees than their domestic counterparts (Altbach, 2004; Lee, 2014). Moreover, institutions are introducing alternate modes of delivery of education, as they offer distance and online learning (British Council, 2018; Camilleri & Camilleri, 2019; Schofield et al., 2013). Therefore, universities and business schools are increasingly promoting their higher educational services in global markets (Pucciarelli & Kaplan, 2016; De Jager & Gbadamosi, 2010; Friga et al., 2003).

In this light, this contribution uses a generic approach to assess the internal strengths and weaknesses of today's higher education institutions, including universities and colleges. The researcher critically analyses the opportunities and threats of their macro marketing environment. After having reviewed the current situation, he presents contemporary marketing communications tactics that may be used by the HEI leaders to promote their services. In a nutshell, this chapter explains how educational institutions can make use of traditional and digital media to attract students as well as academic members of staff.

Literature review

HEIs, including those operating from the African continent, are facing intensifying competition, as they operate in an international marketing environment (Maringe & Gibbs, 2008). At the same time, they are encouraged to recruit larger, international student intakes as they face financial constraints to survive in a competitive marketplace (Russell, 2005). As a result, universities may diversify their student populations by expanding the recruitment of international students for their home campuses (Lee, 2014), and / or by serving new markets, by entering foreign countries with satellite campuses (Pucciarelli & Kaplan, 2016; Friga et al., 2003). Hence, universities need to adopt a consumerist approach whilst taking into account the environmental factors (Pucciarelli & Kaplan, 2016; Friga et al., 2003).

Relevant academic literature suggests that the HEIs' performance is shaped by many entities at both supranational and national levels (Estermann, Nokkala, & Steinel, 2011; Maton, 2005). Estermann (2017) contended that the universities' political autonomy and academic freedom is a fundamental prerequisite for them, to be able to develop their strategic profiles. The European University Association has called on the national governments to refrain from interfering with the universities' autonomy and accountability (EUA, 2017). The public authorities may also exert their political influence through their funding mechanisms, and concentration processes, that can affect their management. Altbach (2004) argued that institutions ought to design fundraising activities that target companies and alumni. The author contended that HEIs could promote their continuous professional development opportunities as they can deliver courses to executives. Notwithstanding, the challenging economic context can also have an impact on the HEI's financial management, staffing matters and organisational aspects (Estermann, 2017). The universities increased autonomy, self-organisation, and accountability (Hoecht, 2006) has brought some level of privatisation of the higher education sector and has facilitated the entrance of new players (Pucciarelli & Kaplan, 2016).

The university leaders are not always market-oriented, and their institutions may not always be capable of differentiating themselves by marketing their high-quality 'product' (Pucciarelli & Kaplan, 2016; Ivy, 2008). Russell (2005) argued that the classrooms' resources and the effective management of physical assets are also important determinants for the students' perceptions of higher education and service quality. This author referred to specific aspects such as the HEIs' campuses, their infrastructure and surroundings, as well as other evidence that may influence customer perceptions, including; their prospectuses, web sites, exhibition stands, stationery, and business cards. These are essential elements to prospective students, particularly for those who are not able to visit the campus before committing themselves to enrol in a specific HEI.

Kotler and Fox (1995) argued that the general public might usually form images of HEIs that could affect the likelihood of students attending or recommending institutions to others. In a similar vein, Parameswaran and Glowacka (1995) held that higher education institutions need to maintain or develop a distinct image to create a competitive advantage. HEIs need to maintain or develop their corporate image as they want to occupy a position in the minds of their students. Mazzarol's (1998) research reported that the institutions in Australia, Canada, New Zealand, the UK, and US enjoyed a right image and reputation in terms of fostering a culture of innovation, while Bharadwaj, Varadarajan, and Fahy (1993) had emphasised the importance of organisational learning and expertise as a source of competitive advantage. These studies suggested that students' decisions when selecting courses were based on the reputation and experience of the universities' faculty staff (Mogaji, 2016; Beneke, 2011; Van Heerden, Wiese, North, & Jordaan, 2009). The university's service quality relies on 'human actors' who are entrusted to deliver individualised, student-centred experiences (De Jager & Gbadamosi, 2010).

The universities' classes may be composed of diverse students hailing from different cultures, beliefs, and geographical backgrounds. This issue has led to drastic shifts in the students' expectations regarding their classroom experience (Budde-Sung, 2011; Altbach et al., 2009; Friga et al., 2003). The international students may usually value the educational institutions' quality and reputation as well as the recognition of their qualifications in their own country (Beneke, 2011; Van Heerden et al., 2009; Binsardi & Ekwulugo, 2003; Mazzarol & Soutar, 2002). Kotler and Fox (1995) posited that the university's perceived excellence has usually affected the decisions of prospective students and scholars to choose one HEI over another. The authors contended that the HEIs' primary focus of attention should be on increasing their service quality whilst delivering 'perceived excellence'. Customer satisfaction correlates with perceived quality (or, attitude towards HEIs' products), which ultimately affects their profitability (Duque, 2014; De Jager & Gbadamosi, 2010; Mazzarol & Soutar, 2002; Cronin & Taylor, 1992). For this reason, the HEIs need to enhance their prestige (Pucciarelli & Kaplan, 2016). If they do so, international students may be willing to pay higher 'prices'. In a similar vein, Binsardi and Ekwulugo (2003) held that the product and pricing variables ought to be considered when HEIs formulate their market penetration strategies. Eventually, Pucciarelli and Kaplan (2016) went on to suggest that HEIs need to expand interactions with crucial stakeholders whilst co-creating value with them. Like other for-profit businesses, HEIs ought to nurture relationships with a range of stakeholders, including; students and their parents, policymakers, employers as well as with other universities and colleges (Maringe & Foskett, 2002).

Previous literature reported that the best way to attract international students is to lower tuition fees; provide more scholarships, and better service quality to students (Binsardi & Ekwulugo, 2003; Mazzarol & Soutar, 2002). HEIs may also benefit of education marketing (Constantinides & Zinck Stagno, 2011; Maringe & Gibbs, 2008; Hemsley-Brown & Oplatka, 2006; Mazzarol, 1998) and promotions, including; word-of-mouth publicity on positive learning experiences from students themselves, and their friends and relatives. Furthermore, HEIs may resort to integrated marketing communications as they may use broadcast, digital, and outdoor advertising, sales promotions, personal selling, direct marketing, interactive marketing, public relations and publicity, to raise awareness of their educational services (Maringe & Foskett, 2002). The advances in technology can provide significant opportunities for HEIs to leverage themselves through online media (Pucciarelli & Kaplan, 2016; Njenga & Fourie, 2010). HEIs may be in a position to address the increasing demand for distance learning education that cannot be fully met through offline channels Schofield et al., 2013). The use of digital media can also result in significant cost savings, as the transition from physical to digital solutions improves efficiency and effectiveness (Moore & Kearsley, 2011). Notwithstanding, today's students are becoming very acquainted with the use of ubiquitous technologies in the realms of education (Camilleri & Camilleri, 2017, 2019; Njenga & Fourie, 2010). Therefore, it is in the interest of HEIs to keep up to date with the latest developments in the marketing environment.

A critical analysis of the HEIs' marketing environment

The researcher has outlined a non-exhaustive list of the HEIs' strengths and weaknesses. It also shed light on possible opportunities and threats from political, regulatory, socioeconomic, and technological issues (Helms & Nixon, 2010; Marginson, 2006).

A SWOT analysis of the HEIs' strategic orientations

Strengths

- HEIs raise their financial capital requirements by charging tuition fees to full time, part-time, and distance learning students; Government-funded HEIs may provide free or reduced tuition fees.
- Many international courses are taught in English; The English language has become an essential lever for international student mobility (ICEF, 2017).
- Several HEIs provide work-integrated education; they deliver pragmatic, application-oriented programmes. The students are/may be expected to

undertake industry placements as part of their studies. Therefore work-integrated education (WIE) may be a component of the HEIs' curriculum.

- Work-integrated education supports students to become all-around professionals with an appropriate level of operational experience. It equips students with a thorough understanding of the business and industry's operations. WIE would usually take place in an organisational context that is relevant to the students' future employment prospects. At the same time, the students would obtain communicative and transferable skills that will be valuable for their development. The focus is to help them acquire a range of valuable generic abilities, including people-skills through interactions with peers, subordinates, and supervisors. After their working period, the students will be in a position to apply the theories that they have learnt in real-life settings. Hence, students develop their knowledge and skills in a professional environment, whilst increasing the chances of their employability prospects (Kolb & Kolb, 2005).
- HEIs are increasingly establishing international collaboration agreements with other educational institutions, across borders. They enable student exchange programmes and field trips. The classroom teaching is enriched with student exchanges and field trips that provide students relevant on-the-job training.
- HEIs are building their alumni networks over the years. Many of their students have become business and industry professionals.
- HEIs are often engaging with business and industry as they provide their consultancy and research services.
- HEIs offer Executive Development Programmes to industry practitioners, allowing them to update their skills, and to broaden their knowledge.

Weaknesses

- Many HEIs are not managed as profitable organisations;
- HEIs' academic employees may become members of trade unions. The unions can use their bargaining power on the university's administration;
- HEIs can be slow to respond to the ongoing changes in the business and industry. They may need to adapt their curricula and courses to meet the prospective employers' requirements better;
- The HEIs' academic members of staff may have long contact hours with their students (when compared to other institutions);
- The HEIs' academia are not always publishing adequate and sufficient research (when compared to other institutions);
- The HEIs' prospective students may be attracted to competitive institutions who are offering cheaper tuition fees. The international prospects will consider the HEIs' locations and their living expenses;

- The HEIs' international marketing efforts may be focusing on limited catchment areas. They may be overlooking promising markets (Constantinides & Zinck Stagno, 2011).

Opportunities

- HEIs may use educational technology to improve their students' experience. Educational technologies could enhance the quality of online courses, particularly those that are offered to part-time, or distance learning students.
- HEIs can utilise blogs, RSS feeds, podcasts, wikis, electronic fora, webinars, et cetera to reach their target audiences. They may use social media and word-of-mouth marketing by communicating student testimonials, online reviews and ratings, in order to attract students from different markets.
- HEIs could incentivise their educators and researchers to participate in academic conferences and to publish their work in highly indexed journals.
- The setting up of research (or special interest) groups could improve collaboration and teamwork amongst the HEIs' members of staff.
- HEIs' academics should be encouraged to become members in editorial boards of leading journals.
- HEIs can offer high-level consultancy and professional advisory services to private and public organisations.
- HEIs may organise international conferences and fora that can be used as a platform for insightful exchange amongst academics, industry practitioners, and tourism policymakers.
- HEIs can engage with alumni by involving them in social events, webinars, and continuous professional development programmes.
- Industry professionals can be invited to speak to students on specific subject lectures. These experts may help students gain a deeper understanding of the industry.
- HEIs' academia should be encouraged to share their research expertise with business and industry to pioneer developments. They should promote their research outputs (Duque, 2014; Parameswaran & Glowacka, 1995). Relevant research can enhance industry performance and influence policy making.
- HEIs can extend collaborative agreements in many areas, with reputable education institutions.
- HEIs can obtain quality assurance and accreditations from international awarding bodies, for their educational programmes. The recognition of their courses would necessitate a thorough assessment of their leadership, curriculum programmes and skills, assessment methods, project work, student placements, student support, feedback and resources, et cetera.

- The HEIs' international admissions pages should evidence their 'global perspective' and could highlight their extensive range of services they offer to international students. For example, their course prospectus should be available in different languages.
- There is an increased demand for higher education from mature students as the concept of life-long learning is being promoted in developing and advanced economies.
- There are still untapped markets in Asia where students can't access quality education at home. There is a business case to attract students from Africa as the continent's youth population is rising (British Council, 2018; Camilleri, 2016a,b).
- The HEIs' international students could be used as brand ambassadors and should be featured in their digital media.
- HEIs may be supported by student scholarships (from governments, foundations, or NGOs) and sponsorships that may be donated by industry partners.

Threats

- Many HEIs' national governments have already decreased (or cut) their public funding to HEIs (Estermann, 2017; Estermann, Nokkala, & Steinel, 2011; Hoecht, 2006; Maton, 2005). Therefore, HEIs may have to raise their capital requirements through tuition fees and fundraising activities.
- There is a very competitive environment (in the global market). HEIs are increasingly targeting international students from many markets.
- Many countries (including developing economies) have improved (or are improving) their educational systems. However, there may be students who decide to go abroad because they believe that there is neither capacity nor high-quality education at their home country (ICEF, 2017).
- The ageing populations in many parts of the world, their greater life expectancies, coupled with lower fertility rates, means that populations in many countries are getting older. At the same time, the 15-to-24-year-old cohorts are shrinking. This key college-aged demographic will peak in Asia somewhere around 2020. Then it will start a gradual decline from that high point (British Council, 2018).
- There may be political, socio-cultural, and legal factors affecting the marketing of HEIs. International students may face travel restrictions. Rigorous travel formalities including the issuance of national visas and immigration policies, can affect the students' choice of their prospective HEI.
- Reduced scholarships and student exchange programmes from foreign governments can have an impact on the number of students who may afford international mobility.
- A growing number of Asian students are choosing to stay within their own region to study, and students from other countries – including

African nations – are adding Asian destinations to their list of attractive options. Asian countries, including China, Japan, South Korea, Singapore, and Malaysia, amongst others, are increasing their capacity to absorb international students. Students and families are placing more emphasis on value, and on the return on investment from overseas education. Therefore, students may opt to study close to their home.

- There are growing indications that major employers are placing less emphasis on reputable HEIs and their brand identities (ICEF, 2017).

The HEIs' integrated marketing communications

The integrated marketing communications campaigns of HEIs ought to be based on clear strategies that will help them achieve their goals and objectives. Different promotional tools are distinct from each other in terms of their purpose. Therefore, the HEIs' marketing managers need to coordinate their various promotional activities into a concerted and organised manner. They have to allocate adequate financial resources in support of every marketing activity so that all touchpoints will convey consistent messages to the desired target audience (Bonnema & Van der Waldt, 2008). Hence, HEIs ought to consider their (i) market, (ii) mission, (iii) message, (iv) media, (v) money and (vi) measurement, whenever they use their marketing communications tools:

The market

The market includes both competitors as well as customers. The competitors are other HEIs who are targeting prospective students. The customers include domestic and international college students, as well as employees who pursue life-long learning opportunities and continuous professional training and development.

The mission

The marketing objectives may include increased sales volumes, market share, return on investment, and profitability. The communication objectives may include; raising awareness of a product or service, increasing the consumer knowledge of the product features and attributes, improving the consumers' preferences and convictions towards the product, and entice customers to make their purchase decisions, amongst others (Ivy, 2008). The latter objectives are related to the hierarchy of effects model, which map out the response process of prospective customers before their actual purchase. One premise of this process is that the marketing communications take time to yield results. Another aspect of this model is that; different elements of IMC can be beneficial and targeted explicitly at integral steps in the response process. For example, advertising is an excellent tool to raise awareness and to convey information on a product or service. Public relations may be used to generate interest and desire. Personal selling through open-day events (which would necessitate face-to-face interactions) may be used to convert preference and conviction into purchase behaviours.

The message

The HEIs ought to adapt their promotional content to different markets. Educational institutions would better use the local language of their prospective students. They should consider their prospects' socio-cultural norms, beliefs, and expectations before formulating their marketing messages. Hence, HEIs may decide to test their promotional content with various groups of students in order to ensure that their message is clear and compelling for the target market, before launching their marketing campaigns (Bonnema & Van der Waldt, 2008). Afterwards, HEIs may be in a position to communicate their strategic messages that promote the specific aspects of their quality educational services, for example; (i) their student-centred teaching culture; (ii) the provision of work-integrated education for full time students, as part of their academic work; (iii) ambitious objectives that are intended to attract the best employees and to retain them; (iv) nurturing human resources, through ongoing training opportunities and continuous professional development; (v) significant investments in appropriate cost-effective enhancements to the extant infrastructure in support of research, scholarship, and creativity; (vi) incentive research output and improve its impact, particularly in the fields of critical importance, for societal benefit; (vii) forging collaborative relationships with other HEIs to enhance the quality and stature of academic disciplines or fields; (ix) engagement with stakeholders, including the government and its policy makers, as well as with business and industry; (x) encouraging undergraduate students to pursue post-graduate studies; implementing strategically focused; (xi) fostering a diverse workplace, student body, and staff in terms of gender, race, and ethnicity; (xii) recruiting new PhDs and 'rising stars'.

The media

The marketers who possess a generous budget may have access to an arsenal of communication options, including electronic media (TV and radio), print media (newspapers and magazines), direct-mail solicitations, telemarketing, personal selling, public relations, and the web, amongst others. One medium is seldom enough to reach segments. The choice of media depends on a number of factors, including: (i) the markets which are being targeted; (ii) the combination of media which will be the most effective to the target markets; (iii) the amount of money that is dedicated to the marketing communications budget, which can be affected by the decisions made in (i) and (ii).

Advertising

HEIs can advertise in print media in different countries. Newspapers and magazines can report news releases that promote the HEIs' credentials, in terms of quality educational programmes, high-impact research, as they may provide relevant information on the institutions' engagement with stakeholders, including business and industry. Moreover, digital advertising can deliver effective results for the marketing of HEIs, for far less of an investment. For example, the Pay-Per-Click (PPC) advertising is often used to target potential markets, as the sponsor only incurs an expense when prospects click on the online banner. However, before launching the PPC campaigns and their related analytics, the HEIs should improve their landing pages to specific sites that would appeal to online prospects; who are seeking information on particular degrees and academic programmes.

Direct marketing via digital and mobile technologies

The HEIs' website should be accessible through different devices; via desktop computers, smartphones, tablets, et cetera. The online content should be optimised for mobile-device usage as many international students are mobile-exclusive. Hence, HEIs should communicate relevant details of their selling propositions, in different languages. They can provide information on course admissions; collaborative agreements with stakeholders; student mobility; research opportunities; et cetera. International students will also require factual data, on tuition and bench fees, as well as on study and work permits, amongst other issues.

The HEIs' web sites could offer personalised, interaction facilities in real-time, through live chat services. They can use web-conferencing via easily accessible tools like Skype or Google Hangouts to engage with prospective students in their queries or to address their concerns, share documents or videos, and guide them through relevant webpages, via co-browsing. HEIs can organise webinars for parents and prospective students, with admissions and faculty employees in multiple languages. Moreover, the HEIs' website could feature student testimonials, including; reviews and ratings that may serve as proof that they are providing an adequate level of service to their scholars. The positive experiences from the students themselves will help them attract new ones.

The HEIs' web sites should be structured and well-designed with a good selection of high res-images, video, et cetera. They may also incorporate the Google Maps Street View or Oculus Rift virtual reality technology as they allow prospects to visualise the premises of their prospective campus. Attractive websites could entice visitors to fill their subscriber list to receive electronic newsletters and promotional material, via email. This direct marketing tactic enables HEIs to communicate directly with prospective students through a variety of media, including; by electronic newsletters, mobile messaging apps, websites, online and offline catalogues, promotional letters, amongst others. The HEIs' direct marketing seeks to create one-to-one personal relationships with prospective students. Its underlying goal is to generate a response from the prospects themselves.

In this day and age, the engine behind direct marketing is usually a sophisticated database. The collection of data is growing at an exponential rate as it is continuously stored, in massive amounts, by search engines, including Google and Bing, amongst others. The advances in technology are increasingly allowing marketers to know more about their audiences. For instance, marketers are benefiting from the growth of geo-location data services like satellites, near-field communication and global positioning systems that track the users' movements that measure traffic and other real-time phenomena. New anonymous cookie-less data-capture methods are connecting the consumers' data with geolocation-based data. These methods are increasingly empowering marketers as they use Google's and Bing's Business Solutions, to hyper-target online users with real-time mobile ad campaigns to drive conversions. For example, the HEIs' marketers can use Google AdWords to know about the most popular search terms, as they could identify which ads are converting prospects. AdWords identifies the combinations of keywords and messages that are the most effective in particular markets. Besides, Google Analytics enables the HEIs to have an accurate picture of their web activity. As a result, they will be in a position to track and monitor their online marketing effectiveness whilst segmenting and customising communications.

User-generated content, interactive marketing and social media

HEIs can also use external websites and online portals that feature user-generated content that promotes higher education courses in different contexts. For example, Wikipedia pages can reach broad audiences, and they enjoy high credibility with search engines.

Moreover, HEIs can engage with prospective students through conversations, informal surveys, and informational posts that are intended to improve interactions with online users. Communications on social networks, including Facebook, Instagram, Snapchat, Twitter, and Linkedin, amongst others, can be used to filter unqualified prospects. These networks may reveal exciting insights on the prospects' language proficiencies, interests and their perception of the HEIs' brand image (Beneke, 2011). Social media provides an opportunity to HEIs to improve their brand awareness. Therefore, they should establish their presence on social media platforms in different markets. HEIs are increasingly relying on the most popular social networks as exciting prospects may be intrigued to share and spread promotional content, online. Such digital marketing stimuli may result in social contagion through e-mails, posts, likes, tweets, mentions, et cetera. This would lead to a viral dispersion of the HEIs' marketing messages as effective marketing campaigns may trigger a strong emotional response among prospects. Therefore, HEIs may leverage themselves through word-of-mouth (WOM) publicity on social networks. For instance, they could join WeChat and Sina Weibo to target Chinese prospects.

Public relations and publicity

The testimonials of students or alumni would probably reveal meaningful information on the quality of educational institutions or the effectiveness of their curriculum programmes. These communications may be available in different languages in order to provide peer affirmations to a wide array of local and international students. The videos of the students' referrals that are not scripted may appear as more authentic than professionally edited marketing material. Such word-of-mouth publicity may prove to be more credible and trust-inspiring than academic awards, accreditations, or past statistical information. HEIs may feature the success stories of their former alumni who are now engaged in key government or corporate positions. They may provide internship programmes to their former HEIs' students. At the same time, they may benefit from a talent pool of promising students.

HEIs can improve their brand equity by organising public relations activities on campus, including; summer camps, open-day events, et cetera. They can attract international students from different markets to follow academic courses in specific disciplines.

Personal selling

Inevitably, the positive or negative word-of-mouth publicity could affect the prospective students' perceptions of HEIs. Therefore, front office employees in the admissions department would be in an excellent position to engage in two-way communications with potential students. The HEI's admissions department must be aware that they are 'selling' the university when they provide their technical support to prospects, applicants, and admitted students with their queries. They may also need to be proficient on how to handle complaints. Therefore, front office employees ought to be monitored and evaluated regularly.

The money

How much will be budgeted for each marketing tool? Many HEIs may rely on the budget allocation from their national government. Alternatively, they may be receiving some financial support from alumni, corporations, foundations, et cetera. HEIs should continuously seek new and diversified funding sources and methods. Their potential sources of income may include; tuition fees for courses, national and international research grants from institutional funding, as well as 'other' income sources that could be obtained from consultancy, conferences, specialised courses, knowledge exchange/technology transfer, et cetera

(Njenga & Fourie, 2010). They could engage in collaborative agreements with reputable research institutes to benefit from the pooling of institutional resources and expertise.

The measurement

Very often, HEIs claim that their graduates are finding rewarding careers following the completion of their degrees. These statements need to be substantiated with evidence. The students' career outcomes are often considered as one of the most critical factors that will influence student decision-making. This is particularly true for many disciplines and recruitment markets. Therefore, HEIs should regularly monitor their progress against their set priorities, commitments, and aims by using relevant performance indicators, benchmarks, and targets.

HEIs should measure the performance and successes of their marketing strategies. Key metrics could analyse and measure; student enrolment ratios, graduate rates, student drop-out rates, the students' continuation of studies at the next academic level, the employability index of graduates. Other metrics may involve the calculation of their costs per credit, costs per degree and student-faculty ratio, amongst others.

HEIs may want to find out the students' opinions and perceptions towards their host institutions. This data can be used to identify the HEIs' strengths and identify other areas that may require further improvement. Qualitative research may shed light on the HEIs' progress on planned goals, objectives, and strategic initiatives. These insights could provide valuable data on the students' opinions and perceptions of their learning environments. Conversely, HEIs may explore the students' attitudes through quantitative research that will analyse courses (including undergraduate, graduate, and professional). Survey instruments could measure the students' satisfaction with teaching; research opportunities. They could reveal the students' attitudes on international and public engagement opportunities; ease of taking courses across boundaries and investigate whether there are any administrative/bureaucratic barriers at their respective HEI.

Other metrics may evaluate the HEIs' strategic priorities and initiatives; including ongoing assessments of academic and administrative staff, and their retention rates. They may track changes in faculty size; outline the age distribution of academic employees; diversity of students and staff, in terms of gender, race, and ethnicity, et cetera. HEIs could examine discipline-specific rankings; and may involve a continuous scrutinisation of courses, research output, reviews of expenditures per academic member of staff, et cetera.

Also, more and more institutions are keeping a track record of their alumni, although they may not always differentiate between the outcomes for domestic and international students. However, they will probably report on the cohort of students' career progression following the completion of their education. HEIs often mention specific companies that have employed their graduates.

Besides, HEIs may gather data on the international students' attitudes towards housing and determine if they are happy in their new location.

HEIs may have a good reputation in specific regions or countries (Beneke, 2011). Nevertheless, international students will usually rely on the international rankings to quickly understand the quality of their potential host institution and its educational programmes. They may come across league tables, such as the Academic Ranking of World Universities from Shanghai Jiao Tong rankings; Times Higher Education World University Rankings; 'Professional ranking' of world universities from the École des Mines de Paris or QS rankings, amongst others. These rankings usually adopt several metrics and key performance indicators to differentiate amongst HEIs.

Conclusions and implications

In recent years, there were significant changes in the governance of HEI systems in developed as well as in developing countries. Many renowned universities and educational institutions have already introduced marketisation policies as they compete for domestic and international students. At the same time, the marketisation of higher education has become less dependent on state control and government intervention. In response to these challenges, HEIs are resorting to contemporary marketing strategies and tactics to garner a larger share of the international market (Mogaji, 2016). Many universities are increasingly crunching big data and analytics to tap into new market segments in different contexts; as well as laid-out integrated marketing communications plans are providing the right pathways for growth.

This chapter's SWOT analysis has suggested that HEIs' long term sustainability is dependent on the recruitment of international students and faculty employees. Therefore, international HEIs operating in different markets, including those that are located in the African continent, should formulate strategic plans in order to increase their international student figures, enhance research collaborations, foster student mobility in exchange programmes, and forge partnership agreements with business and industry. HEIs ought to invest in resources, competences and capabilities to attract domestic and international students (and staff) to improve their financial and strategic performance.

Not all HEIs, colleges and business schools are responding to the political, socioeconomic, and technological changes promptly. Arguably, those HEIs who are still benefiting of public funding, will not have an urgency to differentiate themselves from their competitors. However, autonomous institutions are in a better position to leverage themselves through effective marketing communications. This way, universities and colleges hailing from different contexts may be in a position to compete in a global market environment and to increase their brand equity amongst international students. Of course, the educational institutions need to ensure that their quality claims are substantiated, year after year.

References

Altbach, P. G. (2004). Globalisation and the university: Myths and realities in an unequal world. *Tertiary Education and Management,* 10(1), 3–25.

Altbach, P. G., Reisberg, L., & Rumbley, L. E. (2009). Trends in global higher education: Tracking an academic revolution. A Report for UNESCO World Conference of Higher Education. Retrieved from www.cep.edu.rs/public/Altbach,_Reisberg, _Rumbley_Tracking_an_Academic_Revolution,_UNESCO_(2009).pdf.

Beine, M., Noël, R., & Ragot, L. (2014). Determinants of the international mobility of students. *Economics of Education Review,* 41, 40–54.

Beneke, J. H. (2011). Marketing the institution to prospective students: A review of brand (reputation) management in higher education. *International Journal of Business and Management,* 6(1), 29–44.

Bharadwaj, S. G., Varadarajan, P. R., & Fahy, J. (1993). Sustainable competitive advantage in service industries: A conceptual model and research propositions. *The Journal of Marketing,* 57(4), 83–99.

Binsardi, A., & Ekwulugo, F. (2003). International marketing of British education: Research on the students' perception and the UK market penetration. *Marketing Intelligence & Planning,* 21(5), 318–327.

Bonnema, J., & Van der Waldt, D. L. R. (2008). Information and source preferences of a student market in higher education. *International Journal of Educational Management,* 22(4), 314–327.

British Council. (2018). International student mobility to (2027). Local investment, global outcomes. Retrieved from https://ei.britishcouncil.org/educationintelligence/ ei-feature-international-student-mobility-2027-local-investment-global-outcome.

Budde-Sung, A. E. (2011). The increasing internationalization of the international business classroom: Cultural and generational considerations. *Business Horizons, 54*(4), 365–373.

Camilleri, M. A. (2016a). Corporate sustainability and responsibility toward education. *Journal of Global Responsibility,* 7(1), 56–71.

Camilleri, M. A. (2016b). Reconceiving corporate social responsibility for business and educational outcomes. *Cogent Business & Management,* 3(1), 1–14.

Camilleri, M. A., & Camilleri, A. C. (2017). Digital learning resources and ubiquitous technologies in education. *Technology, Knowledge and Learning,* 22(1), 65–82.

Camilleri, M. A., & Camilleri, A. C. (2019). The students' readiness to engage with mobile learning apps. *Interactive Technology and Smart Education.* doi:10.1108/ITSE-06-2019-0027.

Constantinides, E., & Zinck Stagno, M. C. (2011). Potential of the social media as instruments of higher education marketing: A segmentation study. *Journal of Marketing for Higher Education,* 21(1), 7–24.

Cronin Jr, J. J., & Taylor, S. A. (1992). Measuring service quality: A reexamination and extension. *Journal of Marketing,* 56(3), 55–68.

De Jager, J., & Gbadamosi, G. (2010). Specific remedy for specific problem: Measuring service quality in South African higher education. *Higher Education,* 60(3), 251–267.

Duque, L. C. (2014). A framework for analysing higher education performance: Students' satisfaction, perceived learning outcomes, and dropout intentions. *Total Quality Management & Business Excellence* 25(1–2), 1–21.

Estermann, T. (2017). Why university autonomy matters more than ever. *University World News,* 454. Retrieved from www.universityworldnews.com/article.php?story= 20170404132356742.

Estermann, T., Nokkala, T., & Steinel, M. (2011). University autonomy in Europe II. The scorecard. Brussels: European University Association. Retrieved from http://agir-ups.info/wp-content/uploads/2013/01/University_Autonomy_in_Europe_II_-_The_Scorecard.sflb_.pdf.

EUA. (2017). EUA calls on governments to refrain from interference in university autonomy. Retrieved from www.eua.be/activities-services/news/newsitem/2017/04/03/eua-calls-on-governments-to-refrain-from-interference-in-university-autonomy.

Friga, P. N., Bettis, R. A., & Sullivan, R. S. (2003). Changes in graduate management education and new business school strategies for the 21st century. *Academy of Management Learning and Education*, 2(3), 233–249.

Helms, M. M., & Nixon, J. (2010). Exploring SWOT analysis–where are we now? A review of academic research from the last decade. *Journal of Strategy and Management*, 3(3), 215–251.

Hemsley-Brown, J., & Oplatka, I. (2006). Universities in a competitive global marketplace: A systematic review of the literature on higher education marketing. *International Journal of Public Sector Management*, 19(4), 316–338.

Hoecht, A. (2006). Quality assurance in UK higher education: Issues of trust, control, professional autonomy and accountability. *Higher Education*, 51(4), 541–563.

ICEF. (2017). Mapping the trends that will shape international student mobility. Retrieved from http://monitor.icef.com/2017/07/mapping-trends-will-shape-international-student-mobility/.

Ivy, J. (2008). A new higher education marketing mix: The 7Ps for MBA marketing. *International Journal of Educational Management*, 22(4), 288–299.

Kolb, A. Y., & Kolb, D. A. (2005). Learning styles and learning spaces: Enhancing experiential learning in higher education. *Academy of Management Learning & Education*, 4(2), 193–212.

Kotler, P., & Fox, K. F. (1995). *Strategic marketing for educational institutions*. New York: Prentice-Hall.

Lee, J. T. (2014). Education hubs and talent development: Policymaking and implementation challenges. *Higher Education*, 68(6), 807–823.

Marginson, S. (2006). Dynamics of national and global competition in higher education. *Higher Education*, 52(1), 1–39.

Maringe, F., & Foskett, N. (2002). Marketing university education: The southern African experience. *Higher Education Review*, 34(3), 35–51.

Maringe, F., & Gibbs, P. (2008). *Marketing higher education: Theory and practice*. London: McGraw-Hill Education.

Maton, K. (2005). A question of autonomy: Bourdieu's field approach and higher education policy. *Journal of education policy*, 20(6), 687–704.

Mazzarol, T. (1998). Critical success factors for international education marketing. *International Journal of Educational Management*, 12(4), 163–175.

Mazzarol, T., & Soutar, G. N. (2002). 'Push-pull' factors influencing international student destination choice. *International Journal of Educational Management*, 16(2), 82–90.

Mogaji, E. (2016). Marketing strategies of United Kingdom universities during clearing and adjustment. *International Journal of Educational Management*, 30(4), 493–504.

Moore, M. G., & Kearsley, G. (2011). *Distance education: A systems view of online learning*. Belmont, CA: Cengage Learning.

Njenga, J. K., & Fourie, L. C. H. (2010). The myths about e-learning in higher education. *British Journal of Educational Technology*, 41(2), 199–212.

Parameswaran, R., & Glowacka, A. E. (1995). University image: An information processing perspective. *Journal of Marketing for Higher Education*, 6(2), 41–56.

Pucciarelli, F., & Kaplan, A. (2016). Competition and strategy in higher education: Managing complexity and uncertainty. *Business Horizons*, 59(3), 311–320.

Russell, M. (2005). Marketing education: A review of service quality perceptions among international students. *International Journal of Contemporary Hospitality Management*, 17(1), 65–77.

Schofield, C., Cotton, D., Gresty, K., Kneale, P., & Winter, J. (2013). Higher education provision in a crowded marketplace. *Journal of Higher Education Policy and Management*, 35(2), 193–205.

Van Heerden, N., Wiese, M., North, E., & Jordaan, Y. (2009). A marketing perspective on choice factors considered by South African first-year students in selecting a higher education institution. *Southern African Business Review*, 13(1), 39–60.

7 Social media for universities' strategic communication

Temitope Farinloye, Thomas Wayne, Emmanuel Mogaji, and Josué Kuika Watat

Introduction

Nowadays, information and communication technologies in general, and Web 2.0 technologies in particular, have become the first concern of young people as well as adults. Social networks have taken the lead in terms of number of users on all continents. Their use is often associated with the exchange and sharing of different content, with Internet users who can subsequently accept in friendship.

The African continent has recorded since 2010 an explosion in the use of mobile phones, gravitating around 65% according to the International Telecommunications Union (ITU, 2018). A mobile phone is, therefore, an essential tool for Internet users who wish to have access to technological innovations, communicate with their friends, and share diverse contents (Aker & Mbiti, 2010; Bonjawo, 2002). This is necessarily the consequence of obsolescence of fixed telephone lines and also the acquisition of computers that can sometimes be expensive (Oyelaran-Oyeyinka & Lal, 2005).

Social media has seized the academic world and education for more than a decade. Some universities, institutes, and training centres have created some kinds of social media intending to simplify communication, better-coordinating exchanges and learning, with relevant stakeholders (Gachago & Ivala, 2012; Watat, Wamba, & Kamdjoug, 2018). Social media has demonstrated its strengths in connecting several stakeholders, including students to each other, teachers to themselves, students and teachers, all the entities in the university, as well as external actors (Junco, Heiberger, & Loken, 2011). This link creates a community of people who share the same interests, the same challenges, and the same objectives, to help one another and create social cohesion.

Social media is transforming how consumers interact with brands and how brand-related content is consumed (Mogaji, 2016). The advent of readily available social media applications has created opportunities for dialogic and more interactive engagement (Bonsón & Ratkai, 2013). Universities are not excluded from using social media to engage with their stakeholders. Unlike most other brands, universities do have a diverse range of stakeholders which inadvertently influences their communication strategies, suggesting the need to recognise and embraces the benefits and opportunities that social media can bring as a tool.

Universities communicate with prospective students for student recruitment purposes, they communicate with current students through providing updates, and they also communicate with the public and funders about their research activities and innovation. While recognising these diverse communication strands, this chapter aims to address and explore the universities' strategic communication while using social media.

Given that the European and American universities are widely in the lead in terms of marketing strategies and communication via social media, it is clear that African universities are lagging (Altbach, Reisberg, & Rumbley, 2019). In a study in 2015, ARCES reports that 97% of French universities and colleges of higher learning use social media (Küster & Vila 2006; Peruta & Shields, 2017). Very few African universities have communication strategies and are present on social media, whereas Africa has one of the highest rates of social media use, given that young people are strongly represented. For many African institutions, social media is limited to entertainment and friendly exchanges. The 'strategic communication' aspect is strongly neglected. Social media is exponentially invading many parts of African society, and education is the most affected sector. This is because the majority of Internet users in Africa are mostly young, and this amount has doubled since 2010 (Kemp, 2018).

Previous academic studies have explored social media in the context of marketing communication strategies by universities to reach prospective customers, social media for brand engagement and social media for teaching. While this chapter aims to provide a holistic view, it will also be specifically focusing on social media for communication within the African context and also recognising the challenges that are specific to the continent.

The chapter highlights the purpose of social media, arguing that it is not just for marketing communications, but a dialogical engagement between a university and its stakeholders. The stakeholders and their expectation within the context of the university system, are also discussed to understand the content creating and scheduling strategies to be implemented. The chapter further explores selected social media network sites that are often used by universities. Also, there is recognition of the human resources in achieving the set objectives for the social media strategy.

Specifically, this chapter has three objectives:

1. To understand the benefits of social media for strategic communication by universities.
2. To recognise the African context that makes strategic communications on social media unique.
3. To offer recommendations on how African universities can adopt social media for strategic communication.

While acknowledging that this chapter is not empirically driven, it offers implications for managers of universities' social media profile. The chapter highlights best practice for universities, aiming to improve their existing use of social media for strategic communications and those working to develop a new one. The chapter further offers practical action plans and recommendations for managers who aim to develop a new team for social media engagement and those who want to improve their team's performance.

Theoretical framework

Usually, any organisation or university that uses social media, whether for profit or not, does so for commercial purposes. It can be to promote their training, the propaganda of its number of graduates and their smooth integration into the professional world, or for the popularisation of its teachings. Dahl's work is based on the assumption that social media is used by the majority of universities for the same purpose – to raise more funds at the university while providing better service to students (Dahl, 2018). Besides, this determination generally involves the strengthening of already existing links between the stakeholders, leading to increased spending (Slaughter & Leslie, 1997). Quantifying this commitment of universities via social media can be done by comparing reactions (follow, like, and retweet on Twitter; I like, I share on Facebook … comments following a topic, or from a given point of view (Dahl, 2018).

Before the advent of the Internet, universities, especially those in the USA, focused their efforts on training and passing on knowledge to students. Marketing and communication strategies, therefore, took a back seat (Veysey, 1981). Shortly before the 1950s, rivalries between universities created a quasi-corporate environment (Blackwell, 1936; Canterbury, 2000). Currents of thought about communication strategies and marketing grew in the 1970s, with the advent of several marketing and strategic theories in universities (Krachenberg, 1972). There has been a massive flow of students attending universities. This was necessary due to the end of the war in Vietnam and the military service made compulsory (Discenza, Ferguson, & Wisner, 1985). It was therefore noticed that there was a disinterest in the progress of an education that trains man through the transmission of humanist culture. On the other hand, they turned to fields that could lead to job opportunities, leaving universities to reshape their job-oriented training and graduation models (Doyle & Newbould, 1980).

The arrival of the Internet and the World Wide Web in the early 2000s has been a boost for universities. Several interdisciplinary research projects, like the works of Klassen (2002) and Gomes and Murphy (2003), have emerged to explain marketing psychology and technological understanding. Most universities in Europe and the USA have a website. These websites served as dynamic showcases, aimed at attracting potential students while encouraging former students to promote their institution (Gomes & Murphy, 2003). In addition to its beginnings, Ganster and Schumacher (2009) state that several universities around the world were late in taking a hand in the use of social media. They felt they were not the target (Raineri, Fudge, & Hall, 2015). However, the social and informational nature of social media such as Twitter and Facebook has been demonstrated several times, and it is observed that several universities have joined such trend (Bélanger, Bali, & Longden, 2014). All in all, it is undeniable to mention the fact that most universities in Africa and the world are modernised by the use of social media for marketing purposes of maintaining its image of brands among stakeholders.

Social media networks

Social media can be defined as a group of technologies that foster engagement where individuals are active participants in creating, organising, editing, combining, sharing, commenting, and rating Web content, as well as forming a social networks through interacting and linking to each other (Chun, Shulman, Sandoval, & Hovy, 2010; Criado, Sandoval-Almazan, & Gil-Garcia, 2013). These technologies include social networking (e.g., Facebook), microblogging (e.g., Twitter) and multimedia sharing (e.g., YouTube). Social media is no longer new. The implementation of content management, engagement, and measurements are the new challenges.

Organisations are increasingly adopting social media for strategic corporate and organisational communication and public relations (Macnamara & Zerfass, 2012). It has been hailed as transformative which allows brands to engage with their stakeholders (Mogaji, Farinloye, & Aririguzoh, 2016). Universities are not exempted in using it as well for strategic communications to engage with stakeholders with Internet access. Social media provides a wide range of audio, video, and interactive capabilities without substantial costs (Hrdinová, Helbig, & Peters, 2010).

There are different social media for different purposes, and universities need to choose the platform upon which they want to engage with their stakeholders. This chapter, however, recognises seven social media that are often used by universities. Spencer (2019) and Worthy (2019) of Hootsuite presents a glossary of social media:

Facebook – Presently the largest social networking site in the world and one of the most widely used. It connects friends and relatives to create a network. Brands can have their profile pages and engage with those who have liked their pages. Users can share comments, upload their images, and engage with the university.

Twitter – A social network and media platform where users communicate with 280-character messages, along with photos, videos, and other content. Twitter is known for real-time discussions on breaking news stories and trends. Brands have their profile, (which can be verified), they follow other profiles, and they are followed as well. Brands can send tweets, and they can retweet tweets, converse through direct messages, and reply to tweets.

Instagram – A free online photo-sharing app that is independent of, but owned by Facebook. It allows for the addition of several filters, editing, and sharing options. Brands can have their verified profile and share photographs, video, stories, which they use as a mode of engaging with their followers. Conversations can also be carried out using direct messages, which are private conversations.

Snapchat – A photo- and video-messaging app launched in 2011. It enables the user to chat with friends by using pictures. Users can add filters, text, drawings, or emoji to their content before sending it to their recipients. Individual messages last only up to 10 seconds before they are entirely removed from the company's servers. This feature gives the user control over their post and makes it unique and attractive to its users.

LinkedIn – Acquired by Microsoft in 2016, LinkedIn is one of the most popular professional social networking sites. It is used across the globe by all types of professionals and serves as an ideal platform to connect with different businesses, locate, and hire ideal candidates. Individuals have their page which serves as an online CV, and they can share video, images and live streams with their connections. Brands as well do have their page, where they share contents, including job vacancies.

WhatsApp – Another social media technology which joined Facebook in 2014 but continues to operate as a separate app, with a laser focus on building a messaging service that works fast and reliably anywhere in the world. This is linked with specific telephone numbers and allows chat and phone calls. More than 1 billion people in over 180 countries use WhatsApp. Businesses do have their pages and can communicate with brands. It is often integrated as a chatbot and AI assistance on websites.

YouTube – Operating as one of Google's subsidiaries, YouTube is the world's largest video-sharing social networking site that enables users to upload and share videos, view them, comment on them and like them. This social network is accessible across the globe and even enables users to create a YouTube channel where they can upload all their personally recorded videos to showcase to their friends and followers.

The stakeholders

For effective communication to take place, it is essential to identify the key players within the communication cycle. A university has many stakeholders with varying interests and commitments. Thus, identifying the right communication media for a specific stakeholder is essential to elicit stakeholder engagement (Payne & Calton, 2017). This section identifies three forms of stakeholder engagement identified by Mogaji (2019) and how it influences the strategic communications of the universities. These are:

1. Recruit – These are communications geared towards prospective students and their parents. The aim of communicating with these stakeholders is to recruit students. The university may use their social media profile to provide prospective students and their parents with relevant information so that they can make an informed choice. For prospective students, this may include the support available for filling out the application form, invitation to Open Day, comments and testimonies from present students, sharing images of the campus, and the student life. This also includes an opportunity to ask questions and engage through messengers, chatbot or by replying to comments or tweets. This strategic communication also involves sharing the story of an alumnus who has successfully graduated from the university.
2. Retain – These are communications geared towards stakeholders who are already within the university. This includes the staff and the students. The present students are considered the most significant stakeholder in the university. They need to know the events and activities that are going on within the campus. They need to be informed in case of an emergency. Dabner (2012) reported how the University of Canterbury, New Zealand, used social media as a channel to carefully control their response to an earthquake that affected their city. This provides further evidence that social media can effectively support information sharing, communication and collaboration in higher education contexts, particularly in times of crisis. Likewise, staff needs to be engaged with as part of this group of stakeholders. Research activities and achievements of staff may be shared on social media.
3. Report – These are communication aimed at stakeholders that need to be updated about the progress within the university. These include alumni that need to know what is going on within the university and how best they can contribute back to the university. Besides, the funders and research partners need to be updated about research activities. These are groups of stakeholders that have interest in the university, and there are possibilities for engagement on social media.

It is essential to recognise that these stakeholders have different expectations from the university, and the university should be able to communicate with them almost at a personal level, which includes sharing information that is relevant to each group. It is, however, possible that some information might be relevant to all the stakeholders at once.

The purpose

With the understanding of these different stakeholders and their expectation, universities need to identify their purpose on the network, as the purpose of adopting social media abounds. Though primarily it is all about communications, it is varied across different sectors and industry. The way a FTSE 100 uses social media will be different from a charity organisation. They both have different values and objectives. Likewise, their target audience and stakeholder interested in their social media posts are different. This will suggest the need for them to adopt different communication strategies.

As stated earlier, universities do have diverse stakeholders, and each stakeholder expects different communications. A prospective undergraduate student may not find tweets about the latest research findings very relevant, compared to a tweet about the Open Day. While recognising this broad spectrum of expectation, universities need to understand that their purpose on social media is not just for marketing purposed, but for engagement – a dialogical engagement between the university and their stakeholders

From a practical perspective, being on social media may indicate an intention to actively engage with the stakeholders (Lovejoy & Saxton, 2012). It is, however, paramount to be strategic about this. The fact that every organisation is on social media is not enough justification to jump on the bandwagon without having clear objectives and goals.

Social media can be used as a tool for student recruitment, perhaps moving away from the idea of prospectuses and websites. Social media also can offer insight into university life, and students can engage with admission staff through chats and direct messages.

Likewise, social media can be used as a tool to promote research activities and innovation. As an effort to highlight achievements and contribution, universities can use their social media pages to promote their latest research findings, their research team, and activities that are being carried out within the university.

Additionally, alumni often want to keep up with what is going on in universities. They are still a part of the stakeholders that need to be engaged with; either because they may be interested in postgraduate studies, they may be interested in mentoring students, establishing industry partnership, or making financial contributions. Social media can be used for alumni engagement and as a fundraising tool.

For universities with a large following of students, social media updates can be used as a crisis communication tool. Perhaps if there is an emergency on the campus, social media becomes handy. The official university handle can be used to provide updates and keep everyone informed about the situation of things.

Besides, universities are always seeking to sell their brand to potential students. According to Kishun (2011), there is a considerable increase in the number of African students enrolled in foreign universities outside their country of origin. This migration, coupled with accelerated population growth, is leading some countries to increase their demand for higher education through the creation of new academic institutions. Thus, in the face of increasing competition, universities are required to review their communication and product promotion strategies if they hope to achieve their goals and disseminate their products to any potentially interested student. For an institution to stand out from others through its strategies and its quality of communication, the public it targets, as well as the products presented, it must watch over its branding. This will lead to making the institution unforgettable in the minds of the stakeholders and allowing them to discover more. The university owns and is responsible for the brand it conveys to stakeholders. It is considered by McAlexander, Koenig, and Schouten (2006) as a community of brands where connected stakeholders are gathered.

It is important to note that the student engagement on universities' social media platform is also essential. Allowing students to co-create the content, using hashtag and sharing pictures of their experience on campus. This is not just limited to Instagram. Students can share their experience of Open Day, clearing or exam pressure on YouTube, providing relevant content for prospective and present students.

The purpose of social media is more than just communicating to make sales, and it is about building relationship, engaging with stakeholders, providing relevant content and a reason for them to want to engage. It is not surprising to see that students' tweets at their universities to make complains or ask question and universities are expected to respond to their concerns.

With the understanding of different stakeholders in the university and their expectation with regards to communications, it is not surprising to see universities creating different profiles, on different social media network, to communicate with their stakeholders. While there is the primary account often used by the university, there are other profiles for student unions to communicate with the students, faculties profile to communicate events and activities going on within the faculty. There may also be a profile page for research groups, which communicates what they are doing within the group.

Harmonising these different profiles is, however, very important. Firstly, to avoid parody account which may confuse the stakeholders. Secondly, consistency in the description and header images should be considered, perhaps if they can have similar form of header. Thirdly, aligning with the leading university account (including it in their description) is essential as well.

The African challenge

Various challenges are militating against successful integration of most social media for strategic communications in Africa. These highlighted challenges are from the perspective of the university as they make effort to engage with their stakeholders.

1. The Motivation to Engage – There appeared to be a lack of motivation by African universities to engage on social media. There are challenges with the content to be updated, the frequency, and the relevance of the

content. Marketing to reach prospective students is often limited because the universities are oversubscribed. If universities, especially the public universities, do not market, they are guaranteed of recruiting their students.

2. The Content Creation – universities in the developed world showcase their facilities, campuses, and students having a good time around their campus. However, there is a challenge with African universities with regards to what they can showcase. There are funding challenges, and the facilities are often in poor state which cannot be showcased. Research activities are limited.

3. The Technical Skills – Olaleye (2017) reported the lack of creative designs in African universities, highlighting the limited technical skills to adopt social media for effective communications with stakeholders.

4. Internet Bandwidth – Africa is still considered an emerging market, with the rate of Internet penetration still quite low as compared to her Western counterparts (Wawira, 2017). By June 2019, Internet World Stats estimates a 39.8% Internet penetration rate in Africa, contributing to only 11.9% of the world users (IWS, 2019). This means that most people are still offline. While the universities are willing to engage, the challenges of Internet bandwidth inhibits the stakeholders, especially the prospective students who have limited access to the Internet.

5. Languages – Linguistic mismatch is another challenge towards the process of strategic communications with stakeholders in Africa. In some regions of Tunisia and Algeria, students are taught in Arabic while some books are written in French instead of English, which is a universal language (Ndofirepi,Farinloye & Mogaji, 2020). In the south of Africa, especially South Africa where the constitution recognises 11 official languages, the adopted language of communication can pose a challenge as they try to engage with stakeholders.

The managerial implication

Designated team

The human resources in achieving the social media objective are acknowledged. There should be a dedicated team responsible for social media engagement. This may be within the communications team or the marketing team (Department of Public Relations & Communications). Importantly, if possible, bring together a multi-functional team, including all stakeholders from communication, legal, technology, human resources, and programme units (Hrdinová, Helbig, & Peters, 2010). With such a big team, it is essential to have some responsibility for managing the social media strategies, to coordinate different activities from different platforms, and to make sure they are all aligned towards the strategic direction of the university. There should be a designated online spokesperson to reply to messages or enquires which may be out of scope for staff (or students) who manage these accounts. It is essential to recognise that there will be trolls online sending abusive and vile messages, therefore measures for support must be in place for staff reading these messages. Staff should not take these personally.

The content creating strategy

The content creating strategy is also essential. The designated team should take responsibility for content creation and engagement on social media platforms. Managers should consider the personal characteristics of the stakeholders when designing marketing strategies (Adefulu et al., 2019; Dwivedi et al., 2018).

Contents provided on social media should aim at communicating the universities' brand value and key messages to the stakeholders. The content strategy provides an effort to present content in meaningful, useful, and relevant contexts within the user experience. It is essential to recognise the different characteristics of stakeholders through research and provide personalised experience for them. The strategy should ensure that the right content reaches the right stakeholder at the right time and for the right reason.

The idea of having different social media platform for different university groups is supported. However, messages should be coherently and consistently provided. The contents must be aligned with the strategic direction of the university. It must also align with the brand identity of the university. If possible, the username should present an alliance with the university. Account profile information should clearly state the purpose of the account and the hours during which it is monitored.

While the list is inexhaustible, there are some content strategies that can be considered by the university.

Images of Campus – These are images or video showing different buildings and facilities, for example, the library, lecture theatres, iconic buildings, accommodation, and the landscaped gardens and other naturel elements on campus. These images can be taken during different times of the day and during different seasons. Creation of user-generated content should also be encouraged where the university allows the students to share pictures of campus using branded hashtags, and cultivating a more inclusive and diverse campus community.

Images of Mascot or Brand Identity – Universities can use their social media platform to integrate their brands and create more awareness. Often universities have mascots or animals that represent the university. Images of these mascots can be taken around the university. This could also be with students at different occasions, like graduation or Open Day. Brand identities like the school anthem, logo, sports team uniform, souvenirs and other brand items, can also be showcased on the platform. Likewise, changes to the university's brand identity can be announced. When a university changes its logo, updates should be shared on its social media platform.

Images of activities on Campus —These are images or video of events such as Open Days – showing present student participating, wearing their branded T-shirt, and helping prospective students and parents who have come visiting. Images during graduation, showing excited graduates and their family are also examples of images of activities on campus. Universities can also share and retweet these images that have been created by the students on their account. Student union activities on campus should also be featured, to give an insight into life as a student. This can be from the student union profile, but can also be shared by the university's main profile. Special guest visiting the university can also be featured on the university's social media profile.

Images of activities outside the Campus – This gives the university the opportunity to tell its story in a different context, an opportunity to share what life is like outside the university, and how its students can stand out. A very good example is sports events, perhaps winning a competition, or other student activities that showcase the university among other universities. It showcases the ability of the university to stand out and excel outside its comfort zone.

Images of Host Community – Acknowledging that universities are situated in a location with their own identity and has been found to influence student choice, it is important for universities to create content around their location in order to showcase what they have to offer. These images can include a known landmark, transport connection, social life and activities around the city.

Student Stories – This can be a short video for Instagram or a longer video for YouTube whereby the students shares their stories about how they considered the university, the admission process, and the support they have received in order to settle down very well. This can also involve featuring students from diverse backgrounds, like international students, students with a form of disability, or a different culture to cultivate and showcase a more inclusive and diverse campus community. This will give insight into the university and be able to assist others who are thinking of coming to the university.

Staff Stories – Like student sharing their stories, staff can also share their story on the university. Explaining their research to non-experts and highlighting the impact their research is making in the community. The professional and support services staff such as the facilities manager, marketing communications team and librarians can also give insights into their day and effort they are making in enhancing the students' teaching and learning experiences. This could be a video or a profile picture that is followed up with a story or a blog post.

Alumni Stories – This highlights the success stories of alumni as a way of encouraging present and prospective students to work harder and achieve their goals. The university can also use this to reinforce their values and support they provide for their students, in other to achieve greatness. These videos can be uploaded on LinkedIn among other platforms, as it is considered a social media networking site for professionals. Also, it can be shared elsewhere. The

University of Toronto shared a video on Instagram where they took pride in the fact that their alumni include four prime ministers, two governors-general and two astronauts. This kind of message arouses a positive attitude towards the university's brands.

Infographics – These are graphics illustration that can be used to keep the stakeholders updated about development in the university. These are often suitable for Twitter and Instagram. An example could be the latest ranking of the university and the progress the university has made on the league table. The university can also showcase the number of followers on the platform as a means of credibility and appreciate those who are engaging with them. Step-by-step insight into problems faced by students can also be graphically presented. This can also provide insight into activities for prospective students as they settle down on campus. Quotes from individuals or other motivational quotes can also be shared on the platform as a means of motivating the students.

Help Guides and Supports – Universities can provide content around help guide and support available for students –both present students and prospective students. Prospective students may be interested in how to book accommodations, access the library and eLearning platform, how to submit their assignment, or deal with stress during exams. Universities can gain insight from their research, understand what problems students encounter, and provide help and support to solve those problems. Prospective students can be provided with tips and advise on how to navigate the application process successfully. This can also include Webinars, Question and Answer session with the university's management team, the Head of Department, or Live Chats. Here students can call in or chat to get answers.

Listicle – This is a piece of writing or other content presented wholly or partly in the form of a list. It evolves from the concept of the help guides and support, but instead of having a long blog list, it provides short bullet-point insight. This can be used to give students' insight into the university. Prospective students and their parents may be interested in Top 10 reasons why they should consider the university, or Top 10 things that the student enjoy about the university. These articles can be made available on different social media platform and accompanied with relevant images. It is aimed at effectively and promptly engaging with the stakeholders who might not want to read a long blogpost.

Invitation – There are many events and activities going on in the university, from graduation to Open Day to Taster days and conferences. To keep stakeholders up to date about these events are important. Information about these events can also be shared on the social media platform. Likewise, photography and video from the events can also be shared to further engage with the stakeholders. Branded hashtags for events are also essentials in order to track and measure the level of engagement.

The execution, creation, and management of these content is essential in order to present a coherent strategic communication successfully. The team need to recognise that the implementation of this strategy requires time. It is no use having a profile and not engaging with other users or update with relevant content. Efforts should be made towards achieving a structured approach to creating and managing timely postings of these social media contents. As part of the content strategy, the team should monitor references to the university on social media and the Internet, and act accordingly. This might suggest a timely response while the momentum is still on. The strategy should include overall objectives, Key Performance Indicators (KPIs), an outline of measurement methods and explain how social media communication is integrated with the university's strategic plans (Macnamara & Zerfass, 2012).

Ecityinteractive (2019) describes the idea of content governance, which illustrates how digital content in a presented in a controlled and orderly fashion. This helps in visualising the content creation workflows. Identifying what tasks need to be done, who is responsible for such tasks, and what tools are necessary to support these activities. Importantly content governance recommends the Plan > Create > Edit > Approve Publish > Review workflow.

While recognising that social media offers the opportunity to engage, it is essential to note that responses of stakeholder to the content may change the direction of the conversation. Other users on the social media profile can comment online, post videos and photos, and tag the university. This highlights the possibilities of losing control over messages, and this has been cited as the major obstacle and risk in using social media (Macnamara & Zerfass, 2012). The 'loss of control' can expect the social media team to react professionally promptly to take back control of the conversation. Not surprisingly some social media like YouTube and Instagram have the tool to disable comments.

Challenges with Internet bandwidth and access should be considered as this presents a practical implication for content design, size of images, and duration of videos. Likewise, while there is a limitation with subtitles during live events, for the sake of accessibility, all audio and video content in the social media campaign must have subtitles.

Verified account

It is also important to work towards getting their profiles verified and engaging more with the stakeholders as there are many parody accounts. These parody accounts do not represent the university and can confuse the stakeholders who are willing to engage (Mogaji & Erkan, 2019). Often, these parody accounts, especially on Facebook, share irrelevant posts, and as the pages are often created to attract followers and used for advertisements and sponsored post. Universities, starting with their social media strategy, need to search for any existing site claiming to be the official profile for the university. This is another reason for the universities to take ownership of their social media profile and take charge of their communication strategies, as prospective students may not be able to identify the real profile by a simple search on the social media platform.

Technical skill training

To maintain the accounts, training should be towards improving the technical skills of the team, such as familiarisation with different software and tools. Social media analytics, to understand the key drivers of engagement, is essential. The team should endeavour to measure the impact of their campaigns, track the performance of posts, and discover what resonates with the stakeholders by tracking performance at the post level. These insights can be used to create better content, inform campaign strategy, and better engage your stakeholders. Tools for the entire publishing process should be considered based on the significant number of stakeholders to engage with.

Soft skill training

Staff training is essential and should be ongoing. Staff should be made aware of the basic etiquette of customer services, even though they are behind the scene. Likewise, for accounts to be managed by students, they should be trained on conduct and practices on social media while representing the university. The fact that they are conversant with social media in their personal life does not exclude them from proper training. Students, especially managing social media accounts related to the university brands, should make the effort to separate it from their accounts. While employees who are 'official' Twitter users for the university are identified as such, they must focus solely on engagement and not unnecessary banter which may bring the university into disrepute. Sometimes this banter can be very humorous and go viral. While there is a positive twist to that, staff should be very mindful. It is becoming a common practice that university staff on social media, especially Twitter, are including the caveat that their social media postings are theirs – and theirs alone – and not associated with the university, as an effort to differentiate themselves from the university. While some students may contribute to the university's official social media activities as part of their role, they should be well trained and supported through the process

Coordinated media profile

Considering that there are social media profiles from different faculties, departments and group in the university, it is essential to coordinate and ensure all profiles reflect the values of the university. As social media presences and postings of employees can be problematic for organisations (O'Connor, Schmidt, & Drouin, 2016), there should be a central control team, developing guidelines to guide employee content and bringing the guidelines to the attention of the employee. Likewise, there should support for the administrator of the social media profile that will be associated with the university and those who have the intention to develop theirs.

The social media policy

With different stakeholders to be engaged with, different messages from different channels, and different profiles disseminating information, it is essential to put policies and guidelines in place. Hrdinová et al. (2010) differentiated between social media policies and guidelines – guidelines provide advice on how to best use social media tools to achieve the desired result, while policies, on the other hand, represent official positions that govern the use of social media by employees in the organisation.

Hrdinová et al. (2010) analysed various government social media policies to identify the core elements of a social media policy, and they identified eight essential elements for a social media policy. These are: 1) employee access, 2) account management, 3) acceptable use, 4) employee conduct, 5) content, 6) security, 7) legal issues, and 8) citizen conduct. Pomerantz et al. (2015) also analysed social media policies for American institutions and found that they addressed three categories which are the appropriateness of posts (e.g., appropriate content, appropriate tone), representing the institution (e.g., branding, public image, posting in the institution's name), and ensuring that posts comply with the law.

This highlights the importance of this policy to guide the staff and protect the university's brand reputation. The social media policy should set expectations for everyone involved within the university's social media, and universities need to do significantly more to inform staff and students involved in social media policies. Likewise, the guideline should identify the designated person who can speak on behalf of the organisation in social media and under what circumstances (Macnamara & Zerfass, 2012).

There should be contingency plans for continuity in case staff leave, and they do not leave with the password. Staff are trained on tools to engage effectively and professionally. The ever-changing landscape of the social media environment should be acknowledged. Staff must keep themselves updated with developments, and likewise the policy should reflect these changes. Moreover, as with any other policy, social media policies should be reviewed periodically (Hrdinová, Helbig, & Peters, 2010) to ensure that they continue to reflect the universities' changing strategy and priorities.

Conclusion

This chapter recognises the importance of social media in communicating with stakeholders. Universities are also known to use social media to communicate. While recognising the challenges in communicating with a diverse audience, this chapter explores the challenges of African universities as they use social media to engage. The high cost of devices, lack of infrastructure, and low bandwidth and access to Internet (Oji, Iwu, & Tengeh, 2017), the linguistic challenges (Ndofirepi & Mogaji, 2019) and lack of strategic ideas for content creation affecting how African universities use website for strategic communications.

In view of various technological evolutions and the expansion of teaching according to methods more and more adapted to realities, the ever-increasing rivalries between universities and higher education institutions inevitably lead them to review the methods used to implement cutting-edge communication strategies to better position themselves in the minds of their stakeholders, regardless of the geographical area in which they are located (Bower, 2001; Wolff, 2002). For example, building an active and strong community through social media is an ideal option if universities want to attract more students. However, more importantly, to retain them so that they can, in turn, spread the reputation of the institution. Through social media, universities will perfect the experiences of their students, since they will adapt to the realities and tools they use widely (Bosch, 2009). They will also improve their communication with former students and thus increase the development of their brand. Social media also improves the marketing identity of the university and perpetuates the dedication of students by taking into account the desires and aspirations of newcomers to the digital world. McAlexander, Koenig, & Schouten, (2005) have demonstrated in their work that adherents of a robust, effective and popular academic brand congregation tend to develop positive attitudes towards the university. Thus, there are often alumni and other stakeholders making donations to the university or still promoting the university in various secondary schools to attract potential students (Chisenga, 2006). The brand community, therefore, includes all stakeholders who are interested in the brand according to its relevance, and also the various relationships that make them particularly interested in using the brand.

Right or wrong, it is therefore clear that Web 2.0 technologies represent a real and robust challenge for the African education system as it exists today (Abugre, 2018). They are seen as having an impact on the supply of education and training. Whatever their nature or type, social media is out of step with the current educational foundations in Africa. Indeed, the use of social media in education in Africa is conditioned by the fact that the student must first be an 'active co-producer' of knowledge rather than a 'passive consumer' of content. Besides, training must be a 'participatory social process' (Lee & McLoughlin, 2011). That is why there are two streams of thought: those who believe that social media can be used to strengthen relationships between stakeholders and improve the functioning of the university in its current form, and those who are rather demoralising, believing that social media is created to disrupt students and replace the essential vision of the university. The continued and rapid proliferation of social media is a clear challenge to the future of university provision and training in higher education in Africa. In the case of already existing technologies, empirical and practical studies remain mostly speculative rather than affirmative and concrete. Let us note nevertheless, the existence of an emerging and very promising literature which testifies to the benefits of the use of social media in the education. One can list the benefits associated with Facebook usage for learning and assimilating lessons, where still is the need to integrate Twitter into the collaborative process and communication between students and teachers.

The chapter offers managerial implications for university managers who want to adopt social media for effective strategic communications. The challenges are presented as it requires a considerable amount of effort for planning and human resources. However, the opportunity abounds to effectively communicate the universities' values aligned with the strategic plans and engaging with the stakeholders with personalised content.

A content creation was provided which highlights how universities can create content to share on social media. These content creation ideas include images of the campus, the facilities and the host community. Likewise, there are stories told by staff, students and alumni, full of emotions and positive narratives, providing informative, relevant, useful and timely information for existing students and prospective students through blogs, help guides and infographics.

While this information can be shared through various university social media handles, the designated team needs to make sure the profile accounts are well managed and aligned with the values of the university. The chapter recognises that there are also several risks associated with the use of social media which could ultimately impact on the university's reputation and this suggests the need to have a social media policy to guide and assist that staff and everyone involved in the universities' social media. Regular updates to the policy are recommended as social media are ever-changing.

Even though the chapter is not backed upon by any theoretical underpinning or empirical research, it offers practical implications based on academic research and practices to inform the strategic use of social media for communications in the university. This is not just limited to African universities, but other universities can find the content relevant and applicable. It is, however, noted as well, that social media use by a university is not solely meant for marketing purposes. Building a community through engagement and interaction is essential towards achieving the overall goal of the university.

References

Abugre, J. B. (2018). Institutional governance and management systems in Sub-Saharan Africa higher education: Developments and challenges in a Ghanaian research university. *Higher Education*, 75(2), 323–339.

Adefulu, A., Farinloye, T. & Mogaji, E. (2019). Factors influencing post graduate students' university choice in Nigeria. In E. Mogaji, F. Maringe, & R. E. Hinson (Eds.), *Higher education marketing in Africa: Explorations on student choice*. Cham, Switzerland: Springer.

Aker, J. C., & Mbiti, I. M. (2010). Mobile phones and economic development in Africa. *Journal of Economic Perspectives*, 24(3), 207–232.

Altbach, P. G., Reisberg, L., & Rumbley, L. E. (2019). *Trends in global higher education: Tracking an academic revolution*. Rotterdam: Brill.

Bélanger, C. H., Bali, S., & Longden, B. (2014). How Canadian universities use social media to brand themselves. *Tertiary Education and Management*, 20(1), 14–29.

Blackwell, R. E. (1936). College recruiting: Salesmanship or guidance?. *The School Review*, 44(6), 417–424.

Bonjawo, J. (2002). *Internet: A chance for Africa*. Paris: Karthala.

Bonsón, E., & Ratkai, M. (2013). A set of metrics to assess stakeholder engagement and social legitimacy on a corporate Facebook page. *Online Information Review*, 37(5), 787–803.

Bosch, T. E. (2009). Using online social networking for teaching and learning: Facebook use at the University of Cape Town. *Communicatio: South African Journal for Communication Theory and Research*, 35(2), 185–200.

Bower, B. L. (2001). Distance education: Facing the faculty challenge. *Online Journal of Distance Learning Administration*, 4(2), 1–6.

Canterbury, R. M. (2000). Higher education marketing: A challenge. *Journal of Marketing for Higher Education*, 9(3), 15–24.

Chun, S., Shulman, S., Sandoval, R., & Hovy, E. (2010). Government 2.0: Making connections between citizens, data and government. *Information Polity*, 15(1–2), 1–9.

Criado, J. I., Sandoval-Almazan, R., & Gil-Garcia, J. R. (2013). Government innovation through social media. *Government Information Quarterly*, 30(4), 319–326.

Dabner, N. (2012). 'Breaking ground' in the use of social media: A case study of a university earthquake response to inform instructional design with Facebook. *The Internet and Higher Education*, 15(1), 69–78.

Dahl, S. (2018). *Social media marketing: Theories and applications*. Newbury Park, CA: Sage.

Doyle, P., & Newbould, G. D. (1980). A strategic approach to marketing a university. *Journal of Educational Administration*, 18(2), 254–270.

Discenza, R., Ferguson, J. M., & Wisner, R. (1985). Marketing higher education: Using a situation analysis to identify prospective student needs in today's competitive environment. *NASPA Journal*, 22(4), 18–25.

Dwivedi, Y. K. et al. (2019). Artificial Intelligence (AI): Multidisciplinary perspectives on emerging challenges, opportunities, and agenda for research, practice and policy. *International Journal of Information Management*. doi:10.1016/j.ijinfomgt.2019.08.002.

Ecityinteractive. (2019). Building a content for higher ed. ecityinteractive.com. Retrieved from https://cnr.ncsu.edu/wp-content/uploads/2014/05/ebook-Content-Strategy-Higher-Ed.pdf.

Gachago, D., & Ivala, E. (2012). Social media for enhancing student engagement: The use of Facebook and blogs at a university of technology. *South African Journal of Higher Education*, 26(1), 152–167.

Ganster, L., & Schumacher, B. (2009). Expanding beyond our library walls: Building an active online community through Facebook. *Journal of Web librarianship*, 3(2), 111–128.

Gomes, L., & Murphy, J. (2003). An exploratory study of marketing international education online. *International Journal of Educational Management*, 17(3), 116–125.

Hrdinová, J., Helbig, N., & Peters, C. S. (2010). *Designing social media policy for government: Eight essential elements*. Albany, NY: Center for Technology in Government, University at Albany.

ITU. (2018). *Measuring the information society report.* Geneva, Switzerland: International Telecommunication Union. Retrieved from https://www.itu.int/en/ITU-D/Statistics/Documents/publications/misr2018/MISR-2018-Vol-1-E.pdf.

IWS. (2019). Internet user in the world. Retrieved from www.internetworldstats.com/stats.htm.

Junco, R., Heiberger, G., & Loken, E. (2011). The effect of Twitter on college student engagement and grades. *Journal of Computer Assisted learning, 27*(2), 119–132.

Kemp, S. (2018). Global digital statshot essential insights into internet, social media, mobile, and E-commerce use around the world. Retrieved from https://wearesocial.com/blog/2018/01/global-digital-report-2018.

Kishun, R. (2011). Student mobility trends in Africa: A baseline analysis of selected African countries. In R. Bhandari & P. Blumenthal (Eds.), *International students and global mobility in higher education: National trends and new directions* (pp. 143–165). New York: Palgrave Macmillan.

Klassen, M. L. (2002). Relationship marketing on the Internet: The case of top-and lower-ranked US universities and colleges. *Journal of Retailing and Consumer Services, 9*(2), 81–85.

Krachenberg, A. R. (1972). Bringing the concept of marketing to higher education. *The Journal of Higher Education, 45*(2), 369–380.

Küster, I., & Vila, N. (2006). A comparison of marketing teaching methods in North American and European universities. *Marketing Intelligence & Planning, 24*(4), 319–331.

Lee, M. J., & McLoughlin, C. (2011). *Web 2.0-based e-learning: Applying social informatics for tertiary teaching.* Hershey, NY: Information Science Reference.

Lovejoy, K., & Saxton, G. D. (2012). Information, community, and action: How non-profit organizations use social media. *Journal of Computer-Mediated Communication, 17*(3), 337–353.

Macnamara, J., & Zerfass, A. (2012). Social media communication in organizations: The challenges of balancing openness, strategy, and management. *International Journal of Strategic Communication, 6*(4), 287–308.

McAlexander, J. H., Koenig, H. F., & Schouten, J. W. (2006). Building relationships of brand community in higher education: A strategic framework for university advancement. *International Journal of Educational Advancement, 6*(2), 107–118.

Mogaji, E. (2016). This advert makes me cry: Disclosure of emotional response to advertisement on Facebook. *Cogent Business & Management, 3*(1), 1177906.

Mogaji, E. (2019). Strategic stakeholder communications on Twitter by UK universities. *Research Agenda Working Papers, 2019*(8), 104–119.

Mogaji, E., & Erkan, I. (2019). Insight into consumer experience on UK train transportation services. *Travel Behaviour and Society, 14,* 21–33.

Mogaji, E., Farinloye, T., & Aririguzoh, S. (2016). Factors shaping attitudes towards UK bank brands: An exploratory analysis of social media data. *Cogent Business & Management, 3*(1), 1223389.

Ndofirepi, E., Farinloye, T., & Mogaji, E. (2020). Marketing mix in a heterogenous higher education market: A case of Africa. In E. Mogaji, F. Maringe, & R. E. Hinson (Eds.), *Understanding the higher education market in Africa.* London: Routledge.

O'Connor, K. W., Schmidt, G. B., & Drouin, M. (2016). Helping workers understand and follow social media policies. *Business Horizons, 59*(2), 205–211.

Oji, O. N., Iwu, C. G., & Tengeh, R. (2017). Social media adoption challenges of small businesses: The case of restaurants in the Cape Metropole, South Africa. *African Journal of Hospitality, Tourism and Leisure, 6*(4), 1–12.

Olaleye, S. A., Sanusi, I. T., Ukpabi, D. C., & Okunoye, A. (2018). Evaluation of Nigeria universities websites quality: A comparative analysis. *Library Philosophy and Practice (e-journal)*, 1717. Retrieved from https://digitalcommons.unl.edu/libphilprac/1717.

Oyelaran-Oyeyinka, B., & Lal, K. (2005). Internet diffusion in sub-Saharan Africa: A cross-country analysis. *Telecommunications Policy*, 29(7), 507–527.

Payne, S. L., & Calton, J. M. (2017). Towards a managerial practice of stakeholder engagement: Developing multi-stakeholder learning dialogues. In J. Andriof, S. Waddock, B. Husted, & S. Rahman (Eds.), *Unfolding stakeholder thinking* (pp. 121–135). London: Routledge.

Peruta, A., & Shields, A. B. (2017). Social media in higher education: Understanding how colleges and universities use Facebook. *Journal of Marketing for Higher Education*, 27(1), 131–143.

Pomerantz, J., Hank, C., & Sugimoto, C. R. (2015). The state of social media policies in higher education. *PLoS One*, 10(5), e0127485.

Raineri, E., Fudge, T., & Hall, L. (2015). Are universities unsocial with social media?. In *Technology, innovation, and enterprise transformation* (pp. 164–179). Hershey, PA: IGI Global.

Slaughter, S., & Leslie, L. L. (1997). *Academic capitalism: Politics, policies, and the entrepreneurial university*. Baltimore, MD: The Johns Hopkins University Press.

Spencer, J. (2019). 65+ social networking sites you need to know about. Retrieved from https://makeawebsitehub.com/social-media-sites/.

Veysey, L. (1981). *The emergence of the American university*. Chicago, IL: The University of Chicago Press.

Watat, J. K., Wamba, S. F., & Kamdjoug, J. R. K. (2018). Use and influence of social media on student performance in higher education institutions in Cameroon. Paper presented at the Americas conference on information Systems (AMCIS2018). Retrieved from https://aisel.aisnet.org/amcis2018/Education/Presentations/24.

Wawira, J. (2017). Challenges facing Africa's digital marketing. Retrieved from www.hospitalitynet.org/opinion/4081553.html.

Wolff, L. (2002). The African virtual university: The challenge of higher education development in sub-Saharan Africa. *TechKnowLogia, International Journal of Technologies for the Advancement of Knowledge and Learning*, 4(2), 23–25.

Worthy, P. (2019). The ultimate list of social media definitions you need to know in 2019. Retrieved from https://blog.hootsuite.com/social-media-glossary-definitions/#W.

8 Social media for universities' strategic communication

How Nigerian universities use Facebook

Sunday Olaleye, Dandison Ukpabi, and Emmanuel Mogaji

Introduction

Firm effective and coordinated communication is essential for positive image perception among its different stakeholders (Van Riel & Fombrun, 2007). Scholarly evidence suggests that one of the metrics of measuring effective communication is when feedbacks are received from the intended target audience (Kreuter, Farrell, Olevitch, & Brennan, 2013). Over time, universities in developing countries primarily rely on the traditional mode of communication with different stakeholders (Anene, Imam, & Odumuh, 2014). A university has many stakeholders with varying interests and commitments. Thus, identifying the right communication media for a specific stakeholder is essential to elicit stakeholder engagement (Payne & Calton, 2017).

Social media has assumed a critical interaction medium for organisations. Social media is a group of Internet-based applications built on ideological and technological foundations that allow the creation and exchange of user-generated Internet content (Kaplan & Haenlein, 2010). It offers abundance of services which include; social networks (Facebook, Instagram, Myspace, and LinkedIn), micro-blogs (Twitter, Plurk, and Friend Feed), reviews and ratings (Yelp, Amazon, and Trip Advisor), video (YouTube, Snapchat and Vimeo) and lots more. While there are different electronic media sites, social media is growing every day. Nigeria in September 2015 had 97,210,000 Internet users, more than 52% of its population (Internet World Stats, 2016). A staggering 73% of all adults are now using a social media site worldwide. With massive growth and close to one billion users all over the world and 15 million users in Nigeria, Facebook alone has created a new communication channel that is to be reckoned within less than ten years, becoming one of the biggest communication channels in the world today (Callaghan, 2013; Hauger, 2014).

According to the stakeholder theory, an organisation consists of multiple stakeholders who are impacted by the operations of the business (Freeman, Wicks, & Parmar, 2004). The interest of a specific stakeholder depends on values and benefits derived from the business (Hart & Sharma, 2004). Thus, while the organisation seeks to balance the interest of every stakeholder, it must prioritise the interest of critical stakeholders over those who hold peripheral stakes in the organisation. Within higher educational institutions, balancing the interest of internal and external stakeholders is a recipe for engagement, growth, and success (de la Torre, Rossi, & Sagarra, 2018). To achieve this, the higher educational institution must maintain adequate and consistent communication with these interest groups. Several studies have examined modes and methods of HEIs communication with stakeholders. In a study of communication methods adopted by universities in Czech Republic David and Martina (2011) found that universities rely exclusively on marketing tools (advertising, promotions, and so on) for communicating with their stakeholders.

Similarly, Verma and Dahiya (2016) examined gender differences in the perception of the use of information and communication in Indian universities and found that gender was not a significant factor in the perception use of information and communication as a medium with internal stakeholders. Finally, Quadri and Idowu (2016) investigated the use of social media by libraries of selected Nigerian universities and found a high level of awareness of the use of social media by the different institutions. To the best of our knowledge, it is not evident in literature how the engagement between universities and its stakeholders proceed on the social media platforms particularly from a developing country perspective. Accordingly, the objective of our study is to a) examine the use of social media by the universities in Nigeria; b) investigate the level of activity of Nigerian universities on social media; and c) to analyse stakeholder responses to the social media content by the universities. Thus, with our study, practitioners, scholars, and other stakeholders would be abreast of the level of penetration and use of social media by the universities in Nigeria. Thus, our study proceeds as follows.

Theoretical development and literature review

Stakeholder theory

Stakeholders intervention has become a global issue in higher education institutions (HEIs), and different authors have contributed to the literature of stakeholders in HEIs. For example, Vargas, Lawthom, Prowse, Randles, and Tzoulas (2019) developed new insights into sustainable development through stakeholder networks for organisational change in HEIs while Casablancas-Segura, Llonch, and Alarcón-del-Amo (2019) used latent class segmentation technique for public universities based on their stakeholder orientation. Later study motivates the universities to be stakeholder-oriented. Also, Le (2019) analysed the stakeholder's perception in Vietnam universities regarding their involvement in translation studies course and discovered that stakeholders' feedbacks have been helpful in different subjects of their Bachelor of Arts training program. The involvement of strategic engagement in academic library was emphasised by (Harland, Stewart, & Bruce, 2019) and established a strategic framework for engagement with stakeholders. Due to the inevitability of stakeholders in HEIs, Edwards, Venugopal, Navedo, and Ramani (2019) addressed the needs of diverse stakeholders and touched on three key ways of managing the stakeholders through planning, implementation, and monitoring. Stakeholders are a multidimensional phenomenon in HEIs as Alexander and Hjortsø (2019) examined the tensions and contradictions of stakeholders in participatory curriculum development. Unlike the earlier mentioned authors, Wood & Su (2019) focused on parents as a specific stakeholder, and their findings show that HEIs parents desired to be treated as an essential stakeholder that can contribute to the teaching excellence in England HEIs. Dobija, Górska, and Pikos (2019) also participated in the discussion of stakeholders in HEIs as they showed how the internal organisational processes change due to the response of external demands in Polish universities and concludes that the influence of influential stakeholders constitute changes in performance measurement and performance information while Radinger-Peer (2019) confirmed the influence of multi-stakeholder in universities regional engagement.

The relevance of stakeholders to the survival of HEIs especially the universities is crucial, and Guerrero-Villegas (Aguilera-Caracuel & Guerrero-Villegas, 2019, p. 196) described stakeholder as 'an individual or a group that can affect or be affected by the actions taken by the firm in pursuit of its objectives'. According to Vargas et al. (2019), the inclusion of stakeholders in the affairs of HEIs could improve decisions that fostered sustainable development and proposed that future research dwell on quality, processes of stakeholder participation in organisational change.

The stakeholders depend on the policy concerned with HEIs. Casablancas-Segura, Llonch, and Alarcón-del-Amo (2019) clustered stakeholders in HEIs into high stakeholder-oriented and low stakeholder-oriented and in the same line, Guerrero-Villegas (Aguilera-Caracuel & Guerrero-Villegas, 2019) group them into core stakeholders, strategic stakeholders, and environmental stakeholders and described the stakeholders that possess the attribute of legitimacy, power, or urgency as latent stakeholders while the latent stakeholders could be sub-classified as dormant, discretionary, demanding, dominant, dangerous, dependent, definitive, and non-stakeholders.

The non-stakeholders are nominal. Dobija, Górska, and Pikos (2019) found that the design of performance measurement and performance information could be influenced by the external pressures of dominant stakeholders and compared the private and public HEIs based on isomorphic pressures of coercive, normative, and mimetic. The public universities are more coercive than private universities. Private universities are high in normative and low in public universities while the public universities are low in mimetic and moderate in private universities. Since the priorities of stakeholders are competing and complementary, Edwards et al. (2019) suggest stakeholders' identification, activities identification, stakeholders' engagement plan, identify the core team members that will interact with the stakeholders, device a means of feedback and summarise the stakeholder analysis and communication plan. These mentioned tasks will help in sorting out the problem of overlapping and diverging interests of various stakeholders. The influence of stakeholders in HEIs impact both theory and practice.

The stakeholder is held beyond shareholders. A stakeholder involves a person or group of persons affected directly or indirectly by the operations of the business. Thus, the success of the business lies in satisfying these multiple interests (Freeman, 2010). Donaldson and Preston (1995) identified three components of the stakeholder theory: normative, descriptive, and instrumental. The normative stakeholder theory outlines how organisations should treat their stakeholders while descriptive describes how organisations should manage different stakeholders.

Similarly, the instrumental stakeholder theory prioritises the relationships with stakeholders that are critical to the achievement and objectives of the company (Freeman, 2010). Similarly, there are internal and external stakeholders (Cardwell, Williams, & Pyle, 2017) and the organisation must identify their various interests to be able to satisfactorily perform to their expectations (Van der Zee, Gerrets, & Vanneste, 2017). The stakeholder theory has gone through some refinements and applied in different contexts. Mason and Simmons (2014) conceptually applied the stakeholder theory in the context of corporate social responsibility. They argue that firms would successfully be perceived as responsible corporate entities by taking into account their different stakeholders in formulating their corporate social responsibility objectives.

In the management of universities, there are internal stakeholders (students and staff) while external stakeholders 'can be broadly defined as individuals and groups having interests in HEIs but without an immediate linkage with them' (Musiał, 2010, p. 46). The advent of new technologies such as social media has opened fascinating frontiers through which these different stakeholders engage with HEIs (Sashi, 2012; De Vries & Carlson, 2014). Accordingly, through these platforms, HEIs have been able to communicate effectively and gauge the feelings of their stakeholders through their feedbacks. The effective deployment of social media would enhance a higher level of engagement and involvement by the stakeholders of the HEIs. From the internal stakeholder perspective, students and staff would be able to know the goings-on in the university by regularly postings these happening on their universities' social media pages (Dabner, 2012).

Similarly, university administrators would be able to understand the mood and feelings of its internal stakeholders when they utilise these social media platforms. Many incidents of strikes and students unrest happened due to lack of opportunity for these internal stakeholders to be heard by university administrators (Odu, 2014). Similarly, from the external stakeholder perspective, some vital information such as inventions, research breakthroughs, recruitment exercises can quickly reach these stakeholders faster than the traditional means of communication. It is pertinent to state that it is not enough to launch these social media platform, but continuous use and monitoring feedbacks across the stakeholders are most important. The effective use of these platforms would enhance robust university-stakeholder relationship.

Methodology

An inductive, generic, qualitative approach

An inductive, generic, qualitative approach in a netnography context is adopted to achieve the aim of this study. This approach 'seeks to discover and understand a phenomenon, a process or the perspectives and worldviews of the people involved' (Caelli, Ray, & Mill, 2008, p. 3). While the netnography offers a 'form of ethnographic research, adopting the participant-observational approach and taking online interactions as its fieldwork' (Kozinets, 2010, p. 1). The online community is advancing as a research stream for qualitative scientists and netnography is one of the recommended approaches for exploring diverse cultural dispositions of online communities and interpreting the results in a descriptive or analytical format (Kozinets, 2015).

It should also be noted that the participants (stakeholders) were not part of any interview or laboratory setting to understand how they engage with the university or vice versa. Stakeholders were not asked any questions about their relationship with the university, and there were no concerns about confidentiality and anonymity because, unlike interviews, their comments were publicly displayed online (Mogaji & Farinloye, 2018).

All indicators of engagement and communication between the university and the stakeholders were derived from subsequent analysis of their online comments to the universities' profile pages. This approach followed the methodology adopted by Mogaji et al. (2016) to understand consumers attitude towards bank brands. The level of engagement between the university and stakeholders is understood through observation and thematic analysis of the social media post.

The sampled universities

There are 174 Universities in Nigeria (Mogaji, 2019a). However, not all of them have a social media profile. By 1 April 2019, only 125 Universities in Nigeria had a Facebook profile, of which only 5 have a verified Facebook page. These universities are Covenant University, Ota, Federal University of Technology Akure, University of Port Harcourt, Osun State University, and the American University of Nigeria. These verified pages have the blue checkmark which identifies a verified Facebook page; the verification adds credibility to the page, ranked higher on the list of searched items. It builds trust with your audience, and the audience knows they are getting factual information from a verified and official source (Sorensen, 2018). Also, critical metrics of Facebook engagement were explored to increase the sampled universities. The study used LikeAlyzer open software to calculate the engagement rate of Facebook users (Olaleye, Sanusi, Ukpabi, & Okunoye, 2018). The university with the highest comments per post (University of Maiduguri), highest reactions per post (Kola Daisi University) and highest shares per post (Summit University Offa) were included in the sampled universities. In total, eight universities were sampled. Five universities for being the only universities verified by Facebook, three for being the most active based on the Facebook metrics.

Data collection

Two sets of data were collected to achieve the aims of this study. The first data were the official postings on the Facebook pages of the eight universities. These data were collected to examine how universities are using social media. The other data were the user-generated contents in the form of comments from the Facebook pages of these universities. These data were collected to analyse how stakeholders are responding to the social media posts of these universities. These data were collected between 1 October 2018 and 31 April 2019 using NVivo12, a qualitative content analysis tool that incorporates a new web browser plug-in called NCapture, which is capable of capturing social media data (in RAW format). This plug-in is capable of downloading social media data for further analysis by the software NVivo. It facilitates the taking of publicly available data without programming expertise and arranges it into exportable spreadsheets. It also offers a variety of visualisation tools, including word-cluster analysis, treemaps, charts, and word-frequency arrangements (Lane & Menzies, 2015; Mogaji & Farinloye, 2017). Posting data-screening processes were put in place to inspect the extracted posting, identifying outliers and dealing with incongruent comments (Mogaji & Farinloye, 2018). Profane comments, comments that were not in English or those that contain swear words, were removed before coding.

Data analysis

In total, 1,209 postings (from the universities) and 5,205 comments (from stakeholders) were extracted and thematically analysed. Braun and Clarke (2006)'s thematic analysis approach was used to analyse both the postings and comments. Themes were inductively extracted. The inductive analysis involves coding the data without trying to fit it into a pre-existing coding frame (Braun & Clarke, 2006). This form of thematic analysis is data-driven. The data was read over and over again to gain a better understanding of the engagement between the universities and stakeholders. Braun and Clarke (2006) suggested that 'Immersion usually involves "repeated reading" of the data and effectively reading the data - searching for meanings, patterns, and so on.'

Codes were inductively generated as there was not pre-existing coding frame. A short description (often one or two words) was given to each tweet, gathering all the references to a specific topic on the postings. At this stage of the analysis, these codes were fluid, changing, and emerging. Codes were redefined, new ones were created, codes were merged and split to account for new ideas as the coding progresses. The next step involved identifying and describing links and relationships between codes. Codes were categorised, and themes generated based on the relationship between the codes, the frequency of the codes and the underlying meaning across the codes.

The themes were shared with the co-author to review and refined the themes. It became more evident that some of these themes were closely related. Initial codes were examined, trends patterns and the most frequent and significant themes were explored. There were regular debriefing sessions between the first author doing the analysis and the other co-authors. Themes were frequently discussed and revised. The meetings also provide a sounding board and opportunity for peer scrutiny. Also, a detailed account of the methods, procedures, and decision points in carrying out this study was documented in the form of an 'audit trail' as advised by Shenton (2004). The assurance of analytic rigour to ensure that data was not selectively used and that the researcher's position did not overpower the participants' voices can be evidenced from the audit trails. Key themes were determined after the discussion. This step was followed by the theoretical coding which connects

Table 8.1 Selected Nigerian universities on social media

FACEBOOK

University	Facebook	Comments per post	Shares per post	Reactions per post	Administrator
Covenant University **Verified**	119.315	0.81	3.97	24.27	Staff/Student/ Public
Federal University of Technology, Akure **Verified**	90.396	12.93	14.28	151.66	Staff/Student/ Public
University of Port Harcourt **Verified**	71.905	0.58	0.66	10.08	Staff/Student/ Public
Osun State University **Verified**	50.526	12.14	4.21	63.47	Staff/Student/ Public
American University of Nigeria **Verified**	43.453	0.52	1.88	13.14	Staff/Student/ Public
University of Maiduguri	41.176	59.98	33.38	124.45	Staff/Student/ Public
Kola Daisi University	5.161	7.42	6.38	512.52	Staff/Student/ Public
Summit University Offa	1.621	9	49.57	197.71	Staff/Student/ Public

the core categories to create the narrative proposition and stakeholder theory for universities on social media.

Results

This section presents results of the thematic analysis of the posts by the universities, which indicate how they are using social media and comments by the stakeholders, which highlights how they are engaging with the universities' posting.

Universities' posting

The universities are using their social media profile for various purposed, targeting different stakeholders but predominantly prospective students who are interested in higher education. Five key themes emerged from the analysis of how the universities are using Facebook for their marketing communication strategy.

Inform

Universities were using social media to inform prospective students about their desires to welcome them to their university. They presented information about the availability of spaces to study for a degree, screening exercises around the country to recruit prospective students and also provide admission requirements and criteria. Some universities take pride in their achievements as they present themselves to students.

> Meet us in Jos this Saturday. The University leadership will be available to attend to your inquiries on admissions, academic programs, tuition fees, campus life and more.
>
> Admission is still ongoing for the 2018/2019 academic session into 100 & 200 levels, JUPEB and remedial at the Kola Daisi University, Ibadan.
>
> Meanwhile, this is to inform interested applicants that opportunities still exist for qualified applicants to study at Covenant University, as the final screening exercise has been scheduled for this weekend July 12 and 13th respectively. Visit the Admission Website for more details.

Likewise, the universities use their social media platform to inform present students about developments going on within the university. They inform them about resumption dates, events like convocation and matriculation, dignitaries visiting the campus, and also announcements around examinations.

> Provisional examination Time-table for 2018/2019 academic session GST Unit …
>
> (Updated) Education: First-semester examination time-table for degree students 2018/2019

All Fresh and Returning Students should visit bit.ly/2ObqDQf in preparation for the Resumption of 2018/2019 Academic Session. Compulsory!
Date; Returning students: August 12, 2018
Freshers: August 15, 2018

The Vice-Chancellor of Covenant University, Professor \o "Rẹmi Atayero" Rẹmi Atayero decorating the Executive Vice-Chairman/CEO, National Agency for Science and Engineering Infrastructure, Professor M. S. Haruna and Business Development and Relationship Manager, Development Bank of Nigeria, Mary Esther Ezeadi, during a courtesy visit to Covenant University Vice-Chancellor's Office after making presentations at the 2019 International Conference on Sustainable Development in Africa …

Motivate

Universities in Nigeria are making an effort to motivate their students by sharing contents which can encourage them to work harder and achieve excellent results. There were postings about the best graduating students, alumni that have a successful business and present students that have won an academic or sports competition. Universities push this narrative to encourage and motivate their students.

FUTA undergraduates win Microsoft competition … Win All Expenses Paid Trip to Microsoft's Headquarters in Redmond, USA
Congratulations to the overall best graduating student in Covenant University … from the dept. Of architecture with 4.97GP.
Ajibua Michael Alayode, Director, Sports and Chief Coach of the FUTA Football Club is among the 24 selected coaches of tertiary institutions nationwide who attended the "Coaching The Coaches" Clinic in Lagos Organized by the Higher Institutions Football League (HiFL) in partnership with Manchester City Football Club of England.

They also provided motivational quotes and prayers for the students. On the first day of the month, there were postings about the new month, greetings, wishing the students all the best and hoping they have a blessed month.

Reflect this weekend over Dean Bullock's powerful quotes.
Gossip is verbal poison. It seeks to defame & discredit others. It is hurtful & dangerous. It is the quickest way to destroy trust and friendships. Do not take it lightly. You may think it is harmless, but you're ruining someone's reputation. You'll pay a high price for it in your Lifetime Even in Paradise HALLH Says.
This February will usher you with new experiences. Happy New Month

The greatness of AUN does not only depend on the quality of our diverse degree programs or our faculty or this beautiful infrastructure but also the motivation, dedication, and hard work of you, the student.

Update

These are often targeted towards present students and staff who are considered internal stakeholders. These types of posts include the event that will be held on campus, a forum or announcements, Pictures and images of events that have happened such as inaugural speeches, graduation, and matriculation. This type of post is about updating the stakeholders about activities going on campus. The university also uses its social media to wish their staff happy birthday or announce the death of a colleague. KolaDaisi University predominantly did this posting strategy. Often, they showed a picture of their team, tag their social media handle and wish them a happy birthday. Other universities also use this strategy to showcase their staff contribution and achievements.

Osun State University recorded a victorious outing by winning four medals at the just-concluded annual university sports competition organised by the Nigerian University Game Association (NUGA).

The outstanding virtues of an elder statesman, teacher, and author, Basorun Seinde Arogbofa were extolled by dignitaries at a book launch held to commemorate his 80th birthday at the main Auditorium of the Federal University of Technology, Akure, FUTA.

Our Vice-Chancellor @ 61. Today we celebrate Professor Joseph Adeola Fuwape, Vice-Chancellor FUTA on the occasion of his 61st birthday. May the Good Lord continue to grant you good health and the wherewithal to take our University to Greater heights. Congratulations Mr Vice Chancellor.

The sudden death of our students shocks me – SUG President. The President, Students' Union Government, Comrade Farouq Muhammad Ahmad receives with sadness, the terrible news of the ghastly motor accident that claimed the lives and injured many UNIMAID Students on their way back to Gombe.

Report

Unlike the updates provided by the university for the internal stakeholders, the universities use their Facebook to report what is going on within the university. This posting strategy is an attempt to flaunt their achievements for external stakeholders to see. These are targeted towards parents who may be looking at a prospective school for their children, staff who are looking at changing the university and considering the university as a better option, the regulatory bodies, employers, press, and the general public. The university showcases its world league table ranking, and they showcase their latest research funding from international organisations. Appearance in the media like television interview or newspaper coverage are also shared on their Facebook page. This type of messages appeared to be an attempt to create a narrative about a successful university which everyone should be a part of.

> Samuel Adeyanju graduated with First Class from the Department of Forest and Wood Technology in 2016. In 2017 Adeyanju and nine other Alumni of FUTA won 10 out of the 12 MasterCard's Foundation Scholarships allocated to Nigeria. He is currently a Masters student at the University of British Columbia (UBC) Canada. He was in Nigeria recently to undertake practical fieldwork along with some other engagements. In this interview, he talks about the scholarship, his experience and his vision for the future.
>
> Happening now: 10th Commencement Ceremony and the inauguration of Dr Dawn Dekle officially as AUN's 4th President. Over 150 graduating students will be conferred with Bachelor's Degrees, Post Graduate Diplomas and Masters Degrees You can catch the live broadcast on the African Independent Television (AIT) and Gotel Television.
>
> Prolonged Exposure to Radiation Can Lead to Cancer, Others – FUTA Don — Leadership Newspaper

Share

This posting strategy is when the university is not posting content they have created, but instead, they are sharing information from other sources. This approach was predominantly adopted by the University of Port Harcourt sharing information from the World Health Organisation. This posting strategy can have a negative effect when most of the stakeholders do not find it relevant. This negative effect was evident from the comments under those posts. Students felt that such information was not necessary when the university has not provided information about examinations and other things that are more important to them. Universities are using this strategy to keep their profile active and engage with other stakeholders who might find such information relevant.

> Support Mums to breastfeed anytime, anywhere. We can all help make society breastfeeding-friendly - WHO.

Stakeholders' comments

This section of the analysis shows how the stakeholders are engaging with the posting from the universities.

Ask

Prospective students use the social media platform to ask the university about various questions regarding their admission. They ask about admission requirements, fees, and insight into the institution. The stakeholders believe they can directly engage with the university and request specific information. Students ask if their qualifications can secure them admission into the university, they ask for an update about their admission, especially those who have submitted their form and attend the screening exercise. Some prospective students also ask about the cost of an application form, if the government approves the university, scholarship offers, and resumption dates. Parents as well were asking questions on the behaviour of their children. Present students seldom ask questions as there is little evidence of them interacting with the post to ask question that relates to their current needs as students.

> I want to ask if a returning student can pay part of the school fees and the procedure.
>
> Pls help ooooooh, I was given admission but was unable to pay acceptance fee due to nationwide strike(banks) with 2wks ultimatum, Any other way apart from using bank.
>
> Hello #CovenantUniversity, I am an applicant to the institution for 2019/2020 session. I have not been receiving emails through the email address I presented during my application whereas other applicants like me do receive. I only ask other people to hear from them whatever message has been passed, please help me out.
>
> Please my spiritual referee has not filled her part, and I did not see my name on the first list do I stand a chance of seeing it on the second list.
>
> Please, friends and colleagues I have a question to ask. Why is this that my UTME screening is showing me that Jamb number has already been registered and I have made my payment. It has refused to allow me to continue with registration.

Advice

On the other hand, present students are more likely to provide answers and guidance instead of asking questions. They serve as an online influencer that can give advice and answer questions being asked by the prospective students. Though disappointing to note that the universities infrequently engage and answer the questions that are being asked, the present students and other prospective students take up that role – they provide advice and answers to students and parents inquiring about the location of screening, information about admission, resumption date, and lifestyles in the university.

> During my time a very similar case took place, I wrote the last supplementary exams but still got admitted on the 1st batch list a week after I took CUSAS.

It is completely normal to feel nervous before an examination. What you can do to reduce test anxiety. Breathe, be prepared, practice with your study group. Have a positive mental attitude. Good luck in your midterm exams.

Acknowledge

These are comments that indicate an understanding of the postings by the university. The stakeholders are acknowledging the message the university is sending to them. They often say OK or mention another of the friends to see the message as well. There are indications that these are present students. As an indication of acknowledgement, some stakeholders do say *Congratulations, Happy for you*, and *well done*, especially when information about a successful student is shared, or pictures of the graduation are shared.

Appreciation

For stakeholders who appreciate the universities post and find it relevant, they tend to be appreciative and say *Thank you*. While present students are acknowledging the posts, prospective students are more likely to appreciate posts that provide information. These appreciation comments are often on posts that offer an update about the admission process, the admission criteria, screening venue, and scholarship opportunities. Prospective students feel they can make use of the information and tends to be grateful.

Advertise

Disappointedly, some use the comments section of the universities' post on Facebook to advertise their goods and services. The presence of these advertisements is an apparent lack of control and monitoring from the part of the page administrators. Sometimes these advertisements are relevant to the students, such as helping them with the admission process to some other universities, extra classes to improve grades or helping with admissions and travel plans to universities outside Nigeria. However, there are others like bitcoin, foreign exchange training, and car sales. These advertisements in the comment section can sometimes hijack the conversation and distract the readers from the message of the initial post.

> They are Legit, They are TRUSTED … BRING YOUR BITCOIN at a low rate depending on volume …

> *I buy 100 USD for 350/$ and 1000 for 356/$ … They also Trade cards too at best current rate*
> Contact—070**********
> Do not be left out people are making money in this 2018 already … This is for business-minded persons.

DROP YOUR WHATSAPP NUMBER IF YOUR INTERESTED. BITCOIN AVAILABLE FOR SALE, INTERESTED BUYERS SHOULD WHATSAPP (+23470**********")

Discussion and conclusion

Social media is transforming how consumers interact with brands and how brand-related content is consumed (Mogaji, 2016) and universities are not excluded from using social media to engage with their stakeholders. The advent of readily available social media applications has created opportunities for dialogic and more interactive engagement (Bonsón & Ratkai, 2013). To understand how universities in Nigeria are engaging with stakeholders on social media, the study examined social media profiles of 125 universities on Facebook, Twitter, and Instagram. The study was set out to accomplish three main aims. Firstly, to examine the use of social media by the universities in Nigeria; Secondly, to investigate their level of activity and lastly, to analyse stakeholder responses to the social media content. The study was anchored on the stakeholder's theory which recognises the success of the business lies in satisfying the multiple interests (Freeman, 2010) within a business. In the case of a university, these interests vary and communicating with them is essential.

Findings of the study revealed the use of social media which highlights the initial challenge of which of the social media platform to use, while the study focused on 125 universities, only a few of them have a presence on the three media considered (Twitter, Instagram, and Facebook), perhaps as an indication of the challenges in effectively managing all the profiles. There were concerns about the nature of the post on these social media profiles. They do not appear strategic enough to engage with the diverse stakeholder of a university. The information posted is often information-focused aimed explicitly to students and staff. The engagement rate is also meagre. The American University of Nigeria with the highest rate has 11%.

The targeted audience is also worthy of consideration as the study recognises the diverse nature of university stakeholders. The most crucial content entails inaugural lecture, universities ranking, workshop, reunion, travel, symposium. These understandings can explain the low engagement rate. Often the student (and sometimes the parents) are the primary audience while other stakeholders are often excluded in the communication. This gives an indication of the universities' awareness of their stakeholders and how best to curate content to engage them with. There are little or no engagement between the university and the alumni, the host community, funders, and other research organisations.

With a specific focus on Nigeria as a developing county, it is essential to consider the context in with the universities relate with their stakeholders and perhaps gives an insight into their level of engagement on social media. Firstly, Internet user penetration in Nigeria is a concern. In 2019, 56.4% of the Nigerian population were Internet users (Statista, 2019), though this is growing, it is still a challenge especially for prospective students and other stakeholders who may want to engage. Secondly, public universities in Nigeria are underfunded from both the Federal and State Government. The funders, regulators (like National Universities Commission) and research organisation are key stakeholders, but often there is no engagement on social media as indicated by the analysis of the frequent messages. Often there is no posting about community services, research activities and impact but more of updates to strike. Lastly, admission spaces are oversubscribed as the demand for university places is higher than the supply and therefore there is hardly interest in marketing communications campaign because they are always guaranteed a steady supply of prospective students. This is, however, different from the private universities who are competing with prospective students who have not secured admission or willing to attend the government universities. The private universities are often more motivated to engage with stakeholders, share their research achievements, provide updates about activities and events on campus.

Notwithstanding these contextual challenges, understanding consumer behaviour on social media is vital for the successful development of an appropriate channel that reflects stakeholders' varied requirements (Dwivedi et al., 2019; Shareef et al., 2016). As with many consumers, there are high expectations on social media (Ukpabi et al., 2019) from students especially when engaging with the universities, and they want answers to their questions

Theoretically, this chapter makes three key contributions. First, it extends the knowledge of the use of social media by universities, moving beyond the use of websites as strategic, interactive stakeholder engagement tools. This study recognised that social media applications present communication opportunities that differ from universities' websites (Lovejoy & Saxton, 2012) as it offers more flexibility and engagement between the universities and their stakeholders.

Second, the study extends the application of stakeholder theory to include university conversations on social media, especially regarding the higher education institutions from a developing country perspective. It recognises a different structure of stakeholders, the universities' peculiar challenges, and the developing country perspective. Third, while acknowledging the unique and dynamic nature of stakeholders on social media, the study adopts a unique methodology to capture the usage of social media by the university and explored their level of activity and analysed stakeholder responses. Methodologically, the study contributes to the literature on social media research.

Managerially, the current study offers implications that highlight the need for managers of universities' social media profile to understand their essence of having a social media presence. This is expected to feed into their social media strategy. From a practical perspective, being on social media may indicate an intention to actively engage with the stakeholders (Lovejoy &

Saxton, 2012), it is, however, paramount to be strategic about this. The fact that every organisation is on social media is not enough justification to jump on the bandwagon without having clear objectives and goals.

Universities need to understand their stakeholders to engage and communicate with them properly. As there are internal and external stakeholders (Cardwell, Williams, & Pyle, 2017), the university must identify their various interests to be able to provide the relevant content that they can engage with satisfactorily. Managers need to understand the expectation of the prospective students who needs information about the courses offered by the university, the expectation of current students who needs an update about what is going on at the university and alumni who are looking forward to opportunities to develop and contribute back to the university.

Importantly as well, this suggests the need for content creation strategy. Managers must be aware that stakeholders are not just consumer of the content but also actively participate in creating and shaping it (Bonsón & Ratkai, 2013; Mogaji & Farinloye, 2018). With the understanding of the stakeholders, relevant contents should be created by the universities' communications team and be co-created with stakeholders. These contents should go beyond the usual update about activities on the campus but something which is more strategic, scheduled and engaging with the stakeholders. This is anticipated to increase the engagement level, and build communication, gain insight into the level of engagement and be able to target them with more relevant information.

The more extensive range of functionality on different social media platform is recognised. For example, Twitter is restricted to 280 characters; cross-posting from Facebook will truncate the message on Twitter. Managers need to be conversant with these functionalities and use it effectively (Mogaji, 2019b). One size does not fit all in social media, and each site is used correctly to engage with the stakeholders.

It is also essential to work towards getting their profiles verified and engaging more with the stakeholders as there are many parody accounts. These parody accounts do not represent the university, and it can confuse the stakeholders willing to engage (Mogaji & Erkan, 2019). Often, these parody accounts, especially on Facebook share irrelevant post and as the pages are often created to attract followers and used for advertisements and sponsored post, this is another reason for the universities to take ownership of their social media profile and take charge of their communication strategies as prospective students may not be able to identify the real profile by a simple search on the social media platform.

Analytics to understand the key drivers of engagement is essential (Mogaji, 2019c). Managers should be endeavouring to measure the impact of their campaigns, track the performance of posts and discover what resonates with the stakeholders by tracking performance at the post level. These insights can be used to create better content, inform campaign strategy and better engage your stakeholders. Tools for the entire publishing process should be considered based on the significant number of stakeholders to engage with.

There should be a dedicated team responsible for social media engagement, and this may be within the communications team or the marketing team (Mogaji, 2019b). The social media policy should guide the team, and there should be contingency plans for continuity in case staff leave, everyone should have access to the password, staff are trained on tools to engage effectively and professionally. Staff are aware of the basic etiquette of customer services even though they are behind the scene. These are essential points to be considered by universities when putting a social media team together.

There are limitations to this study, however. The study restricted itself to the analysis of social media pages of Nigerian universities. It is acknowledged that not all the universities are using social media and even for those analysed, not all of them are using the three social media networks analysed. Other social media pages haven't been explored, such as YouTube, etc. The results cannot be generalised to other sectors. The study has offered insights into communications strategies of universities on social media, albeit quantitively; future research should try to analyse the content and frequency of the post to understand how each stakeholder are being targeted and the nature of their contents. The distinctions between different university typology can also be explored.

References

Aguilera-Caracuel, J., & Guerrero-Villegas, J. (2018). How corporate social responsibility helps MNEs to improve their reputation: The moderating effects of geographical diversification and operating in developing regions. *Corporate Social Responsibility and Environmental Management*, 25(4), 355–372.

Alexander, I. K., & Hjortsø, C. N. (2019). Sources of complexity in participatory curriculum development: An activity system and stakeholder analysis approach to the analyses of tensions and contradictions. *Higher Education*, 77(2), 301–322.

Anene, J., Imam, H., & Odumuh, T. (2014). Problem and prospect of e-learning in Nigerian universities. *International Journal of Technology and Inclusive Education (IJTIE)*, 3(2), 320–327.

Bonsón, E., & Ratkai, M. (2013). A set of metrics to assess stakeholder engagement and social legitimacy on a corporate Facebook page. *Online Information Review*, 37(5), 787–803.

Braun, V., & Clarke, V. (2006). Using thematic analysis in psychology. *Qualitative Research in Psychology*, 3(2), 77–101.

Caelli, K., Ray, L., & Mill, J. (2008). 'Clear as mud': Toward greater clarity in generic qualitative research. *International Journal of Qualitative Methods*, 2(2), 1–13.

Callaghan, M. I. A. B. (2013, 2 May). Facebook's declining user growth rate, pictured. *The Wall Street Journal*. Retrieved from http://allthingsd.com/20130502/facebooks-declining-user-growth-rate-pictured/.

Cardwell, L. A., Williams, S., & Pyle, A. (2017). Corporate public relations dynamics: Internal vs. external stakeholders and the role of the practitioner. *Public Relations Review*, 43(1), 152–162.

Casablancas-Segura, C., Llonch, J., & Alarcón-del-Amo, M. D. C. (2019). Segmenting public universities based on their stakeholder orientation. *International Journal of Educational Management*, 33(4), 614–628.

Chan, H. K., Wang, X., Lacka, E., & Zhang, M. (2016). A mixed-method approach to extracting the value of social media data. *Production and Operations Management*, 25(3), 568–583.

Dabner, N. (2012). 'Breaking ground' in the use of social media: A case study of a university earthquake response to inform educational design with Facebook. *The Internet and Higher Education*, 15(1), 69–78.

David, S., & Martina, R. (2011). Marketing communications mix of universities-communication with students in an increasing competitive university environment. *Journal of Competitiveness*, 3, 58–67.

de la Torre, E. M., Rossi, F., & Sagarra, M. (2018). Who benefits from HEIs engagement? An analysis of priority stakeholders and activity profiles of HEIs in the United Kingdom. *Studies in Higher Education*, 5, 1–20.

De Vries, N. J., & Carlson, J. (2014). Examining the drivers and brand performance implications of customer engagement with brands in the social media environment. *Journal of Brand Management*, 21(6), 495–515.

Dobija, D., Górska, A. M., & Pikos, A. (2019). The impact of accreditation agencies and other powerful stakeholders on the performance measurement in Polish universities. *Baltic Journal of Management*, 14(1), 84–102.

Donaldson, T., & Preston, L. E. (1995). The stakeholder theory of the corporation: Concepts, evidence, and implications. *Academy of Management Review*, 20(1), 65–91.

Dwivedi, Y. K. et al. (2019). Artificial Intelligence (AI): Multidisciplinary perspectives on emerging challenges, opportunities, and agenda for research, practice and policy. *International Journal of Information Management*. https://doi.org/10.1016/j.ijinfomgt.2019.08.002.

Edwards, R. A., Venugopal, S., Navedo, D., & Ramani, S. (2019). Addressing needs of diverse stakeholders: Twelve tips for leaders of health professions education programs. *Medical Teacher*, 41(1), 17–23.

Fereday, J., & Muir-Cochrane, E. (2006). Demonstrating rigor using thematic analysis: A hybrid approach of inductive and deductive coding and theme development. *International Journal of Qualitative Methods*, 5(1), 80–92.

Freeman, R. E. (2010). *Strategic management: A stakeholder approach*. Cambridge: Cambridge University Press.

Freeman, R. E., Wicks, A. C., & Parmar, B. (2004). Stakeholder theory and 'the corporate objective revisited'. *Organization Science*, 15(3), 364–369.

Harland, F., Stewart, G., & Bruce, C. (2019). Leading the academic library in strategic engagement with stakeholders: A constructivist grounded theory. *College and Research Libraries*, 80(3), 319–339.

Hart, S. L., & Sharma, S. (2004). Engaging fringe stakeholders for competitive imagination. *Academy of Management Perspectives*, 18(1), 7–18.

Hauger, K. K. (2014). *ABC I sososialmedier: #sosialmarkedsforing*. Kampanje.

He, W., Wu, H., Yan, G., Akula, V., & Shen, J. (2015). A novel social media competitive analytics framework with sentiment benchmarks. *Information & Management*, 52(7), 801–812.

Internet World Stats. (2016). Usage and population statistics. Retrieved from http://IWS.com/Africa.htm.

Jogulu, U. D., & Pansiri, J. (2011). Mixed methods: A research design for management doctoral dissertations. *Management Research Review*, 34(6), 687–701.

Kaplan, A. M., & Haenlein, M. (2010). Users of the world, unite: The challenges and opportunities of social media. *Business Horizons*, 53(1), 59–68. doi:10.1016/j.bushor.2009.09.003.

Kozinets, R. V. (2010). *Netnography: Doing ethnographic research online.* Thousand Oaks, CA: Sage.

Kozinets, R. V. (2015). *Netnography.* London: John Wiley.

Kreuter, M. W., Farrell, D. W., Olevitch, L. R., & Brennan, L. K. (2013). *Tailoring health messages: Customizing communication with computer technology.* London: Routledge.

Lane, M., & Menzies, V. (2015). An analysis of user engagement in student Facebook groups. *Student Success*, 6, 93–98.

Le, T. D., Dobele, A. R., & Robinson, L. J. (2019). Information sought by prospective students from social media electronic word-of-mouth during the university choice process. *Journal of Higher Education Policy and Management*, 41(1), 18–34.

Lovejoy, K., & Saxton, G. D. (2012). Information, community, and action: How non-profit organizations use social media. *Journal of Computer-mediated Communication*, 17(3), 337–353.

Mason, C., & Simmons, J. (2014). Embedding corporate social responsibility in corporate governance: A stakeholder systems approach. *Journal of Business Ethics*, 119(1), 77–86.

Mogaji, E. (2019a). Type and location of Nigerian universities. Research Agenda Working Papers, 2019(7), 92–103. Retrieved from https://ssrn.com/abstract=3442737.

Mogaji, E. (2019b). Strategic stakeholder communications on Twitter by UK universities. Research Agenda Working Papers, 2019(8), 104–119. Retrieved from https://ssrn.com/abstract=3445869.

Mogaji, E. (2019c). Branding private universities in Africa: An unexplored territory. Research Agenda Working Papers, 2019(9), 120–148. Retrieved from http://dx.doi.org/10.2139/ssrn.3457571.

Mogaji, E., & Farinloye, T. (2017). Attitudes towards brands and advertisements: Qualitative and thematic analysis of social media data. In B. Rishi & S. Bandyopadhyay (Eds.), *Contemporary issues in social media marketing* (pp. 206–216). London: Routledge.

Mogaji, E., & Farinloye, T. (2018). Attitude to brands and advertisement: Qualitative and thematic analysis of social media data. In B. Rishi & S. Bandyopadhyay (Eds.), *Contemporary issues in social media marketing* (pp. 206–216). London: Routledge.

Mogaji, E., Farinloye, T., & Aririguzoh, S. (2016). Factors shaping attitudes towards UK bank brands: An exploratory analysis of social media data. *Cogent Business & Management*, 3(1), 1223389.

Musiał, K. (2010). Redefining external stakeholders in Nordic higher education. *Tertiary Education and Management*, 16(1), 45–60.

Odu, O. M. (2014). Management of students crisis in higher institutions of learning in Nigeria. *International Letters of Social and Humanistic Sciences*, 15, 31–39.

Olaleye, S. A., Sanusi, I. T., Ukpabi, D., & Okunoye, A. (2018). Evaluation of Nigeria universities websites quality: A comparative analysis. Retrieved from https://digitalcommons.unl.edu/libphilprac/1717.

Pandey, A. C., Rajpoot, D. S., & Saraswat, M. (2017). Twitter sentiment analysis using hybrid cuckoo search method. *Information Processing & Management*, 53(4), 764–779.

Payne, S. L., & Calton, J. M. (2017). Towards a managerial practice of stakeholder engagement: Developing multi-stakeholder learning dialogues. In J. Andriof, S. Waddock, B. Husted, & S. S. Rahman (Eds.), *Unfolding stakeholder thinking* (pp. 121–135). London: Routledge.

Quadri, G. O., & Adebayo Idowu, O. (2016). Social media use by librarians for information dissemination in three federal university libraries in Southwest Nigeria. *Journal of Library & Information Services in Distance Learning*, 10(1–2), 30–40.

Radinger-Peer, V. (2019). What influences universities' regional engagement? A multi-stakeholder perspective applying a Q-methodological approach. *Regional Studies, Regional Science*, 6(1), 170–185.

Rohm, A., Kaltcheva, V. D., & Milne, G. R. (2013). A mixed-method approach to examining brand-consumer interactions driven by social media. *Journal of Research in Interactive Marketing*, 7(4), 295–311.

Sashi, C. M. (2012). Customer engagement, buyer-seller relationships, and social media. *Management Decision*, 50(2), 253–272.

Shenton, A. K. (2004). Strategies for ensuring trustworthiness in qualitative research projects. *Education for information*, 22(2), 63–75.

Snelson, C. L. (2016). Qualitative and mixed methods social media research: A review of the literature. *International Journal of Qualitative Methods*, 15(1). doi:1609406915624574.

Sorensen, A. (2018). Credibility of your page. Retrieved from https://socialnicole.com/verify-facebook-page/.

Statista. (2019). Internet user penetration in Nigeria from 2017 to 2023. Retrieved from https://www.statista.com/statistics/484918/internet-user-reach-nigeria/.

Tavana, M., Momeni, E., Rezaeiniya, N., Mirhedayatian, S. M., & Rezaeiniya, H. (2013). A novel hybrid social media platform selection model using fuzzy ANP and COPRAS-G. *Expert Systems with Applications*, 40(14), 5694–5702.

Ukpabi, D., Karjaluoto, H., Olaleye, S., & Mogaji, E. (2019). Influence of offline activities and customer value creation on online travel community continuance usage intention. In J. Pesonen & J. Neidhardt (Eds.), *Information and Communication Technologies in Tourism 2019* (pp. 450–460). Cham, Switzerland: Springer.

uniRank. (2019). Universities search engine. Retrieved from www.4icu.org.

Van der Zee, E., Gerrets, A. M., & Vanneste, D. (2017). Complexity in the governance of tourism networks: Balancing between external pressure and internal expectations. *Journal of Destination Marketing & Management*, 6(4), 296–308.

Van Riel, C. B., & Fombrun, C. J. (2007). *Essentials of corporate communication: Implementing practices for effective reputation management*. London: Routledge.

Vargas, V. R., Lawthom, R., Prowse, A., Randles, S., & Tzoulas, K. (2019). Sustainable development stakeholder networks for organisational change in higher education institutions: A case study from the UK. *Journal of Cleaner Production*, 208, 470–478.

Verma, C., & Dahiya, S. (2016). Gender difference towards information and communication technology awareness in Indian universities. *SpringerPlus*, 5(1), 370.

9 Digital marketing communication strategies for private universities in South Western Nigeria

Omolola Oluwasola

Introduction

The emergence of information, communication and technology (ICT) has altered marketing practices, promotion, and service delivery in education and virtually all other fields. This alteration is more noticeable at a time like this when constant interaction and communication is very germane to university marketing. Education, being a tool for socio-economic development of a nation has become a global public service that the government of every country strives to provide for its citizenry. Formal education is the catalyst for sustainable human and national development worldwide. No doubt, the university education system has enhanced communication, cultural, socio-economic, political, scientific, and technological developments all over the world, including Nigeria.

The Nigerian government at both state and federal levels has attempted in diverse ways to promote education; however, as much as the government tried and participated in education, inadequate funding, surging students' enrolment figures, the inadequate number of schools are some of the significant challenges faced by the education sector. Most of the government-owned higher institutions of learning are grossly underfunded, understaffed, under-equipped, and overloaded. These challenges of higher education in the country perhaps explain the incessant industrial actions by the Academic Staff of Universities Union (ASUU). These inadequacies have led to the liberalisation of the education sector which allows private investors' participation in providing tertiary education. In 2019, there are a total of 174 universities in the country, 43 federal, 52 state, and 79 private universities with private universities outnumbering the public schools. The attendant result is stiff competition among private university operators who are now devising creative ways to promote their institutions and services rendered (Mogaji, 2019a).

With this increasing number of private universities in Nigeria, there is a need for more strategic marketing as university aims to reach out to prospective students. Uchendu et al. (2015) pinpoint that the continued existence of any school depends on its capacity to retain current and new customers. The importance of digital technology and the Internet as platforms of marketing communication is growing. More importantly, the media consumption habits of consumers are changing. Consumers are moving from traditional media to digital media. Liza and Jamie (2003) assert that private universities have to use the Internet, social media, and digital marketing initiatives to reach, attract, and subsequently persuade parents and students to enrol in their different universities. Based on this change, organisations are wittingly entering the digital environment. This change has further highlighted the need for theoretical and empirical insight into the use of digital marketing strategies.

Universities are showing interest in using promotional strategies to boost enrolment figures, especially with intense competition that has characterised the sector (Mogaji & Yoon, 2019). Efforts have been made to explore the use of digital technologies in promoting higher education services, especially in other countries like the Netherlands, Australia, and the United States of America. However, in Nigeria, there is limited empirical evidence for the use of digital marketing in the promotion of private tertiary education. This study intends to fill this gap in literature by examining use of digital marketing strategies in the promotion of private higher education of selected private universities in South Western, Nigeria. Specifically, the private institutions under study are Afe Babalola, Caleb University, Covenant University, Elizade University, Fountain University, and Lead City University. These are private university in each of the six South Western states namely: Ekiti, Lagos, Ogun, Ondo, Osun, and Oyo states respectively.

This chapter presents a multi-research study which explores the digital marketing tools private universities deploy to promote their institutions for student enrolment and analysis of various social media used by these universities and their level of engagement. This study contributes to the understanding of digital marketing in African higher education with specific focus on Nigeria, and it presents insights into the challenges and opportunities for digital marketing. The study also provides theoretical and managerial implications which are relevant for academic researcher with interest in marketing higher education in Africa and university managers and policymakers intending to adopt and integrate digital marketing in their enrolment process.

Digital marketing communication tools

The tools used for digital marketing are quite different from what is used in traditional /conventional marketing, although albeit with some resemblance. The classification of promotional tools deployed for marketing communication as paid, shared, earned, and owned media has been a constant practice. This categorisation is taking root in digital marketing channels/ tools. Digital marketing tools are an array of avenues, platforms, and channels available to organisations to drive their digital marketing campaigns. The typology of digital marketing tools is paid, shared, earned, and owned media while a wholesome of the tools fall under convergence of the four categories.

Paid media digital marketing communication tools

These are marketing tools in the form of spaces or content that companies pay certain media owners/ site owners, search engines, and social media platforms and the likes to disseminate their marketing communication commercial messages to create visibility for a company's product, service, and brand. Paid media encompasses traditional forms of advertising, such as print adverts, TV commercials, and billboards, as well as their online equivalents such as display advertisements, pay per click advertising, sponsored social media posts, and so on. (Timson, 2018). These also include all dimensions of online advertising inform of banner advertisements, pop up or pop-under, search engine marketing (on Google, Bing and Opera), video adverts, advertising on the telephone, digital radio, and television.

Owned media digital marketing communication tools

These are corporate channels that a company uses to communicate with customers, employees and other stakeholders about the organisation and its offerings: these include tools such as company websites, content marketing, blogs, and mobile apps. These tools are unique as organisations have great control over their content within the limits of each platform (Pineiro-Otero & Martinex-Rolan, 2016, p. 44) because they offer avenues for most content distributed by the organisation and thus, owned media become the backbone of the digital strategy of a brand. However, because they are biased communication, they do not always have the push or scope needed (Pinnero-Otero & Martinex-Rolan, 2016, p. 45). This is because consumers believe some of the contents in owned media are indirectly trying to persuade them to take action in favour of the organisation

Earned media digital marketing communication tools

These are channels that organisations use to disseminate digital marketing communication messages to their external and internal publics about their firms, products, or brands. Rather than being paid for, earned media tools are 'free tools' because they are information disseminated by journalists, external publishers, or site owners and sometimes customers. Earned media tools are more or less third-party enabled channels/tools that are deployed without any financial commitment. Other digital marketing channels that fall under the earned media typology include influencers marketing, online public relations, online word of mouth, product reviews, and maybe search engine optimisation. According to Marx (2018), earned media is publicity gained from word of mouth, online reviews, and blogger, press, and influencer relations. It is a third-party endorsement of an organisation.

Shared media digital marketing communication tools

Shared media, also known as social media, has become one of the most popular and cost-effective marketing communication platforms. It includes publishing or posting to social networking/sharing sites, such as Twitter, Facebook, LinkedIn, and Pinterest. Shared media also include retweets, shares, and viral marketing

Convergence media digital marketing communication tools

This media is used to describe the combination of paid, owned, shared, and earned media for marketing communication. 'Advertising or paid' media has traditionally led marketing initiatives, both online and offline, but advertising no longer works as effectively as it did unless supported by additional marketing communication promotional tools/channels. Shared, owned, and earned media are vital to campaigns, helping to spread brand messages across a myriad of complicated routes that consumers follow across devices, screens, and media. Earned, shared, and owned media have become so integral to successful marketing efforts that they are now aligning with paid media to create possible new media combinations. Owned plus paid; owned, shared plus paid; or earned plus owned. Paid plus owned plus earned media plus shared models are now becoming functional.

The best practice today is to use a combination of paid, earned, and owned media: To use one media channel to complement another type. Some advertisement (paid) with some company information or product offers on company websites or blog or social media pages (owned media) and maybe some (earned media) public relations interventions or customers word of mouth (WOM). They ought to work hand in hand. Each of these digital marketing tools has its pros and cons, therefore using them in a complementary manner can lead to accomplishing set marketing and organisations goals. They all contribute to the development of the digital marketing strategy (Pineiro-Otero & Martinex-Rolan, 2016, p. 45), for instance, proper management of paid media fosters content for earned media as well as increasing traffic to owned media channels/tools an increase in the web traffic can lead to sales of a firm's product or service offerings. The different digital marketing tools can further be represented by Figure 9.1.

Digital marketing of higher education

Digital marketing is an umbrella term that describes a set of marketing processes that utilises all available digital channels to advance products or services or build a brand/product digitally. Though digital marketing is often referred to as 'e-marketing', 'online marketing', 'internet marketing', or 'web marketing', it, however, goes beyond using the Internet to promote a product or service. This explains why Sathya (2017) reasons that digital marketing is a broad term for the marketing of products or services using digital technologies, mainly, not only on the Internet but also includes mobile phones, display advertising, and any other digital medium. Also, Pride and Ferrel (2016) affirm that digital marketing utilises all digital media, including mobile, interactive channels, especially the Internet to develop communication and exchanges with customers. Digital marketing according to Chaffey, Chadwick, Mayer and Johnson (2009) are marketing communication using electronic media such as the web,

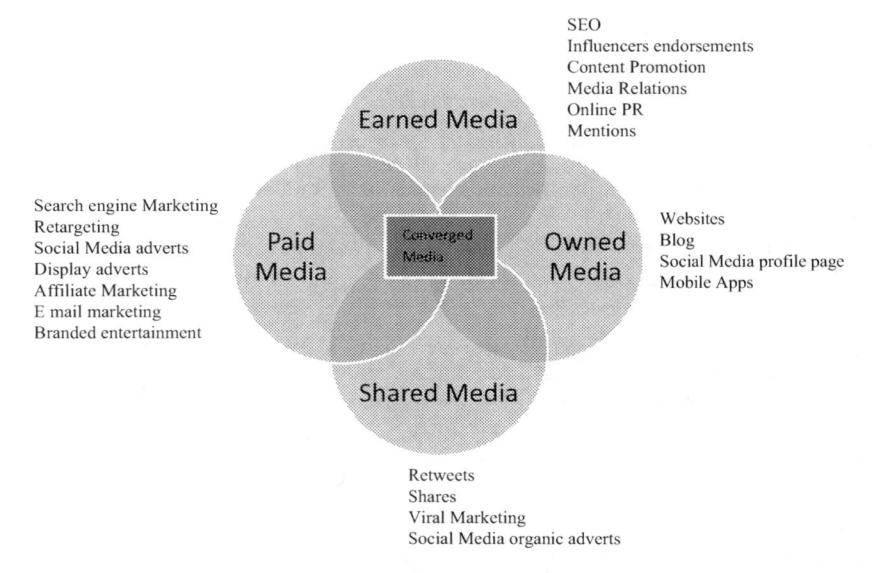

SEO
Influencers endorsements
Content Promotion
Media Relations
Online PR
Mentions

Search engine Marketing
Retargeting
Social Media adverts
Display adverts
Affiliate Marketing
E mail marketing
Branded entertainment

Websites
Blog
Social Media profile page
Mobile Apps

Retweets
Shares
Viral Marketing
Social Media organic adverts

Figure 9.1 Modern means of marketing communication
Source: Author, 2019.

email, interactive television, IPTV, and wireless media in conjunction with digital data about customers characteristic and behaviour.

From the various definitions, it is safe to state that digital marketing is a sub-branch of traditional marketing that uses digital channels to achieve the same goal as traditional marketing, which is to attract new customers and keep old ones by promising superior values. This is only done by engaging the customers with the brand through social media, blogs, forums, email marketing, mobile applications, websites optimisation, and online displays marketing.

Extant literature exists on studies about using digital technology to market tertiary education in other countries. For instance, Adams and Alison (2018) conducted a study on marketing your university on social media; a content analysis of Facebook posts types and formats. The authors sought to examine what social media marketing strategies can spark engagements among students and alumni. The duo found out that user-generated content significantly increased engagement among users. Also, Rayport and Jaworski (2001) posit that organisations must design websites that embody or express their purpose, product, and vision stressing that prospective consumers often visit an organisation's website for information much earlier.

Earlier, Liza and Jamie (2003) conducted an exploratory study of marketing international education online in the Australian market. They sought to establish the role of the Internet in communicating educational opportunities to international students during information search and decision-making. The authors found out that prospective international students do use the Internet in their decision-making process when looking for admission to international universities.

Galan, Lawley, and Clement in 2015 in another exploratory study investigated social media use in postgraduate students' decision-making journey. The authors reported that besides Facebook and YouTube, students were also using blogs in their study search and therefore recommended that education marketers should engage more actively with social media. Also, Pokhrel, Tiwari, and Phuyl (2015) studied the impact of education marketing in enrolment of students at private management colleges in Kathmandu. The authors found out that the words of mouth from family, friends and relatives' recommendations, colleges' websites, and newspapers' advertisements were found to be practical marketing tools for students' enrolment.

Similarly, Constantinides and Stagno (2011) conducted a segmentation study on the potential of social media as instruments of higher education marketing in future university students in the Netherlands. The significant finding reveals that future university students were mostly interested in social interaction and information seeking when using social media. The study established that social media play a secondary role in students' choices when compared to traditional forms of university marketing. Interestingly, the finding from the study is at variance with Liza and Jamie (2003) and Adams and Alison (2018) perhaps because of the demographic characteristics of the future students.

In Kenya, Bowen, Gogo and Maswili (2012) conducted a descriptive study to establish the marketing strategies that attract and increase student enrolment in private universities in the country. The authors' findings showcase that advertising through an institution's website, mass media, social media networks such as Facebook, open day on campus, career fair involvement, encouraging word-of-mouth and alumni support are part of marketing strategies that can offer an opportunity to attract and increase students' enrolment. Concerning Nigeria, Adejuwon, Ilori and Owoso (2013) in their exposition on meeting the demand for post-secondary education in Nigeria: issues and challenges assert that private universities have made an appreciable impact in providing more admission openings albeit for high-income groups. Besides, they posit that world web rankings show that private universities in Nigeria have made an encouraging impact in published materials in such a short period of existence.

Most of the researches have reiterated the need for strategic marketing communication in promoting higher education services (Constantinides & Stagno, 2011; Adam & Alison, 2018). Higher education marketing now involves a blend of promotional channels from traditional advertising using below the line and above the line media to the more recent interactive and digital media. Liza and Jamie (2003) have affirmed that universities, particularly private have used the Internet, social media, and digital marketing initiatives to reach, attract, and subsequently persuade students to enrol in their universities.

Higher education in Nigeria

Nigeria is a federal constitutional republic, a multi-ethnic and multi-religious country comprising 36 states and a federal capital territory Abuja. With approximately 174 million inhabitants, Nigeria, also known as 'Giant of Africa', is the most populous country in the continent. Geographically, Nigeria is situated in West Africa and shares land borders with Republic of Benin (west), Chad and Cameroon (east) and Niger (north). The nation's coast in the south lies in the Atlantic ocean of the Gulf of Guinea. Nigeria has its origin in the colonisation of the region during the late 19th to early 20th centuries by the British. Nigeria was later formed from the combination of two neighbouring British protectorates: Southern Nigeria and Northern Nigeria protectorates. During the colonial masters' era, the British set up administrative and legal structures while retaining traditional chieftains. The country later gained independence on 1 October 1960.

A review of the Nigerian higher education revealed that Yaba Higher College was the first higher institution in Nigeria established in 1932. It was established by the colonial government to train Nigerians in different post-secondary courses leading to disciplines such as teaching, engineering, agriculture but in assisting capacities. The few Nigerians educated than were not trained in the area of technology, as most of them were educated in administrative and civic capacities mainly to assist the colonial masters in administrative duties. Later, Nigerians' agitation for the provision of a more comprehensive higher education led to the constitution of the Asquith and Elliot Commission on higher education in 1943. The report of the commission recommended the need to establish universities in Nigeria, thus giving birth to the University College, Ibadan in 1948 which was initially an affiliate of the University of London.

The National Universities Commission (NUC) of Nigeria is a government agency saddled with the responsibility of promoting quality higher education in Nigeria; the Commission is also responsible for approving all academic programmes run in Nigerian universities and approving the establishment of all higher educational institutions offering degree programmes (Mogaji, 2019a). Nigeria's University education system includes both public and private universities. Both federal and state governments run public universities while the private universities are owned by different religious bodies, individuals, and organisation. Currently, the structure of the Nigeria tertiary institutions is represented in Figure 9.2.

Private higher education institutions in Nigeria

Privatisation has been widely adopted in recent decades not only in higher education but in other public sectors such as telecommunications, oil and gas, media, transportation, energy, power generation and distribution. Privatisation refers to the transfer of shares or assets from public to private sector utilising sale or enactment of enabling government policy/legislation to liberalise or deregulate sole public ownership.

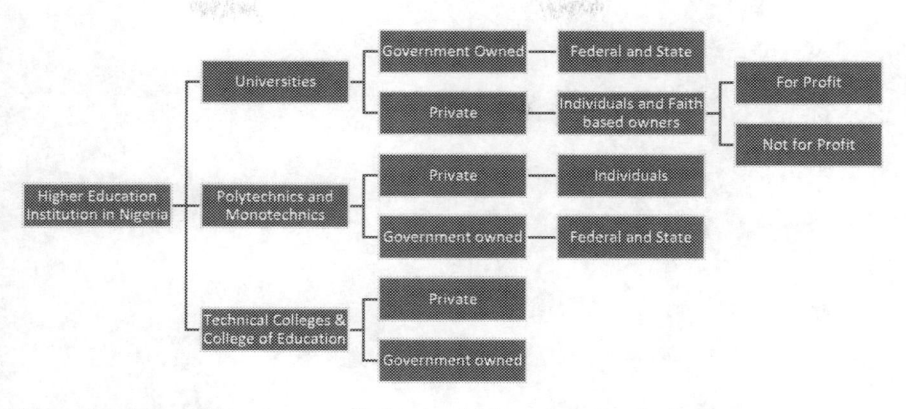

Figure 9.2 Ownership structure of Nigerian higher education institutions
Source: Author

The epileptic academic system occasioned by inadequate funding, incessant strikes by academic staff union of universities (ASUU), population growth and the surging number of candidates seeking admission into the various higher institutions of learning has engineered the need to liberalise the education sector in Nigeria. Private universities are non-public or independent universities, solely owned, financed, and managed by private individuals, denominational or secular boards; often they are operated for profit (Mogaji, 2019a). The idea of private universities was conceived in the 1960s. The idea failed at that time, primarily due to government's intolerance and rejection, and the lack of adequate funds by the proponents (Omomia, Omomia, & Babalola, 2014, p. 155). Typical with all elephant projects and private business entities, the teething problem of gaining financial stability affected the takeoff of some of the first private universities and so, made them defunct.

With the return of democracy in Nigeria, in 1999, under the former civilian president, General Olusegun Obasanjo, the coastline became more evident as private universities in Nigeria received another boost and an upsurge of private universities in Nigeria. Afterwards, first set of private universities were screened in 1999, but only three were approved which are Igbinedion University, Okada, Babcock University, Ilisan Remo, and Madonna University, Okija (Omuta, 2010). The first licensed private university in Nigeria after the return of democracy in 1999 was Igbinedion University, Okada (Owoeye, 2012).

Since then, there arose a tremendous upsurge in the number of private universities in Nigeria after this time, bringing the present number of private universities to 79. Forty-five% (n=79) of universities in Nigeria are private universities. These private universities are, however, more predominantly located in South West (n=36) and South-South (n=14) of the country. There are fewer universities in the North East (n=2) and North East (n=3) of the Country. There are 11 states with no private University. Figure 9.3 illustrates the location of all the private universities in Nigeria. Each square presents a

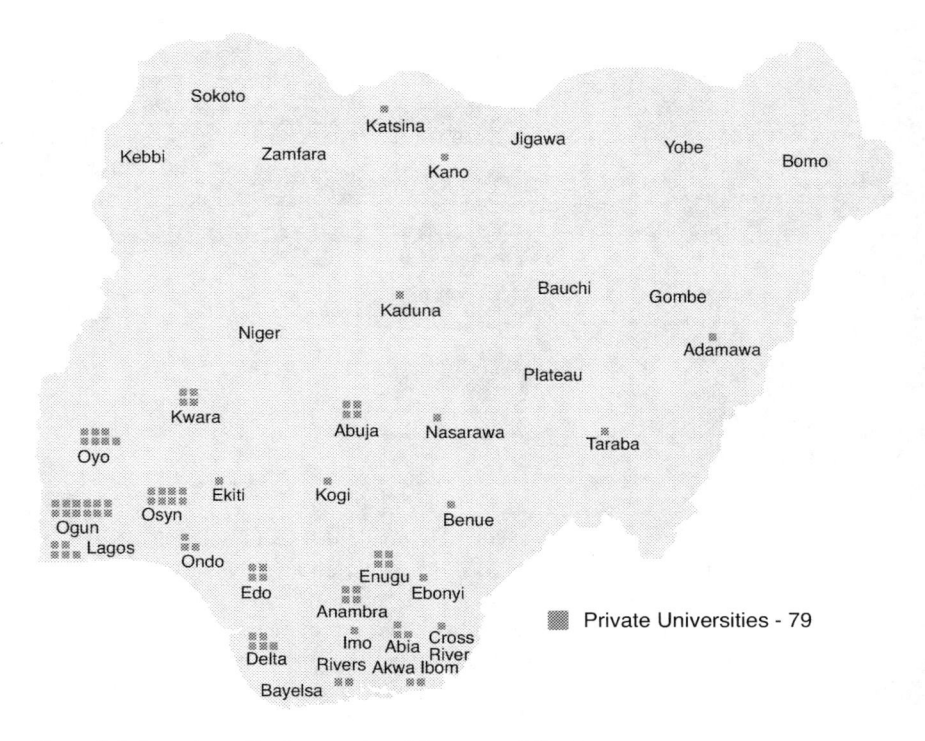

Figure 9.3 Location of private universities across Nigeria
Source: Mogaji (2019a). Used with permission

university. South West (Ekiti, Lagos, Ogun, Ondo, Osun and Oyo) has the highest number of state and private universities. Ogun State, with 12 universities, has the highest number of private universities.

Researchers have established that the survival of many private schools depends on their capacity to effectively use different digital marketing strategies to retain old students and capture new students (Uchendu et al., 2015). With digital marketing, educational institutions now use a different digital platform to strategically showcase their institutions' values, project right image as well as their unique selling point. The use of Internet, email marketing, digital public relations, websites, and social media marketing are not only contemporary means of marketing communication, they are also effective ways to portray an organisation's image to the target market. Understanding how private universities are using these media is essential, and this is the purpose of this chapter.

Theoretical framework

From marketing and communication points of view, the conceptual framework for this study is hinged on the 7Ps of the marketing mix, developed specifically for educational institutions by Kotler and Fox (1995) and the uses and gratification theory propounded by Katz, Blumler and Gurevitch (1974). The scope of education marketing involves element of marketing mix, marketing theory including market strategy, segmentation of target market and market positioning. It also comprises integrating product, price, promotion, place, people, process, and physical evidence in building the overall corporate image to educate, induce, and persuade prospective consumers.

Kotler and Fox (1995) postulate that adopting marketing strategies is an active initiative to overcome the decline in student's enrolment. The scholars affirm that schools that fail to think strategically about their marketing efforts to project favourable image, the unique selling propositions and values of their institutions to the public tend to struggle with a range of issues such as poor enrolment, shrinking operating budget, and image confusion. Therefore, the duo suggested some marketing strategies that schools can use which include advertising, word of mouth, effective use of school website/social media, customisation, competitive pricing, and adequate infrastructure.

Uses and gratification theory also provided theoretical leanings for the study. Uses and gratification theory stipulates that media audience make use of the media for different reasons and does this actively. The theory places much emphasis on the role of the audience making choices and being goal-oriented in his/her media contents consumption behaviour. The proponents of the theory argue that media audiences are active and are exposed to the media willingly based on the intended goal to fulfil identified needs / and thereby get gratification(s). Gratification, on the other hand, implies the satisfaction and rewards obtained by the media audience after the use of mass media or after their exposure to mass media messages or content. It explains motivation behind media use and habits. In other words, people would instead expose themselves to mass media contents and channels based on their interests, habits, and set objectives for achieving satisfaction and pleasure.

Driven by marketing mix variables and the uses and gratification theory, the intertwining of private tertiary institutions' digital marketing communication activities is represented with Figure 9.4.

While organisational operations are prompted by the dictates of the marketing mix to make decisions about what to offer, at what price with what promotional efforts and processes, both organisations and their target audience decisively use the media in a purposive way to satisfy their needs highlighted above and therefore get some gratification. Because of this, the current study sought to establish the use of digital promotional tools by organisations in Nigeria with particular focus on select private universities in the South Western, Nigeria.

Methodology

A multi-study approach was adopted to understand the digital marketing communication strategies for private universities in South Western, Nigeria. Two different studies were conducted one after the other. The study is both

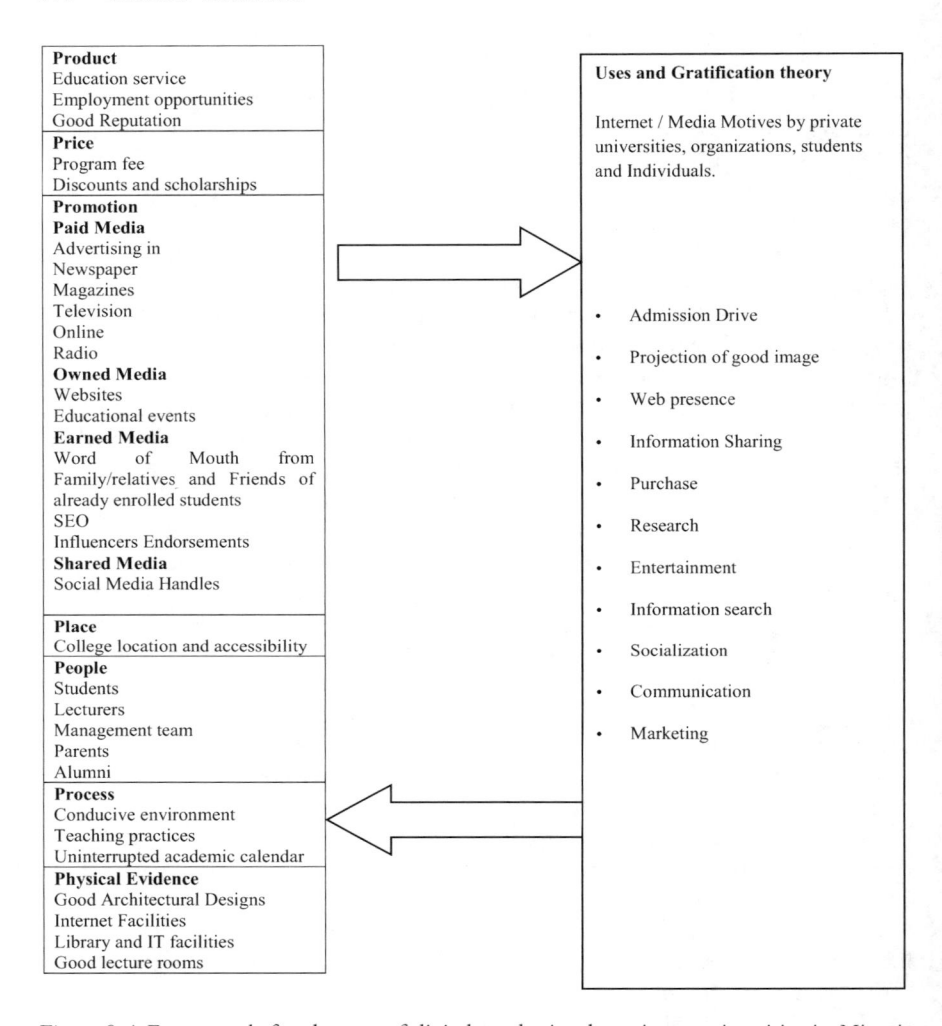

Figure 9.4 Framework for the use of digital marketing by private universities in Nigeria
Source: Author, 2019

source and audience research, which involves an interview with universities' public relations officers and analysis of universities' digital marketing strategies. The sampled universities are from the South Western geopolitical zones in Nigeria. The country has six geopolitical zones. The South Western geopolitical zone was purposively chosen because the geopolitical zone accounts for 36 (45%) of 79 private universities in Nigeria (Mogaji, 2019a). There are six states in the South Western geopolitical zone. One university was randomly selected from five states while Afe Babalola university was purposively chosen for Ekiti State being the only private university in the state. The universities selected are:

1. Caleb University (Lagos State)
2. Covenant University, (Ogun State)
3. Elizade University, (Ondo State)
4. Fountain University (Osun State)
5. Lead City University (Oyo State)
6. Afe Babalola University (Ekiti State)

Study 1: Report of digital marketing communication strategies by universities

Methodology

The first study explores the digital marketing communication strategies by universities through semi-structured interviews with the public relations officers (PRO) of the universities. From the six universities were approached for an interview to understand the digital marketing communications strategies. These officers are the key informant who is responsible for the stakeholder communications in these universities. Key informants from two universities declined the interview. A semi-structured interview was conducted with key informants from the other four universities which Afe Babalola, Caleb universities, Fountain University, and Covenant University. This qualitative methodology offers more in-depth insight and enables the researcher to have a conversation with the participants and gain a better understanding of their experiences regarding the subject matter (Farinloye et al., 2019). The participants were assured of their anonymity (there is more than one PRO in the universities). The participants were asked about the background of the organisation, the digital marketing tools used for promoting the institutions and the challenges they face as they develop strategies to market their universities. The interviews were recorded with participants permission. Interview ware transcribed and thematically analysed accordingly. There was a 'member check' to ensure the credibility and authenticity of this study.

Results

Key themes emerged from the analysis of the interview with the universities' spokesperson. They recognise the need for digital marketing for recruitment purposes. However, there are challenges which are inhibiting a more integrated approach.

THE INTEGRATED APPROACH

The spokesperson identified that private universities are using an integrated digital marketing communications approach which includes email marketing, advertisement placements on blogs and other websites, social media, and the universities' websites. The universities recognises that these platforms offer them the opportunity to engage with prospective students who are savvier about technology.

> Since the world has gone digital, we could not afford to be left behind. So very early in the life of [the University], we had adopted the use of online public relations, display advertising email marketing and the use of social media platforms.
>
> There is a focus on social media. That is very important in reaching our target audience who are always on social media. We do Facebook, Twitter and Instagram advertisements, but Facebook ads are considered most useful to us.
>
> We do use our website, social media, newspapers adverts, email marketing and display adverts on newspaper websites as occasion demands
>
> We use our website, social media like YouTube, Twitter, Instagram, Facebook, LinkedIn. We have also invested in our Search engine optimisation.

However, they also acknowledge that they complement their digital campaign with other traditional media like newspaper advertisements and referrals through word of mouth.

> Currently, the University adopts the Integrated Marketing approach for student enrolment. That is both online, offline, print advert, outdoor, words of mouth, among others.
>
> We do adverts in the newspaper, radio and television but we do not place adverts on newspaper websites.
>
> A mix of digital and marketing and words of mouth but the most effective are words of mouth.

The needed resources

While the respondents reported that they are using digital marketing, the extent to which these digital channels are being used is of concern. The respondents noted that often, they do not have enough resources to do as much as they would like to do with their digital marketing. There is a concern about the shortage of human resources and the technical skills required. Funding (and investment) in tools for analytics and content management are also not forthcoming. Data analytics is essential to understand how users are engaging with the university brands on social media, but that has not been well explored as in most cases the analysis is done manually. This lack of resources highlights an essential limitation for universities as they plan to adopt and integrate digital marketing for their recruiting purposes.

> I know that social media plays a vital role in the promotion of our University and to drive recruitment, but sometimes you do not have the resources and tools to do this effectively.

I am aware of Hootsuite, Buffer and Sprout Social, and often you do not get the full benefit if you are using the paid version. I would like to have Hootsuite Enterprise, but that is not a priority for the University sat the moment.

I can confirm that a University is very expensive to run for private individuals or groups, especially when there is no support from TETFUND to private universities. It could be easy to start but difficult to sustain a private University

The right team

While human resources are a challenge, there is also a challenge in terms of having a dedicated team to work on the digital marketing strategies of the universities. Often the team is embedded within the public relations and recruitment team. These posing and monitoring are done by staff and sometimes students, the university may not always have control over these postings.

Currently, there is no marketing department but subsumed under the PR Unit and Admissions Office.

We do not have a dedicated marketing department for admission drive, but we do draft people from other departments to go to different places when marketing the university for admission.

We do not have a marketing department, but everybody is involved both academic and non-academic staff are encouraged to bring students in.

There is a publicity committee (which is a subcommittee under the Scholastic Aptitude Screening committee of the University). This committee comprises of people drawn from different departments and units, including the media and corporate affairs to market the admission drive.

Study 2: Analysis of digital marketing communication strategies by universities

Methodology

To complement the findings from the participants in Study 1, the second study assesses in real-time, use of digital marketing strategies as well as the digital presence of the six universities selected for the study. The search focuses explicitly on their social media presence, websites, and other digital marketing strategies. This search was used to validate or rebut the claims of the universities' spokespersons that were interviewed. The presence or absence of the universities on five social media was identified. Facebook, Twitter, Instagram, YouTube and LinkedIn were checked in August 2019 to find out if any of the six universities have a profile page.

Results

All the universities sampled had one form or another of social media presence, there are variations, however on the different social media they use. Afe Babalola

University and Covenant University were the only universities that use the five identified social media for communications. Covenant University page has the highest number of likes/followers of over 119,000. Their page was created in July 2012, and it has been verified. Likes on their verified page: Afe Babalola University has just over 700 likes on their page that was created in February 2015, and their page has not been verified yet. Table 9.1 presents the use of social media as a digital marketing tool by selected private universities in South Western, Nigeria.

No doubts the universities have profile pages on these social media but the level of engagement on these social media platforms are considered ineffective and indicates content creation to engage with stakeholders. While Fountain University created its page in 2011, it has not been verified and still has just over 4,000 likes compared to Covenant University which was created in 2012 and now has over 100,000 likes. This lack of engagement and content creation strategy was also seen with Afe Babalola University, which had a post on August 2017 and did not make any post until May 2018. That is about six months without any post on the university's profile.

Even though as Facebook can be considered the simplest form of social media for a brand (Mogaji, 2016), Caleb University and Elizade University do not have a relevant, active, or verified Facebook account. Instead, some pages and accounts were created by individuals to assist students with admission processes. Three of the universities (Elizade University, Fountain University and Lead City University) do not have a relevant, active, or verified LinkedIn profile. Elizade University had the least engagement on social media. They do not have a relevant, active, or verified Facebook, Instagram, YouTube, or LinkedIn account. Elizade University's Facebook page was created since 2014, but there has not been any post. This lack of engagement and content are evidence of lack of resources and team as identified from Study 1, where university officers acknowledge that they have limitations with how much they can commit to their social media campaigns.

Discussion

A multi-study approach was adopted to understand the digital marketing communication strategies for private universities in South Western, Nigeria. The study interviews public relations officer of the universities to understand their digital marketing tool; this was further supported by archival analysis and questionnaire with students. The study provides an overview of the communication strategies being adopted by these universities.

Information obtained from the spokespersons of the universities under study ascertained that indeed, Nigerian private universities know about and in fact, use digital marketing in their marketing efforts especially their institutions' websites although not all the digital marketing tools are being used currently. For instance, influencers endorsement, online relationship marketing, electronic word of mouth, search engine marketing (SEM), Mobile Apps, email advertising and display advertising are either not used at all or underutilised. Besides,

Table 9.1 The use of social media as a digital marketing tools by selected private universities in South Western Nigeria

University	Social media profile pages and activity Level				
	Facebook	*Twitter*	*Instagram*	*YouTube*	*LinkedIn*
Afe Babalola University	760 likes Page created – 20 February 2015	3,750 followers Page created – 18 Sept. 2011	5,334 followers	24 subscribers	64followers
Caleb University	No relevant, active or verified Facebook account	No relevant, active or verified Twitter account	559 followers	No relevant, active or verified YouTube account	165 followers
Covenant University	119,347 likes Verified page Page created – 12 July 2012	32,400followers Verified page Page created – 9 July 2012	10,300 followers	1,823 subscribers	1,503 followers
Elizade University	No relevant, active or verified Facebook account	783 followers Page created –26 August 2012	Not active. No post on page 50 followers	No relevant, active or verified YouTube account.	No relevant, active or verified LinkedIn account
Fountain University	4,477 likes Page created – 8 March 2011	141 followers Page created – 9 May 2013	180 followers	24Subscribers	No relevant, active or verified LinkedIn account
Lead City University	Facebook	Twitter – 272 Page created – 14 Jan. 2015	422 followers	4 Subscribers	No relevant, active or verified LinkedIn account

Uchendu et al. (2015) opined that a useful educational marketing website needs to capture critical customer information such as the products and services offered by a school, especially that the target parents of today belong to a generation that is active in the use of social media. The institutions also admitted that they use traditional media to complement their online presence. Specifically, they mentioned advertisements in the mass media, word of mouth and some press mentions/media relations.

Though the universities have the profile, there is evidence of lack of structure and content development strategies. Some of the institutions' social media profile pages/handles were seen inactive since almost a year ago. This lack of activity and engagement has grave implication for marketing mix model and digital marketing practice which requires constant interaction and engagements with the target audience for best results. Again, the inactivity of these institutions on those platforms also negates one of the assumptions of the uses and gratification assumptions that people and organisations use the media actively to fulfil specific needs and thereby obtain whatever gratification they sought.

The human resources to effectively integrate these digital marketing strategies are recognised. This challenge was also reiterated by the public relations officers who acknowledge that there is a shortage of human resources capable enough to work on the universities' digital marketing strategies. In situations where there are limited funds, universities may not be able to employ a dedicated team for digital marketing, and then they may use staff and students who may not have much expertise. This human resources issue was raised by Wayne, Farinloye, and Mogaji (2020) who questioned the development of the university logos, suggesting that universities' may not be able to outsource the design to a branding agency but ask a member of staff to design a university logo. Also, this aligns with Olaleye et al. (2017) as they reported the lack of creative designs in website of Nigerian University, highlighting the limited technical skills to adopt social media for effective communications with stakeholders. The ability to use tools such as HashtagsForLikes whose algorithm gives the best hashtags for brand, which can help get maximum exposure and reach on social media is essential for the universities, and the financial commitment, however, may be a limitation.

There is limited usage of email marketing and display advertisements; this highlight opportunities for universities to integrate these channels into their marketing communications. Covenant University was the only university which acknowledges that they use email marketing and display advertisements on websites of traditional newspapers as occasion demands to reach out to prospective students.

As illustrated in Figure 9.5, a framework for integrating digital marketing is presented. With universities acknowledging and recognising the value of the integrated digital marketing approach, there is a need to have the needed resources and the right team to support this implementation. Evidence shows that universities have the desires to keep using digital marketing, but if they do not have the right motivation in terms of resources and team to support the drive, it may not work. Besides, there is a close relationship between the resources and the team.

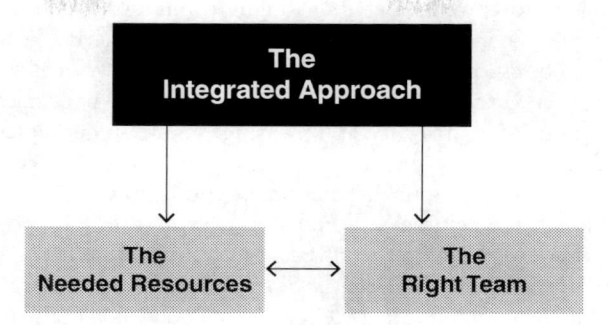

Figure 9.5 Framework for integrating digital marketing communications

While there is a dedicated marketing and communications team for implementing the digital marketing strategies, they should be supported by the required resources to make their work effective. This includes the team members with the right technical/hard and soft skills, which include data analysis, content creation, and customer relationships. Besides, tools, software's and programs needed for content creation, hashtag analysis, and posting across the different platform are essential.

Conclusion

Marketing communication practice is noticeably moving in a digital direction, and those who are mindful of this change will communicate much more effectively than those who do not. The liberalisation/privatisation of the educational sector is one of the significant breakthroughs recorded in Nigeria since the return of democracy. With the privatisation of education, the numbers of private polytechnics and universities have grown in leaps and bounds. Admittedly, some of the institutions have used different marketing communication initiatives to reach out to prospective parents and students through digital technologies, television, newspaper, and radio.

Based on data gathered, it is safe to conclude that the selected universities under study have incorporated technology and digital marketing strategies such as social media, online public relations, and a weblog into their marketing communication efforts particularly the institutions' websites. Nevertheless, the use of digital marketing tools has not been fully explored as there are limitations with the team and their resources. Besides, none of the institutions does influencers' endorsement, no evidence of mobile app and some of the social media pages lacks engagement and activities.

Information gathered from respondents reveal that while they use digital marketing, they still use other traditional media to boost their marketing campaign. The respondents noted prospective students also get to know about the universities' admission opportunities from mass media advertising in newspapers, radio, and television. This understanding suggests the need for other universities, perhaps in Nigeria to complement their online promotional efforts with offline strategies to harness the strength and weaknesses of both channels. This finding aligns with the submission of Mogaji &Yoon (2019) as they analysed marketing communications in universities' prospectuses. While digital media may be becoming the most influential media, universities should still complement it with traditional media like prospectus, newspapers, and billboards. Especially in Africa where there are challenges with Internet access and bandwidth.

Theoretically, this paper makes some key contributions. It provides insight into the use of social media by universities in Africa, it extends the previous works on social media such as Facebook (Adam & Alison 2018), Twitter (Mogaji, 2019b), Instagram (Stuart, Stuart, & Thelwall, 2017) and LinkedIn (Mogaji, 2019c), these studies has also predominantly focused on universities in the developed countries. This present study recognises the challenges universities are facing in developing their social media strategies and the lack of active, relevant, and verified pages of universities. While the proponents of the uses and gratification argued that media audience, universities, in this case, make use of the media for different reasons and does this actively, there are limitations which hinders this usage. This study recognises the gratification as expressed by the university respondents but also the limitations to its usage. The study presents a framework for the integration of digital marketing, recognising the gratification but also the role of the team and the resources needed for an effective campaign. The study also extends the application of the different types of media with focus on social media by universities.

While acknowledging the unique and dynamic nature of digital marketing communication, the chapter offers managerial implications for university managers who want to adopt social media for effective strategic communications. Based on fact gathered, it is recommended that to ensure constant interaction and communication between organisations and their target markets, organisations should make conscious efforts to dedicate employees that will be in charge of the digital channels of their organisations especially their social media handles and other channels for questions and complaints. Besides, there is a need to integrate both offline and online channels for an integrated marketing communication effort for best results. Since research is cumulative, it is suggested that other researchers may explore the place of digital marketing strategies in an organisations' integrated marketing communication plan. Likewise, universities need to understand their stakeholders to engage and communicate with them properly, and perhaps article intelligence can play a crucial role in data aggregation and analysis (Dwivedi et al., 2019).

There are limitations with this study which should receive consideration before generalising any findings. Firstly, the study focuses only on private universities in South Western, Nigeria. These findings may necessarily not be transferable to other parts of the country, and future studies can explore other geopolitical zone or the whole of the country. Secondly, social media data were collected at a time, and there are possibilities to the analysis collected and activities on the profile. Future research can consider a longitudinal study to explore the progress that has been made with digital marketing in African universities.

References

Adam, P., & Alison, B. S. (2018). Marketing your university on social media: A content analysis of Facebook post types and formats. *Journal of Marketing for Higher Education*, 28(2), 175–191. doi:10.1080/08841241.2018.1442896.

Adefulu, A., Farinloye, T., & Mogaji, E. (2020). Factors influencing post graduate students' university choice in Nigeria. In E. Mogaji, F. Maringe, & R. E. Hinson (Eds.), *Higher education marketing in Africa: Explorations on student choice*. Cham, Switzerland: Springer.

Adejuwon, O. O., Ilori, M.O., & Owoso, F. O. (2013). Meeting the demand for post-secondary education in Nigeria: Issues and challenges. *Journal of Sustainable Development in Africa*, 15(4), 143–166.

Adeogun, A. A., Subair, S. T., & Osifila, G. I. (2009). Deregulation of university education in Nigeria: Problems and prospects. *Florida Journal of Educational Administration and Policy*, 3(1).

Atanda, I. A., & Adeniran, F. A. (2017). Towards the effective management of private university education in Nigeria. *International Journal of Advanced Academic Research Arts, Humanities & Education*, 3(3). 7–24. Retrieved from www.ijaar.org.

Bowen, J. D., Gogo, J.O., & R. Maswili (2012). Marketing strategies that attract and increase student enrollment in institutions of higher learning: Case of private universities in Kenya. 2 Annual Conference Proceedings Kabarak University. Retrieved from www.semanticscholar.org/paper/Marketing-Strategies-that-Attract-and-Increase-in-Bowen-Gogo/988135b02daae8587e2cde7eef78ee96a2a996aa.

Chaffey, D., Chadivick, E., Johnson, K., & Maser, R. (2009). Internet marketing strategy, implementation and practice. Harlow: Pearson.

Constantinides, E., & Stagno, M. C. (2011). Potential of the social media as instruments of higher education marketing: A segmentation study. *Journal of Marketing for Higher Education*, 21(1), 7–24. doi:10.1080/08841241.2011.573593.

Dwivedi, Y. K., Hughes, L., Ismagilova, E., Aarts, G., Coombs, C., Crick, T. … & Galanos, V. (2019). Artificial intelligence (AI): Multidisciplinary perspectives on emerging challenges, opportunities, and agenda for research, practice and policy. *International Journal of Information Management*. doi:10.1016/j.ijinfomgt.2019.08.002.

Galan, M., Lawley, M., & Clements, M. (2015). Social media's use in postgraduate students' decision-making journey: An exploratory study. *Journal of Marketing for Higher Education*, 25(2), 287–312. doi:10.1080/08841241.2015.1083512.

Iruonagbe, C.T., Imhonopi, D., & Egharevba, M.E. (2015). Higher education in Nigeria and the emergence of private universities. *International Journal of Education and Research*, 3(2) 49–64.

Katz, E. B., & Gurevitch, M. (1974). Utilization of mass communication by the individual. In J. G. Blumler & E. Katz (Eds.), *The uses of mass communication* (pp. 19–32). London: Faber & Faber.

Kotler, P., & Fox, K. A. (1995). *Strategic marketing for educational institutions*. New York: Prentice-Hall.

Kusumawati, A. (2019). Impact of digital marketing on student decision-making process of higher education institution: A case of Indonesia. *Journal of e-Learning and Higher Education*. doi:10.5171/2019.267057.

Liza, G. & Jamie, M. (2003). An exploratory study of marketing international education online. *International Journal of Educational Management*, 17(3), 116–125, doi:10.1108/09513540310467787.

Marx, W. (2018). B2B PR tips: How to use earned, owned, paid, and also shared media. https://keap.com/business-success-blog.

Mogaji, E. (2016). University website design in international student recruitment: Some reflections. In T. Wu & V. Naidoo (Eds.), *International marketing of higher education* (pp. 99–117). New York: Palgrave Macmillan.

Mogaji, E. (2019a). Types and location of Nigerian universities. Research Agenda Working Papers, 2019(7), 92–103.

Mogaji, E. (2019b). Strategic stakeholder communications on Twitter by UK universities. Research Agenda Working Papers, 2019(8), 104–119.

Mogaji, E. (2019c). Student engagement with LinkedIn to enhance employability. In *Employability via higher education: Sustainability as scholarship* (pp. 321–329). Cham: Springer. doi:10.1007/978-3-030-26342-3_21.

Mogaji, E., & Yoon, C. (2019). Thematic analysis of marketing messages in UK universities' prospectuses. *International Journal of Educational Management*, 33(7). doi:10.1108/IJEM-05-2018-0149.

Omomia, O. A., Omomia, T. A., & Babalola, J. A. (2014). The history of private sector participation in university education in Nigeria (1989–2012). *Research on Humanities and Social Sciences*, 4(18). Retrieved from www.iiste.org.

Omuta, G. E. D. (2010). *The place of private participation in higher Education: A periscope on private universities in Nigeria*. CPED monograph. Benin City: Onokehoraye.

Osagie, A. U. (2009). Private universities: Born out of crises in Nigeria. In A. U. Osagie (Ed.), *Changes and choice: The development of private universities in Nigeria* (pp. 1–18). Benin City: Rawrtune Resources.

Otonko, J. (2012). University education in Nigeria: History, successes, failures and the way forward. *International Journal of Technology and Inclusive Education (IJTIE)*, 1(2), 44–48.

Owoeye, J. (2012). The place of private universities in Nigeria's educational system. Retrieved from www.iuokada.edu.ng/files/b/The%20Place%20of%20Private%20Universities%20in%20Nigeria.pdf.

Pokhrel, S., Tiwari, A., & Phuyal, R. K. (2016). An impact of education marketing on enrolment of students at private management colleges in Kathmandu. Retrieved from www.nepjol.info/index.php/jbssr/article/view/20947/17190.

Pineiro-Otero, T., & Martinez-Rolan, X. (2016). Understanding digital marketing – basics and actions. In C. Machado & P. J. Davim (Eds.), *MBA theory and application of business and management principles*. Cham: Springer. doi:10:1007/978-319-28281-7-2.

Pride, W. M., & Ferrell, O. C. (2016). *Marketing* (18th ed.). Boston: Cengage Learning.

Rayport, F.J., & Jaworski, B.J. (2001). *E-commerce*. New York: McGraw Hill.

Sathya, P. (2017). A study on digital marketing and Its Impact. *International Journal of Science and Research (IJSR)*, 6(2). Retrieved from www.ijsr.net/archive/v6i2/ART2017664.pdf.

Stuart, E., Stuart, D., & Thelwall, M. (2017). An investigation of the online presence of UK universities on Instagram. *Online Information Review*, 41(5), 582–597.

Timson, E. (2018). Understanding Paid, owned, earned and shared media. Retrieved from www.businesswest.co.uk.

Wayne, T., Farinloye, F., & Mogaji, E. (2020). Analysis of African universities' corporate visual identities. In E. Mogaji, F. Maringe, & R. E. Hinson (Eds.), *Strategic marketing of higher education in Africa*. London: Routledge.

Part III

Branding and reputation management

10 University reputation management

Ruth Kiraka

Introduction

Building a reputation is doing ordinary things in an extraordinary way, consistently!

Reputation has existed as an identity influencer almost as long as there have been humans. Although it may not have been defined as such, people tend to trust people who are consistent in their word and actions, are loyal, honest, dependable, and credible. All these characteristics add up to what one might call 'reputation'. Reputation is, therefore, a social construct that represents the opinion of others about a person, institution, or another organised group. Reputation has been highlighted as a driving force behind the success of Fortune 500 companies (McChrystal, 2017). One fundamental sentiment in the corporate setting is that *'Reputation is our most valuable asset.'* However, in the higher education scene, reputation and reputation management have only recently gained traction (Reznik & Yudina, 2018). Beyond rankings and international accreditations, little has been documented on reputation building and management in universities (Aula & Tienari, 2011).

Fombrun and Shanley (1990) defined reputation as the sum of the images of the various constituencies of an organisation. Doorley and Garcia (2015) later defined it this way:

Reputation = Sum of images = Performance (P) (What we achieve) + Behaviour (B) (How we achieve it + Communication (C) (How we communicate) (Adapted from Doorley & Garcia (2015, p. 4))

Building on Fombrun and Shanley's (1990) and Doorley and Garcia's (2015) definitions of reputation, this chapter delves into what constitutes reputation management in a university setting. The chapter discusses the building blocks of university reputation, why it matters, how it influences marketing, how to manage and sustain a university's reputation and the challenges therein, and how to deal with a reputational crisis. The chapter concludes with a comparison of reputation management in a public and private university.

Building blocks of university reputation

For a strong university reputation to be built, Lammers and Guth (2013) suggest that the foundation must be right. They identified three prerequisites for reputation building. First is legitimacy. An organisation must conform to standards of legitimacy, while at the same time setting higher standards for itself. High-quality research and teaching are the basic tasks that give a university its legitimacy. While universities in the developing world have not yet ascended to the top levels of the global rankings concerning research, they are important in their countries and regions – and are steadily improving their reputations and competitiveness on the international stage (Bunting, Cloete, & Van Schalkwyk, 2014). The basic argument is as follows: Research output = research excellence = ranking = global reputation. This argument has been criticised by Overton-de Klerk and Sienaert (2016) because of its narrow focus on *product thinking* (the research output) as the 'king' in reputation building, which suggests '*sameness*' rather than '*distinctiveness*' of the universities. Higher education reputation should never be based upon research or peer reputation alone, although it remains a key determinant of university reputation.

A second one is industry membership, and with the membership comes industry rankings. It is difficult for an entity to claim a good reputation if it is unknown to and respected by its peers. In most countries, there is an umbrella body to which the universities are expected to be members and a government institution that regulates them. In Kenya, all universities must be accredited by the Commission for University Education (CUE). This adds to both the legitimacy and credibility of the university. In the East African context, most universities also belong to the Inter-University Council of East Africa (IUCEA) (membership is not compulsory, and not all qualify). Other university membership bodies in Africa include the Association of African Universities (AAU) and African Research Universities Alliance (ARUA). The third is the geopolitical environment. An organisation may earn a reputation in one environment which is not easily transferable to another. Others have global appeal. The more transferable the reputation (assuming it is a good one), the stronger it is. Overton-de Klerk and Sienaert (2016) argue that for an institution to differentiate itself and have a transferable and robust brand in a highly competitive environment, several things must be combined. These include PhD training, strategic partnerships, global networks, centres of excellence, excellence among staff, research publications, the mission (social contract), distinct market niche, clarity of purpose, accountability to multiple stakeholders, sustainability, and social impact. Very few institutions can meet all these requirements simultaneously, but this broad perspective does give all institutions a fair chance to score well at least on some dimensions. However, it also suggests that if an institution is weak in most of these requirements, it may be challenging to build a strong reputation.

Dowling (2004) identified four components that are the foundation of institutional reputation – character (organisational culture and competitiveness), ability (Board, CEO, employees, resources), products and services (quality, range, value) and behaviour (leadership, financial sustainability). Ragas (2013) later defined three dimensions of institutional reputation, which are reinforced by Doorley and Garcia (2015) **P**erformance + **B**ehaviour + **C**ommunication. The first is *organisational attributes*, referring to the qualities, features, and benefits that derive from engaging with an organisation = Performance. The second is *public esteem* which refers to the degree to which the public likes, trusts, admires, and respects and organisation = Behaviour of the institution. The third is *organisational prominence* (or what is known as 'top-of-mind' awareness) = Communication. Broadly, Dowling's four components fall into the 'organisational attributes' of Ragas' dimensions.

What is more intriguing about Ragas is his external perspective on reputation, that is, as the public perceives it. This external focus is also consistent with Burke (2011) who distinguishes institutional image (reputation) from institutional identity. Institutional reputation is defined as the perceptions and attitudes held by individuals of various stakeholder groups *outside the organisation*. Institutional identity, on the other hand, is about how *insiders to an organisation* assess it. Public perception is important as it forms the foundation of what reputation can do for an organisation – it can either build or destroy it. Indeed, institutional reputations are generally considered as perceptions, aggregation, comparable and mutable intangible parts of the organisation. The reputation can be earned or lost because it is based on perceived status, and often a comparison between different entities (Lammers & Guth, 2013). This suggests that it is incredibly volatile.

The foregoing discussion may be summarised, as demonstrated in Figure 10.1.

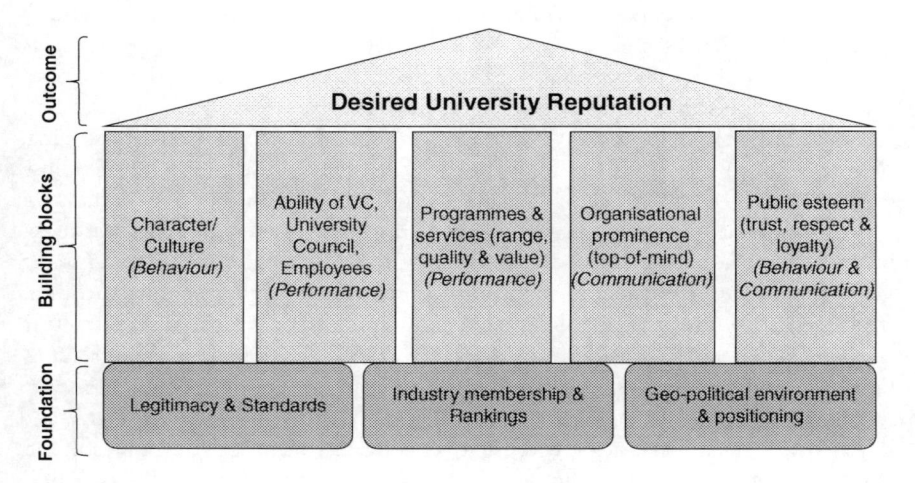

Figure 10.1 Building blocks of university reputation

The value of a good reputation – why it matters

Learning institutions thrive on credibility, a good reputation, and of course, government approval. A good reputation has tangible and intangible benefits. Carpenter and Krause (2012) note that reputation is all the more remarkable because it offers a simplification of complex institutions and is therefore often relied on more heavily than the reality. Universities are large and complex institutions and would, therefore, benefit greatly from having a good reputation. The successful forging of a university's reputation results in building an independent, credible, and sustainable institution. A strong reputation not only serves as a source of competitive advantage, resulting in increased student numbers, visibility, and performance, it is also a valuable political asset, especially for public universities. A strong reputation can be used to generate public support, achieve autonomy and discretion from politicians, and protect the university from political attack (Wæraas & Byrkjeflot, 2012).

Reznik and Yudina (2018) present the case of an excellent reputation within Russian universities. In 2012, the Russian federal government introduced compulsory monitoring of the effectiveness of Russian public and private universities. Based on the results, universities were either classified as 'effective', or 'showing signs of ineffectiveness' rendering reputational damage to those in the latter category. Reputation, therefore, matters because the regulator, in most cases the government, says so. The legitimacy of the institution is enhanced when it has an excellent strong reputation.

Reputation also matters because the consumers of the service say so. Research by Gatfield, Barker, and Graham (1999) on measuring communicative impacts for universities found that the *reputation for quality* of an institution was often more important than its actual quality because it represented the perceived excellence of the institution from the consumer's perceptive – that is the student. This guided the decisions of prospective students to enrol. Thus, building a respected reputation, in this context, gives an institution a competitive advantage.

Burke (2011) identified five reasons why good reputation matters. First, people like to do business with institutions they trust and like. Second, employees are likely to stay longer, be more loyal, and work harder for institutions that have a good reputation. Third, for universities that are seeking to internationalise, attracting global partners is strongly linked to having a good reputation. Fourth, the institution benefits as employees and customers (students) love the learning institution and spread the word, thus attracting the best talent among students and faculty. Fifth, the institution gains reputational capital – this is the ability to differentiate itself from others and develop legitimacy, that helps it to build relationships and grow. Reznik and Yudina (2018) add that a good reputation is essential in attracting investments and ensuring high positions in regional and global university rankings. Additionally, a good reputation helps to sustain an organisation through tough times. It is, therefore, a useful marketing tool.

University reputation and marketing

Between 2016 and 2018, Kenyan universities experienced a significant drop in student enrolments, for direct entry from high schools. The numbers dropped from 169,492 in 2015 to a low of 70,073 in 2017 before rising to 90,744 in 2018 (Commission for University Education [CUE], 2018). This drop was attributed to changes in the primary education national examinations which are the entry requirement to university. However, with about 58 universities scrambling for the dwindling number, the battle has become one of reputation. Additionally, the post-Millennials (that is those born after 1997), who are the target for direct university entry, are social media addicts. They rely a lot on social media and online marketing to get information and make choices about the university to attend.

This increased use of social media and online marketing has given rise to what is now referred to as *reputation marketing*. This involves customers providing real-time feedback on an institution that they have engaged with – feedback that may positively or negatively impact on the organisation's reputation (Daisyme, 2016). What people say online can quickly become the most critical reflection of a university's quality, credibility, and reputation. Daisyme (2016) therefore argues that developing a 5-star reputation should be the number one marketing priority of any organisation. Students and parents want information that will help them feel confident they are making the best decision in choosing a university. *Times Higher Education* [THE], (2019) notes that there are dramatic changes in higher education in the past 10 to 15 years – including the use of social media and the need for impact research, both of which have contributed to the need for effective communication about the work that universities do. It has become so important that universities are recruiting marketing and communications experts at the senior leadership team to address reputation marketing and management.

Consequently, although reputation has always been a significant driver of university success, it has grown in importance as competition has intensified both for students and faculty (*THE*, 2019). A study by Munisamy, Jaafar, and Nagaraj (2014) found that reputation of a university and its programmes was one of the most critical factors in students' decision of a place to study. Hoover (2014) adds that university reputation matters in measurable ways because it directly impacts applications and enrolments of students. Universities must, therefore, provide evidence on which dimensions of reputation matter to prospective and current students to address them.

A study by Azoury, Daou, and El Khoury (2014) and a review article by Lafuente-Ruiz-de-Sabandoa, Zorrillab, and Forcadaa (2018) summarised the following as essential messages that can be derived from a good university reputation. These messages can be used to construct marketing communication:

1. Employers are influenced by the reputation of the universities their new employees attended, and that reputation acts as a summary construct of the

outcome they expect from these employees. As such, a good reputation affects its graduates' labour market prospects.

2. The reputation of a university affects the probability of parents sending their children there.
3. The opinions prospective students gain about a university through personal relationships, and the media affect their intentions of joining the institution.
4. Favourable reputation contributes to payment of a higher price to the institution. Hence those with good reputations can charge higher fees.
5. Institutional reputation is a crucial antecedent of perception of value, overall satisfaction, and loyalty among students, and continues to influence perceptions of lifetime customer value, as graduates continue to associate with their alma mater.

Thus, universities should continuously assess their reputational capital, at least among prospective students, current students, alumni, and employers.

Managing and sustaining university reputation

The cost of recovering a lost reputation can be very high, hence the need to manage and sustain it. A survey of over 800 institutions in the UK found that on average, it would take institutions about 11 years to rebuild their reputation if they had to start from the beginning. If an institution had a strong brand, it might take about four years (Burke, 2011). Verčič, Verčič, and Žnidar (2016) found that there is not much difference between stakeholders on the perceptions or definitions of university reputation, so it should be easy to maintain (at least in theory). Some of the warning signs that the reputation may be at risk include falling employee morale, internal politics that seem more important than doing the job well, the departure of the senior leadership team members and falling credibility of the top management (Burke 2011).

How then should a university manage and sustain its reputation? Doorley and Garcia (2015: 20–21) define *Comprehensive Reputation Management* as a long-term strategy for measuring, auditing, and managing an organisation's reputation as an asset. In this framework, seven components make up the comprehensive reputation management. This section adapts this framework to illustrate how the university reputation may be managed.

First, is *developing a customised reputation template*. This template outlines the essential functions of an organisation that may impact on its reputation. For a university, these may broadly be four divisions:

1. *Academic and Student Affairs* incorporating learning and teaching, admissions, student support services, internationalisation, accreditation, library services, and regional and international faculty and student exchanges.
2. *Research and Extension* that focuses on faculty research and research funding, consultancy and contract research, research partnerships with key stakeholders

including government and the private sector, institutional conferences, technology commercialisation, outreach and service to society.

3. *Planning and Development* that addresses strategy and quality assurance, infrastructure development, fundraising, master planning, partnerships and linkages, and alumni relations.

4. *Administration and Finance* that incorporates budgeting, financial management, human resources, ICT services, security, facilities and maintenance, procurement, and corporate communication.

Different institutions may customise the template as is appropriate, but the message here is to be clear on the different aspects of the university for which it needs to be concerned when discussing reputation management.

Second is the *stakeholder overview*. Each of the critical divisions identified above lists the main stakeholders, as well as the opportunities and threats presented by each. How the university interacts with each stakeholder group is also examined as this forms a reasonable basis for the reputation plan – identifying the needs of each group and areas where the reputation can be enhanced.

The third is the *reputational capital goals*. This represents what the university perceives as essential measures of performance within its industry, or in comparison with competitors. For example, a university may have a goal that seeks to ensure over 80% of graduates are placed in the job market within six months of graduation. Since the focus of reputation is public perception, the reputational goals must focus on outcomes for the external stakeholders – what the university wants to do about graduates, alumni, donors, partners, government, regulator, private sector, and so on. These goals can be measured, monitored, and managed.

Fourth, *reputation audits of internal and external constituents*. This component addresses auditing the status of the university. The internal audit may assess what employees believe to be the reputation of the university and compare that with what senior university management believes to be the reputation. Any gap between the views becomes part of the reputation management plan. The second assessment is an audit of external constituents – students, parents, government, the media, regulator, and any other that the university considers essential. Finally, any differences between the views of internal and external constituents are evaluated add to the reputation management plan.

The fifth is the *reputation management plan*. This is the outcome of the reputation management process – the template, the goals, measures of reputational capital, reputational strengths and weaknesses, reputation challenges, reputational audits, and opportunities available to enhance the reputation. Additionally, budgets, timelines, milestones, and reputation champions are considered. The plan is strategic and seeks to identify initiatives to move the perceptions of the various constituents as close to the university's desired reputation as possible.

Sixth is *accountability or monitoring*. Changes in reputation are measured against the target, using the customised template as a guide. Areas of corrective action are identified, and relevant departments charged with addressing them. Areas of success and outperformance are also acknowledged and celebrated.

Finally, is the *annual audit and assessment*. This is also done according to the reputation management plan. If monitoring has been well done, there should be no surprises here. The annual assessment allows for the review and updating of the plan, including setting new targets where old ones have been achieved. Additional initiatives may also be considered.

In addition to these seven components, there is a need for a *reputation risk assessment* function. This helps to ensure appropriate actions are taken if the reputation is damaged. How quickly an institution recovers depends on how well it undertakes effective measures and communicates to stakeholders. This issue is discussed in some detail later in this chapter.

Reznik and Yudina (2018) argue that there are different levels of responsibility for all the stakeholders involved in the reputation management process. The internal and external stakeholders are interrelated. These interrelations need to be taken into account when implementing the reputation management plan. The relationships are presented in Figure 10.2.

According to Figure 10.2, academic staff are at the heart of a university's reputation as they contribute to each of the core functions. They are supported by both the university administration and non-academic staff. Together, these internal stakeholders produce outcomes that are acceptable to the external stakeholders, resulting in the reputation of the university.

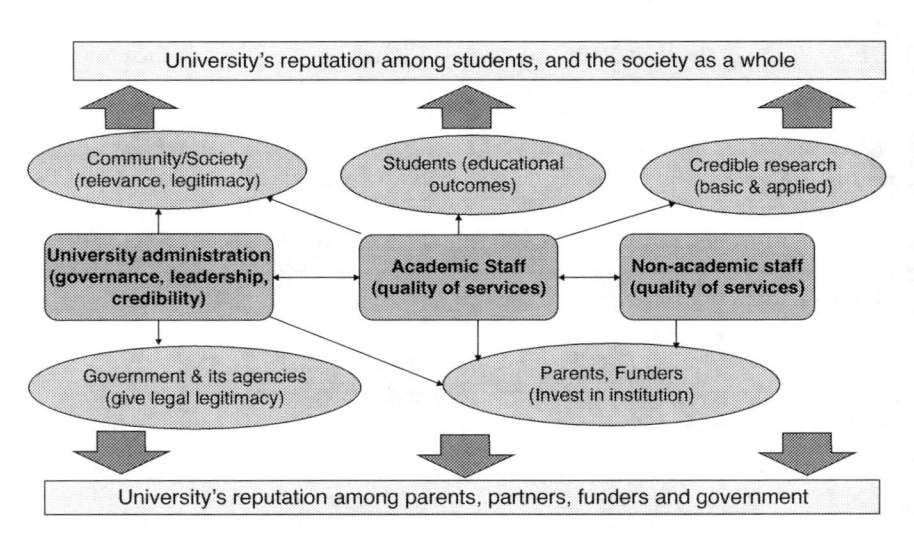

Figure 10.2 University reputational responsibility and outcomes
Source: Adapted from Reznik & Yudina, 2018, p. 382

Challenges in sustaining university reputation

The larger the university, the more critical it is to ensure a good reputation. Increased diversity and internationalisation, and growing staff and student population are generally the outcomes of a good reputation (Reznik & Yudina 2018). A bad reputation impacts people, programmes, and partnerships negatively. Depending on the size of the institution, a bad reputation may even taint the entire higher education scene. However, even small universities have to take care of their reputation. Otherwise, they may never grow and become competitive.

Burke (2011), Carpenter and Krause (2012), Rhee and Hadwick (2011) and Wæraas and Byrkjeflot (2012), identified some key challenges to sustaining reputation that is relevant in a university setting.

1. Not all internal constituents are on the same page. Universities are complex institutions where sometimes there is internal competition for resources, visibility, recognition, and rewards. The silo mentality may be intentional or unintentional. The result is the same: the left hand does not know what the right one is doing, resulting in a reduced overall reputation externally.
2. Difficulty in controlling what different stakeholders will say. Consider a university with 20,000 students. Even if the university management provides a 'university position' regarding a particular situation, between the 20,000 students and social media, there is no telling what twists and turns the story might degenerate into. Sustaining a university's reputation is, therefore, challenging because management has to manage multiple stakeholders' perspectives and needs simultaneously.
3. Sometimes driven by the regulator, universities may emulate the actions and structures of others, because it is easier and safer, often missing out on opportunities to outperform the competition, excel, and break new ground. New initiatives that are backed up by solid research could enhance a university's reputation and possibly introduce different ways of working in the sector, but novelty is not always appreciated (especially by regulators) and can come at a high cost to the university attempting to drive it.
4. External and internal constituencies may not be on the same page. Sometimes, satisfying the needs of one constituent often means upsetting another. For example, students may want small class sizes and individual attention, but these must be balanced against the financial and infrastructure capacities of the university.
5. Decisions or policies are treated as 'irreversible', even when strong incentives to revise them exist. For example, can admission processes or policy approval procedures be made easier, faster, shorter, and more user-friendly?
6. Organisations are systems, which means decisions and actions flow right through every part. If one part of the university is underperforming, this impacts on other parts. Depending on the severity of the under-performance, the entire institution's reputation may be at risk.

7. Reputation can be damaged quickly, owing to increased media scrutiny and fast-paced communication via social media. Even where the media reports may be inaccurate (and there are increasing cases of 'fake news'), it may take while before the university can recover from bad publicity.
8. Reputation stickiness – reputation, whether good or bad tends to be embedded in the minds of stakeholders for a long time. A few Kenyan universities have earned a negative reputation owing to substandard quality. Even when they have hired excellent faculty, or written fundable research proposals, there is still scepticism on the authenticity of the process.
9. There is no possibility of 'product recall'. In the university setting, like any other service provider, service is produced and consumed simultaneously. A poor engagement between a lecturer and students might remain in the minds of those students for a long time – time and money wasted may not be recoverable. Even if financial compensation is offered, the experience may be difficult to erase. This relates to the previous point about reputation stickiness.
10. A university does not operate in a vacuum. If the sector is under reputational threat, the university suffers – the reputational *spillover*. It is not enough to say, 'my university does not do that'. Somehow, the university manager must be ready to address the reputational issue in the sector, even if it may not directly affect their university.

These challenges point to the need for the reputation management plan as it helps to minimise surprises and provides clarity on what to do when faced with a challenge.

Dealing with a reputation crisis

Dealing with a reputation crisis is akin to repairing the image of an organisation. Image repair assumes that reputation is important to stakeholders, and therefore the organisation has a responsibility to repair it. Benoit (2013) notes that the attacks, criticisms, or complaints that have the potential to damage the reputation of an organisation have two essential elements: an offensive act and responsibility for that act. If a relevant stakeholder believes that an offensive act has been committed, then a threat to reputation is likely to occur. Note the emphasis on perceptions: the university's reputation is at risk when relevant stakeholders believe (*perceive*) that it is to blame for the offensive act.

It is also true that institutions that have developed an outstanding reputation (e.g. for high-quality education, high impact research, active student engagement) will have their reputations damaged more severely by a mishap than those that have not put themselves on a 'higher education pedestal'. The higher you go up the reputation ladder, the harder you fall in a crisis. If the damage is also combined with taking too long to respond, or lying or covering up the crisis, the result is a much worse position and a more difficult recovery journey.

Any institution seeking to repair a damaged reputation must balance between the need for speedy communication combined with ambiguity and incomplete information on the one hand and the need to provide accurate and adequate information on the other. More importantly, it must engage its stakeholders in the aftermath of a reputation-damaging event in a way that is acceptable to them (Rhee & Hadwick, 2011).

However, Burke (2011) guides what constitutes an effective response to a reputation in crisis. He identified six critical factors:

1. Assess the incident from the external stakeholders' perspective (especially students and parents), and not the management's. This will help assess just how serious the incident is perceived to be, and therefore the appropriate response.
2. University management must decide how to respond. This includes taking full responsibility for the incident and quickly offering a sincere apology.
3. Recruit others (if needed) to support the management in their response. The support may include crisis management consultants and/or media/communication experts.
4. Disclose details of the crisis as is reasonable. This will limit rumours and false information from spreading.
5. Make progress or recovery visible, to clear the negative reputation and restore the status. This will also help to prove the competence of management if they do a good job.
6. Analyse what went wrong so it will not happen again. This means learning from the incident and documenting essential information and processes for the future. This also includes reaffirming the mission of the university and reigniting its passion for serving and transforming society by providing high-quality education and giving meaning to the lives of its stakeholders.

However, do all adverse incidences of bad press result in reputation crisis? In a university setting, one complaint witnessed often is lateness or absenteeism of faculty from classes. Where such an act is prevalent in an institution, it will probably damage the reputation of that institution. However, there is the second element to this complaint – who is responsible for it? In the Kenyan context, lecturers, especially in public universities are known to go on strike and therefore miss classes. The strikes are often the result of a Collective Bargaining Agreement (CBA) that the government has not honoured. If the students are convinced that the problem is with the government, not the lecturers, then the institutions may not suffer reputational damage as such. Unfortunately, however, responsibility or blame appears in multiple guises. Some may argue that the university should have a mechanism to deal with the faculty challenges without interfering with the learning of the students. In such a case, the reputation of the institution is indeed damaged. The mushrooming of private universities in Kenya was partly in response to the disruptive and unconducive learning environment created by unhappy internal stakeholders in public universities. Reputation-damaging events are therefore interpreted by asking 'Who is responsible'? Where the responsibility lies is where the damage occurs.

However, as illustrated in the section below, public universities in Kenya are large and command a significant share (over 80%) of the total student population.

This is because they are more affordable owing to government funding and have a more extensive range of programmes. They are therefore viewed as 'too large to fail', not to mention they are government institutions, so the government does bail them out as, and when needed. Do they represent some 'monopoly' in the higher education sector in Kenya? Does their reputation matter? Do private universities offer any credible threat to their survival and competitiveness? Is there any incentive for them to focus on reputation management?

Managing reputation in a public or private university – is there a difference? The Kenyan Universities landscape

The university sub-sector in Kenya has grown over the last five decades from one public university in 1970 to 58 chartered public and private universities in 2017. Of these, there are 35 chartered public universities and constituent colleges, and 23 chartered private universities and constituent colleges. This growth has been driven by among other factors, the government's desire to increase access and equity of university education. However, concerns regarding quality and relevance continue to dominate debate on the university sub-sector. Additionally, insufficient funding, inadequate academic staff, and inefficient university systems undermine the ability of the institutions to deliver on their mandate (CUE, 2018) effectively. The number of programmes, students, and academic staff hosted at each category of universities is presented in Table 10.1. Understanding these numbers is essential in discussing reputation management, which as we have seen is about public perception (especially of students, parents, and government).

In addition to the data provided above, the five largest public universities offer 1,420 (36%) programmes and host 235,062 (43%) students and 5,977 (32%) academic staff of the total population (CUE, 2018). This substantial representation of chartered public universities raises essential questions on reputation management at two levels. At one level is to ask what would happen to the staff, students, and programmes of any one of the large universities if it generated a prolonged negative reputation? The other is to ask, what would become of the higher education sub-sector in general if the

Table 10.1 Kenyan universities statistics

University category	No. of academic programmes	No. of students	No. of academic staff
Public chartered	3,272	458,956	13,654
% of total	83.6%	83.9%	72.9%
Private chartered	643	88,360	5,077
% of total	16.4%	16.4%	27.1%
Total	**3,915**	**547,316**	**18,731**
% Total	**100%**	**100%**	**100%**

Source: CUE, 2018.

public universities acquired a negative reputation. In other words, there is both an institution-specific and a sector-wide reputational risk. As argued by Reznik and Yudina (2018) a university which occupies a leading position in a country or region, has to maintain a good reputation, since any negative reputation hurts not only the institution but the country or region as a whole. Burke (2011) describes this as reputation spillover. In the Kenyan scene, therefore, it is evident that the onerous on the public universities to maintain a good reputation is significant, only under their large size.

The webometrics ranking of universities is often used as a proxy for the evaluation of global university performance. Although there are debates on its appropriateness and rigour, stakeholders use it to determine the universities to engage with. Potential students may use it in choosing a university, as it is assumed that the rankings correlate well with the quality of education provided, academic prestige, and therefore overall reputation of the university. Potential partners such as researchers, funders, or international institutions may also use the ranking in selecting their academic collaborators. In Kenya, in the January 2019 webometrics ranking, the first six universities were public universities, and only three private universities were in the top ten (Aguillo, 2019).

Despite what seems to be a distinct advantage of public over private universities, Wæraas and Byrkjeflot (2012) identified reputation management problems that affect public institutions differently from private institutions. First is the *political problem*. Public universities may not entirely have the freedom to choose their identity (who we are) and therefore, their reputation (what we are known for). Second, the public university by nature may have very diverse cultural, structural, and demographic identities imposed on it by government and the management may not necessarily be able to address these in a way that allows everyone to rally behind a single reputation platform. In order to carry out its function of providing the common good – education, the university has to deal with a range of competing and sometimes conflicting priorities, values, and identities, imposed by government. This creates a *consistency problem*. Following from the first two is the *charisma problem*. Ideally, when organisational identity is aligned with image, the institution is trusted, admired, and respected as it creates an emotional bond with its stakeholders – the charisma. Public universities, owing to their large size and public sector tag are often accused of being non-responsive to customer needs or irrelevant. In 2019, 98 university courses in Kenyan public universities were at risk of being scrapped as no students applied for them, again raising questions of relevance and value. They are discrediting of institutions, whether done explicitly or subtly make it more challenging to build the charisma that results in a strong reputation. Paradoxically, the discrediting happens even though many people may be quite satisfied with the services they receive from public universities.

In unpacking this debate further, the author interviewed two senior university administrators – one from a public university, and the other from a private one. Table 10.2 below summarises the issues discussed, and their different perspectives of what university reputation management might look like from their settings.

Table 10.2 Comparing university reputation management in a public and private university

Q1. You are a senior university administrator. From your perspective, how outstanding is university reputation?	
Public university administrator	This has not been an essential consideration until recently, and even then, it is still not something we talk about. Why? Because we have not needed to. By virtue of the fact that we have been around for a long time, are government-funded, we have a diversity of programmes that students want, our programmes are more affordable than those of private universities, and students have generally been sent to us by the universities admissions board, we don't really need to worry too much about our reputation. We are reputable just under being around for long.
Private university administrator	It is imperative. We think about our reputation ALL the time, and I emphasise *all*. Without a good reputation, we would not be in the business of offering higher education. Students and parents come to us because of our reputation for quality of teaching, facilities, learning materials, and sustained culture of high performance.
Q2 What contributes to building a good university reputation?	
Public university administrator	First is our programmes. Having a diverse offering that is attractive to students helps to build the reputation. Second is the faculty. Having adequate faculty in all schools and programmes is essential. Third, research. Our research budget exceeds some universities' entire budget. Having funding enables us to produce high impact research that is commercialised and gives the institution an excellent reputation for relevance and credibility.
Private university administrator	First, the quality of the graduates you produce. If the market likes and recruits them, that speaks to the reputation of the institution. Second, the reputation and qualifications of the lecturers. A university wants academic staff who are qualified, but also prolific researchers and authors — winning a Nobel prize while it is also a great thing. The third is the range and level of educational services. It is good to have diversity, but this must be matched with quality and relevance. There is no point in having many degree programmes that students graduate from and cannot get or create jobs. Another important consideration has an entrepreneurial mindset. This means being innovative in how you do things, but also encouraging entrepreneurship within the student community. That is how we also contribute to employment creation. Scientific achievement – publications, innovations, patents, and commercialisation. This is a difficult one to achieve, but also very important. The reputation of the top management. More often than not, top management means the Vice-Chancellor (sometimes not even the deputies). Having a reputable vice-chancellor is attractive to critical stakeholders.

Q3: In your opinion, who is responsible for maintaining the reputation of the university?

Public university administrator	The university management, of course. It is their responsibility to figure out what needs to be done to ensure a good reputation. However, as I said, we have not focused much on this.
Private university administrator	It is everyone's responsibility. From the security guards at the gate to the subordinate staff, academic staff, up to the Vice-Chancellor and University Council. Everyone has to play their role to ensure the university has a good reputation.

Q4. What are the challenges of maintaining a good university reputation?

Public university administrator	One of the challenges we face as a public university is in consolidating and building consensus around the interests of the stakeholders, especially the University Council. Council members are appointed by the government, with multiple agendas. Some of the agendas derail the university reputation – for example if a Council member wants his/her relative to be admitted to a course for which they are not qualified. In 2017/2018 one of our public universities did not have a Council for over a year owing to these political interests. Appointment to top management positions is also political.
	The other is our large size. This means it takes longer for concerns to be heard and addressed. Bureaucracy stifles creativity and responsiveness.
	It is also true that not everyone understands or appreciates the need to focus on reputation management. Academic staff, for example, think that their job is to teach and do research. That their actions may impact on the university's reputation is often not a consideration.
Private university administrator	As a private university, we are small. Our smallness is both an advantage and a liability. It is an advantage because decisions can be made quickly and issues around reputation addressed in a short time. However, it can also be a liability because a negative incident 'infects' the entire institution quickly.
	The other challenge is that students pay fees directly to the university (unlike in the public universities where they also get government funding). This means there is a certain level of quality and standard they expect and will complain at the slightest challenge. We, therefore, have to be always 'on our toes' so to speak to minimise the likelihood of adverse incidences.
	Private universities in Kenya have been under reputation threat due to bad behaviour by a few. One has been closed, and several others are under threat of being closed or not getting chartered. A number are not financially viable owing to financial mismanagement. (Granted, even public universities have significant financial challenges, but being government institutions, there is an extent to which stakeholders may feel 'safer' dealing with them.) For private universities, though, these scandals and negative publicity paint a picture of weak institutions that may not be sustainable. It is not easy to keep a strong reputation when the peers seem to be struggling.

The above summary of public and private universities perspectives on reputation management paints an exciting picture of the diversity and complexity of the university sub-sector. For public institutions, they look to government and management as the drivers of reputation. In the private sector, they tend to look more inward – staff, students, programmes, quality of education services and responsiveness. This speaks directly to the role that identity plays in thinking about reputation management. For public (government) institutions, it is *someone else*'s responsibility. For private institutions, it is *our* responsibility. Institutions in the same sector have quite different views about reputation management, but this could also be country-specific. It may be interesting to see how this compares with other African countries.

Conclusion

University reputations do matter. Tangible and intangible benefits do accrue to universities with strong reputations. Reputation is an asset that must be managed like any other. All employees in the university have a stake in building and sustaining a good reputation. After all, they have to work there. To be successful in managing and sustaining a reputation, the university must be transparent on its identity (what it stands for), and image (what constituents think). It must also build the infrastructure for a strong reputation – the foundation as well as the building blocks. Where challenges are experienced, or in case of a reputation-damaging event, the university must face them head-on with speed, clarity, and focus. Having a clear reputation plan helps in addressing challenges.

References

Aguillo, I. F. (2019). *Ranking web of universities*. Madrid: Cybermetrics Lab.

Aula, H.-M., & Tienari, J. (2011). Becoming 'world-class'? Reputation-building in a university merger. *Critical Perspectives on International Business*, 7(1), 7–29.

Azoury, N., Daou, L., & El Khoury, C. (2014). University image and its relationship to student satisfaction: Case of the Middle Eastern private business schools. *International Strategic Management Review*, 2, 1–8.

Benoit, W. L. (2013). Image repair theory and corporate reputation. In C. E. Carroll (Ed.), *The handbook of communication and corporate reputation* (pp. 213–221). Chichester: Wiley-Blackwell.

Bunting, I., Cloete, N., & Van Schalkwyk, F. (2014). *An empirical overview of eight flagship universities in Africa: 2001–2011. A report of the Higher Education Research and Advocacy Network in Africa (HERANA)*. Cape Town: Centre for Higher Education Transformation.

Burke, R. J. (2011). Corporate reputations: Development, maintenance, change and repair. In R. J. Burke, G. Martin, & C. L. Cooper (Eds.), *Corporate reputation: Managing opportunities and threats* (pp. 3–43). Farnham: Gower Publishing.

Carpenter, D. P., & Krause, G. A. (2012). Reputation and public administration. *Public Administration Review*, 72(1), 26–32.

Commission for University Education. (2018). *University statistics* (2nd ed.). Nairobi: CUE.

Daisyme, P. (2016). Top 10 tools for reputation marketing. Retrieved from www.entrepreneur.com/article/277197.

Doorley, J., & Garcia, H. F. (2015). *Reputation management: The key to successful public relations and corporate communication*. New York: Routledge.

Dowling, G. R. (2004). Corporate reputations: Should you compete on yours? *California Management Review*, 46(3), 19–36.

Fombrun, C., & Shanley, M. (1990). What's in a name? Reputation building and corporate strategy. *Academy of Management Journal*, 33(2), 233–258.

Gatfield, T., Barker, M., & Graham, P. (1999). Measuring communication impact for university advertising materials. *Corporate Communications: An International Journal*, 4(2), 73–79.

Hoover, E. (2014). *Your college's reputation matters in measurable ways*. Retrieved from www.chronicle.com/article/Your-Colleges-Reputation/144041.

Lafuente-Ruiz-de-Sabandoa, A., Zorrillab, P., & Forcadaa, J. (2018). A review of higher education image and reputation literature: Knowledge gaps and a research agenda. *European Research on Management and Business Economics*, 24, 8–16.

Lammers, J. C., & Guth, K. (2013). The institutionalisation of corporate reputation. In C. E. Carroll (Ed.), *The handbook of communication and corporate reputation* (pp. 222–234). Chichester: Wiley-Blackwell.

McChrystal, T. (2017). A brief history of reputation management. Retrieved from http://blog.uk.reputationdefender.com/a-brief-history-of-reputation-management.

Munisamy, S., Jaafar, N. I., & Nagaraj, S. (2014). Does reputation matter? Case study of Undergraduate choice at a premier university. *The Asia-Pacific Education Researcher*, 23(3), 451–462.

Overton-de Klerk, N., & Sienaert, M. (2016). From research excellence to brand relevance: A model for higher education reputation building. *South African Journal of Science, 112*(5/6), 1–8.

Ragas, M. W. (2013). Agenda-building and agenda-setting theory. In C. E. Carroll (Ed.), *The handbook of communication and corporate reputation* (pp. 153–165.). Chichester: Wiley-Blackwell.

Reznik, S. D., & Yudina, T. A. (2018). Key milestones in the development of reputation management in Russian universities. *European Journal of Contemporary Education*, 7(2), 379–391.

Rhee, M., & Hadwick, R. J. (2011). Repairing damages to reputations: A relational and behavioural perspective. In R. J. Burke, G. Martin, & C. L. Cooper (Eds.), *Corporate reputation: Managing opportunities and threats* (pp. 305–325). Farnham: Gower Publishing.

Times Higher Education. (2019). The world reputation rankings 2019: Strong bonds build strong brands. Retrieved from www.timeshighereducation.com/news/world-reputation-rankings-2019-strong-bonds-build-strong-brands.

Verčič, A. T., Verčič, D., & Žnidar, K. (2016). Exploring academic reputation: Is it a multidimensional construct? *Corporate Communications: An International Journal*, 21(2), 160–176.

Wæraas, A., & Byrkjeflot, H. (2012). Public sector organisations and reputation management: Five problems. *International Public Management Journal*, 15(2), 186–206.

11 Analysis of African universities' corporate visual identities

Thomas Wayne, Temitope Farinloye, and Emmanuel Mogaji

Introduction

Universities are making an effort to present themselves as a unique brand as they reach out to their stakeholders. Branding in universities has become an increasingly topical issue amongst practitioners, as universities invest a vast amount of money in repositioning themselves (Chapleo, 2010). In many countries like the United States of America, the United Kingdom, Canada, Australia, and New Zealand, where universities operate in a market place in which students are consumers of an educational service, there is this increasing marketisation as universities are improving their marketing strategy geared to target prospective students (Roy & Naidoo, 2016). Universities are increasingly recognising the value of marketing (Foroudi et al., 2017), and as they become more marketised, brand building is becoming an essential managerial issue. (Jevons, 2006; Williams Jr & Omar, 2014).

A prominent and public-facing effort towards building a university's brand is the design and development of their logo. Universities around the world are changing their logo to reflect changes and prepare for new challenges. As a brand element, a logo is considered as a graphic representation (Walsh et al., 2010), which can be seen as a source of competitive advantage (Melewar et al., 2006). Logos are used in universities websites, prospectuses, certificates, and souvenirs, where different stakeholders may encounter university logos, and an impression may be made. Given the significance of the logo and building upon the evidence discussed, it is useful to investigate further the concept in order to complement existing studies.

The rationale for the work is that while higher education institutions (HEIs) around the world are behaving increasingly as corporations (Veloutsou et al., 2004) and there is lack of understanding about the brand strategies of African universities, irrespective of the location of the university, the dual identity present in the university – the conflict between the university as a place of learning and a commercial revenue-generating – poses a branding challenge (Alessandri, 2007). There is, therefore, a need to understand better the factors that help to create and build university brands (Khanna et al., 2014), and identify what strategic decisions should be made when designing new or redesigning existing new logos (Kim & Lim, 2019).

Despite the potentially significant role of the favourable university logo, there is no evidence of increasing pressure on universities in Africa to create an appealing corporate logo and strategically communicate it. Likewise, and also, unfortunately, to date, there is a paucity of empirical research within the literature on the visual identities of African universities. Consequently, there is no theoretical underpinning and insight to explain how African universities are defining and visually illustrating their brand identities. Therefore, the development of visual identities – arguably the most prominent manifestation of brand (Marsden, 2019) – remains theoretically underdeveloped.

The purpose of this chapter is twofold: firstly, to develop an understanding of African HEI's brand identity by identifying the types of expressions embedded within the design of the identities, and secondly to develop a conceptual framework which can be used to improve African HEI's brand identity. Using the African higher education sector as an example, this chapter draws on the theories of corporate visual identities to provide a theoretical framework for African universities' corporate visual identities. In so doing, this chapter advances theory in brand identity, design, and development. It also has implications for managers in guiding how HEIs can develop and enhance their corporate visual identities.

This chapter is an initial step to address the call by researchers to study the branding strategies of universities, especially in those in Africa (Mogaji, 2019c). It examines the design of universities' corporate visual identities in Africa, providing guidelines and recommendation for selecting design elements for brand strategies. This chapter studies university logos because they are one of the primary elements of a universities' visual branding strategy within the competitive higher education market. The ultimate goal is to develop managerial guidelines for designing logos for higher education institutions in Africa.

The structure of this chapter is as follows: firstly, a review of literature on corporate visual identities, specifically in HEIs context. Secondly, a discussion of the methodology for the research. Thirdly, the presentation of results and discussions. Finally, a conclusion depicting theoretical and managerial implications and suggested directions for further research.

University as a brand

As higher education is becoming more marketised, various corporate marketing strategies are being employed by universities to make them stand out and effective while competing in the market (Bunzel, 2007). Universities are making effort towards improving the brands and making them more appealing. They are no longer just institutions of higher learning but also businesses striving to survive in the competitive marketplace and aware of critical business metrics (Bunzel, 2007). A university brand is defined as 'a manifestation of the institution's features that distinguish it from others, reflect its capacity to satisfy students' needs, engender trust in its ability to deliver a certain type and level of higher education, and help potential recruits to make wise enrolment decisions' (Ali-Choudhury et al., 2009, p. 14).

A strong brand is the most valuable asset for a university (Robson, Roy, Chapleo, & Yang, 2019) around the world and especially in the UK. Interest in university branding has increased substantially in recent years (Mogaji, 2019) as it is recognised that HEIs, as with any other organisations, have much to gain from developing a strong brand identity (Robson, Roy, Chapleo, & Yang, 2019). Since, universities are under intense pressure to set themselves apart from others, they are rebranding and creating new corporate visual identities, even though not all of them have been all that successful (Mogaji, 2018). Considering that HEIs are making an effort to stand out as a unique brand amongst various competitors and they are increasingly being considered as corporations, branding and reputation management has become a critical part of their business (Chapleo, 2010). No doubt they have been adopting various private-sector ideas such as branding, in order to visibly rebrand; and hence reposition themselves as many universities have been known to alter their visual identity (Mogaji, 2018)

Mogaji (2018) identified two critical motivations for university rebranding. Firstly, universities are rebranding to refresh their brand to become more appealing; universities wants to present themselves as active players in the sector. They want to remain dynamic, contemporary, and relevant. Secondly, some institutions had to rebrand when they were awarded university status. In South Africa, in July 2017, Nelson Mandela Metropolitan University repositioned itself as a global institution by rebranding to become Nelson Mandela University (Gumede, 2017). As one of the newest institutions in the UK, Suffolk (formerly University Campus Suffolk) acknowledge that consistency in how they position and present themselves to the outside world is of utmost importance; hence, they had to rebrand —changing their name and logo (Mogaji, 2018). Likewise, in July 2001, upon attaining university status, Beaver College in the USA officially changed its name to Arcadia University (Williams Jr & Omar, 2014).

While acknowledging that there are many countries in Africa with different higher education markets, branding remains vital within the higher education marketing sector (Lomer, Papatsiba, & Naidoo, 2018), and considerable potential for the application of branding (Furey, Springer, & Parsons, 2014).

There is little evidence of African universities becoming more marketing-orientated in order to attract prospective students, particularly in response to increased global competition. Besides, African universities have their unique challenges, which affects the marketing of higher education. African public universities are often oversubscribed because of accessibility and affordable fees making universities less motivated to engage in marketing activities. However, the influx of private higher education has been changing the market dynamics (Olaleye, Ukpabi, & Mogaji, 2020), with international partnerships with universities in developed countries (German University in Cairo, Lancaster University in Ghana, and Reading's Henley Business School Africa in South Africa) and student desires for quality education. These factors are shaping the higher education landscape in Africa (Ndofirepi, Farinloye, & Mogaji, 2020).

With the consensus amongst academics and practitioners that brands are the most valuable assets for organisations (Madden, Fehle and Fournier, 2006), making efforts to build the African universities' brand is essential, even as the diversity of the sector and the many stakeholders that exist still poses a challenge (Robson, Roy, Chapleo, & Yang, 2019). Developing a strong brand is an essential component of marketing strategy for universities in the competitive market (Watkins & Gonzenbach, 2013). Even as current literature indicates that branding of higher education is in its infancy (Casidy, 2014), there is a shortage of theoretical insight about branding within the African context. African universities, in particular, have not essentially joined the conversation (Mogaji, 2019c). As a result, many gaps remain in our understanding of African HEI marketing in general and explicitly branding.

Corporate visual identity

Brands make effort to distinguish themselves within their market. They create identifiable elements which can be visual, auditory, tactile, gustatory, and olfactory. Though logo is considered the most prominent form of visual identity, other elements can also present visual identification for a brand, such as a store design (Apple Stores) or even staff uniform (flight attendants). Likewise, with the significant increase in social media and TV advertisements, there are possibilities for an auditory version of a visual logo to be considered a corporate identity. This is described as sonic logo (aka 'sogo') (Krishnan, Kellaris, & Aurand, 2012). An example is McDonald's – 'I'm Lovin' It'. Despite the various opportunities and possibilities with brand identity, this study focuses on visual identity.

Corporate Visual Identity (CVI) is defined as the 'way in which an organisation uses logos, type styles, nomenclature, architecture, and interior design in order to communicate its corporate philosophy and personality' (Balmer, 1995, p. 26). The visual identity of a brand is strategically essential in differentiating companies (Hynes, 2009). It 'plays a significant role in the way an organisation presents itself to both internal and external stakeholders' (Van den Bosch et al., 2006, p. 871).

The corporate logo is central at the root of corporate identity as well as the main element of corporate visual identity (Balmer, 2001; Hynes, 2009). It is a significant tangible asset of the organisation (Foroudi, Melewar, & Gupta, 2017). It enhances visibility as well as recognisability of the brand (Balmer & Gray, 2000; Kohli et al., 2002). Despite the importance of logos, the literature on logos remains fragmented (Kim & Lim, 2019). Foroudi et al. (2017) tried to address this issue through their review of literature on logos which revealed that corporate logo is the official graphical design for a company, and the uniqueness of the design requires significant creativity. The notion of a corporate logo is grounded in various subject domains such as marketing and design. The design literature refers to the corporate logo as a set of creative elements that gives prominence to a company's products and services (Mollerup, 1999). While marketers often consider a logo as visual cue help brands communicate their unique identities and capture consumers' attention. (Kim & Lim, 2019).

Logos are also referred to as *aesthetic designations* which are seen by the public and from which they form an opinion (Pratt & Rafaeli, 1997). Marsden (2019) also referred to logo as the corporate brand mark, which a combined unit of a brand name and its visual representation (i.e., logotype and symbol). The corporate logo has various essential elements of design. These include the shape, image, style, and size, as well as the colour(s) used (Hynes, 2009).

Elements of logo

The logo, a form of brand identity, has several components, amongst which are typeface, shape, and colour (Kim & Lim, 2019). Another study has considered brand name and design as logo elements (Foroudi & Nguyen, 2019; Foroudi, Melewar, & Gupta, 2017), Mogaji (2019) however argued that design is not an element nor is design a component of a logo (like colour and typeface), but it is the overarching process of the brand identity development. The design of a logo involves the creative decision of choosing the shape (overlapping circles of Mastercard), the colours (overlapping red and yellow circles) and the typeface (FF-Mark typeface in all lowercase) to make the logo. Likewise, a brand name is not a logo element because the brand name existed before having a logo. Based on this argument, logo as a corporate identity can be expressed through shape, typeface, and colour.

Design is not an element but, instead brings all the elements together to become highly natural and harmonious to achieve specific communication objectives (Van Grinsven & Das, 2016). Perhaps those who considered design as an element (Foroudi & Nguyen, 2019), should consider the shape as an element instead. This can be in form of a circle, square, or an oval. Jiang et al. (2016) suggested that circular shapes are associated with a perception of 'being soft', whereas angular shapes with a perception of 'being hard'. Also, Lieven et al. (2015) found that a heavier and more angular shaped logo increased brand masculinity, whereas a slender and more rounded shaped logo increased brand femininity. Round logos are also viewed as being harmonious and natural, and as a logo element which is an emergent trend that is likely to endure (Walsh et al., 2010). While Luffarelli et al. (2019) found that asymmetrical logos are likely to be more arousing than symmetrical logos, and in turn have a positive effect on consumers' evaluations. With regards to characters, logos depicting characters, places, animals, fruits or any other item are considered more recognisable (Henderson & Cote, 1998).

The typeface is another element of a logo. It is the art of mechanically producing letters, numbers, symbols, and shapes through an understanding of the essential elements, principles, and attributes of design (Solomon, 1986). It is considered the 'the art or skill of designing communication by means of the printed word' (Childers & Jass, 2002, p. 2), and highlights a significant design decision which plays an essential role in the way an organisation presents itself to both external and internal stakeholders (Foroudi & Nguyen, 2019) Typeface plays a crucial role in distinguishing an organisation's visual identity and can become characteristic enough that they can appear on their own without a symbol, for example, the typeface of Coca-Cola (Kapferer, 1994). The typeface is an important component to convey communication goals. A conscious, creative decision is required in selecting the right typeface as a visual identity for a brand. The choice of a typeface can manipulate the meaning of the word it is applied to (Childers & Jass, 2002). University of Greenwich, UK, uses Antonio, a commercial font which they consider to be a strong, punchy typeface used to add visual impact. Mogaji (2018) identified a typology of the typeface. There are the customised fonts (where a typeface is designed explicitly for a brand, for example, the 2012 Olympic typeface), the commercial typeface (brands buy them because it's not commonly available, for example Palatino designed by Hermann Zapf and used by Keele University, UK), and common types (these fonts are available on most, if not all, word processing software and are free to use because they do not require a font licence).

Colour is an integral element of corporate visual brand identity and marketing communications (Marsden, 2019). It induces emotions and moods and influences an individual's perception of a brand. (Foroudi & Nguyen, 2019). Brands can also use colours to position and differentiate themselves in a competitive market. Like Typeface, colour can also remind consumers of certain brands (Singh, 2006). For example, red and yellow for McDonald's, red for KFC, and green for Starbucks. It is therefore not surprising to see universities trademark primary colour which they use on their marketing communication, sports team, and souvenirs. The trademark allows the universities to use a particular combination and shade of colour in their sector. The University of Texas at Austin has the Pantone Colour #159 which they called Burnt Orange, Queens University (Belfast, Northern Ireland) has Pantone 185c called Queen's Red, and University of Greenwich (London, England) has the Greenwich Navy Blue colour (Mogaji, 2018). These colours play a significant role in establishing the universities' identity and should be implemented consistently across all touchpoints (Mogaji, 2019).

With universities under intense pressure to set themselves apart from others, they are rebranding and creating new corporate visual identities (Mogaji, 2018). UK universities rebrand to refresh their brand and be more appealing. They want to remain dynamic, contemporary, and relevant (Sanjit chapter). This opens an opportunity for a better understanding of how other countries, particularly those in the developing economies, are making an effort to create their brand identities.

Methodology

The research was designed to be exploratory, aiming to provide an initial understanding of the different versions of typology used for African universities' brand identities. The research took a predominantly inductive and qualitative approach (Foroudi & Nguyen, 2019). Qualitative seemed to be the most appropriate way to build a picture based on the ideas of informants.

There were three critical stages in the adopted methodology. A summary is presented in Figure 11.1.

Stage 1: Identifying the University – The purpose of the study was to identify the types of expressions embedded within the design of African universities' brand identity. To this end, a broad purposive sample of 200 highest-ranked universities in Africa, according to the UniRank 2019 African University Ranking (UniRank, 2019), were selected for the analysis. These are all universities licensed and accredited by the appropriate higher education-related organisation in each country. These universities are considered the best in Africa, according to the league table, and with the indication that they can give an overview of the brand identity of universities in Africa. As illustrated in Table 11.1, 24 African universities were presented on the league table, that is 44.4% of the 54 recognised African countries. Nigeria has the highest number of universities with 17.5% of the sample (n-35), Egypt followed this with 16.5% (n=33), and Algeria has 14.5% of the sample (n=29).

Stage 2: Identifying the Logo – The second aspect of the selection process involved examining each of the websites of the 200 African universities, to determine which logo they were using on their website that is public-facing. These logos were collected in May 2019. Some universities, while celebrating their anniversary, had modified their logo (such as =the American University in Cairo, Egypt and Stellenbosch University, South Africa). This was collected as their logo for that period. The logos were copied from the website and saved in a serial form as a PDF document. The collected logos are available within an online depository at Mogaji (2019).

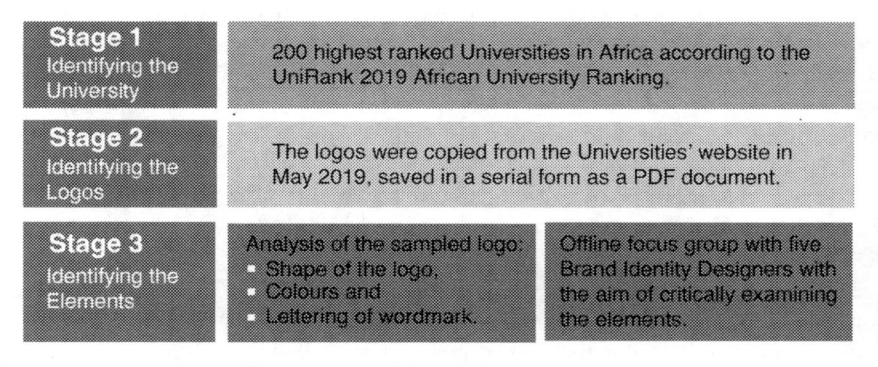

Figure 11.1 Summary of three stages of the methodology

Table 11.1 List of sampled country and numbers of universities

S/N	Country	No of Universities	Percentage
1.	Nigeria	35	17.5
2.	Egypt	33	16.5
3.	Algeria	29	14.5
4.	South Africa	22	11
5.	Botswana	10	5
6.	Morocco	10	5
7.	Angola	9	4.5
8.	Kenya	9	4.5
9.	Ethiopia	7	3.5
10.	Sudan	5	2.5
11.	Tanzania	5	2.5
12.	Ghana	4	2
13.	Libya	3	1.5
14.	Namibia	3	1.5
15.	Uganda	3	1.5
16.	Zimbabwe	3	1.5
17.	Mozambique	2	1
18.	Tunisia	2	1
19.	Mauritius	1	0.5
20.	Réunion	1	0.5
21.	Rwanda	1	0.5
22.	Saint Helena	1	0.5
23.	Swaziland	1	0.5
24.	Zambia	1	0.5
—	TOTAL	200	100

Stage 3: Identifying the Elements – The coding system for this study incorporated a structured approach that drew from the literature and offered a progressive approach that allowed codes to develop layered details from the logo analysis. The PDF documents (in Stage 2 above) was imported into NVIVO, a qualitative analysis software tool (Farinloye, Mogaji, Aririguzoh, & Kieu, 2019). The NVIVO analysis offered a content analysis of the sampled logo. The analysis includes exploring the shape of the logo, the colours, and specific lettering case in a wordmark (Xu, Chen, & Liu, 2017). Following the methodological approach of Henderson, et al. (2004), an offline focus group was organised with five brand identity designers (from Nigeria, Italy, Kenya, UK and Canada) to critically evaluate the design characteristics on different dimensions such as design, subjective familiarity, and recognition. The

designers were informed about the research and consented to participate. The designers were asked to rate the design and select their top 20 logos from the pool of 200 logos, and give justifications for their choices. The first author coordinated the meeting and analysed the minute.

Results

An analysis of the logo of African universities was carried in the first part of Stage 3 of the methodology to understand the recurring themes with regards to the creative elements being used. The analysis revealed the shape of the logos, the colours being used and the typeface. Besides, professional opinions of brand designers were elicited during the second part of Stage 3. The designers critically evaluated these brand visual identities, which informs the theoretical framework for future design consideration.

Logo elements

As earlier argued, there are three elements of a logo – the shape, the typeface, and the colour. These three elements served as the coding framework for the universities' logo, and the results are presented in the subsequent section.

Shape

The shape serves as the containers for the other creative elements that form the logo. The circle was the most predominantly used shape of African universities; 30.5 per cent (n=61) of the sampled logo was in the shape of a circle. This was closely followed by shields – 21.5 per cent (n=43) of the total sample. The shield, however, had different variations, such as inverted shield, flat top, and pointed bottom. There were universities as well that used the coat of arms as a brand identity on their website. While some universities used regular shapes like circles, rectangles, and ovals, some universities used irregular shaped items for the identity. Perhaps that is a creative choice they have made which may have inherent meaning in their culture. This was predominantly from universities from North Africa. Table 11.2 illustrates different shapes of the logo that were used and examples of universities using them.

INTERNAL COMPONENT OF THE SHAPE

While the shape of the logo is recognised as an outline and container for the logo, the internal components are worth considering, as it became a unique feature of most of the African universities' logos. For example, Obafemi Awolowo University had a shape of flat top, round bottom shield, but contained a human face and an icon relevant to knowledge (signified by the book). Another Africa university had the shape of a semi-circle and contained a natural element. There is presence of different elements within the shape, as presented

Table 11.2 Different shapes of logo that were used and examples of universities using them

Shapes		Universities
Circles		The University of KwaZulu-Natal, University of Lagos, Tshwane University of Technology, Mansoura University, Université Kasdi Merbah de Ouargla, Addis Ababa University
Semi-circle		University of KwaZulu-Natal, Université des Sciences et de la Technologie Houari Boumediène, Africa University
Oval		University of Dar es Salaam, University of Zambia
Shields	Flat top and pointed bottom	Rhodes University, University of Ilorin, University of Zimbabwe
	Round top and pointed bottom	University of Botswana, Uganda Christian University, Mount Kenya University
	Flat top and rounded bottom	University of Fort Hare, Obafemi Awolowo University, University of Nigeria
	Round top and round bottom	The University of Ilorin, University of Port HarcourtSohag university
	Inverted shields	Ahmadu Bello University, Zagazig University
Triangle		Libyan International Medical University, Delta University for Science and Technology, Menoufia University, ABM University College
Rectangle		Babcock University, Université Larbi Tebessi de Tébessa, Nahda University, Université Djillali Liabès de Sidi-Bel-Abbès
Octagons		Usmanu Danfodio University, Bayero University Kano, Université Mohammed Premier
Abstract shape		Cape Peninsula University of Technology, Universidade Metodista de Angola, Durban University of Technology, United States International University Africa
Coat of arms		University of Nairobi, Makerere University, Kenyatta University, Vaal University of Technology
Irregular shape		Université Mouloud Maameri de Tizi Ouzou, Université Ibn Tofail, Université 20 Août 1955 de Skikda, Université Larbi Ben Mhidi de Oum El Bouaghi, Université Hassan 1er

in Table 11.3. They include animals and natural elements; perhaps something that aligns with the natural habitats and environments in Africa. Likewise, there were icons relevant to knowledge such as open books, microscope (for sciences and health-related universities), and gears (for engineering and technology universities). Besides, shape of human faces was also presented in the logos.

An example is the Egyptian royalties in Egyptian universities and cultural artefact in Nigerian universities. The University of Benin had the face of a Benin Prince, which illustrated the cultural background of the university in the Benin Kingdom of Nigeria. Also, Obafemi Awolowo University had the face of Oduduwa – who was the first ruler of Ile Ife and progenitor of various independent royal dynasties in Yorubaland in Nigeria where the university is situated.

EXTERNAL COMPONENT OF THE SHAPE

The most prominent external components of the logo are the swirls. These are ribbon-shaped items often below and sometimes above the logo. This is often used to complement the logo and contains information relevant to the brand, such as their name and the motto. University of Zambia, Universidade Pedagógica, and Egerton University had swirls above and below their logo. Universities like Mansoura University, University of Limpopo, Egerton University, and Olabisi Onabanjo University, had their names on the swirls. For

Table 11.3 Different logo shape content and examples of universities using them

Shape Content	Examples	Example of Universities
Animals	Cow, elephant, lion, Eagle	Rhodes University, University of Nigeria, Kwame Nkrumah University of Science and Technology, University of Swaziland
Natural elements	Mountain, sun, trees, plants, water, and leaves	Universiteit Stellenbosch, Africa University, Beni-Suef University, Université de Sfax
Icons relevant to knowledge	Books, microscope, gear	University of Johannesburg, Obafemi Awolowo University, Osun State University, Université Hadj Lakhder de Batna 1
Physical elements	Map, anchor, tractor, lighthouse, flame, and pyramid	Addis Ababa University, University of Pretoria Alexandria University, University of Dar es Salaam
Human face	Founder, royalties of Egypt	Damanhour University, Minia University, Université Hassiba Ben Bouali de Chlef, University of Benin, Universidade Óscar Ribas, Zagazig University

universities with a motto on the swirls, these were sometimes presented in English, like in the case of the University of Lagos, Makerere University, and Obafemi Awolowo University. While the University of Ghana, University of Ibadan, and Vaal University of Technology, amongst others, had non-English motto on the swirls. Modern Sciences and Arts University, however, had an empty swirl.

Colours

African universities appear to be very colourful. Seven per cent of the sample (n=14) only had two colours in their logo. Examples include the University of Johannesburg with orange and white, North-West University, University of Benin and Rhodes University with Purple and white, Université de la Réunion and Nahda University with blue and white, and Walter Sisulu University in black and white. Obafemi Awolowo University has two colours, which are navy blue and yellow. Majority of the logos were very colourful. Ninety-three per cent of the sample (n=186) had more than two colours. This includes the colours that were used in the shape (including icons and coat of arms) and typeface. Durban University of Technology had seven colours – six on the icon and one for the typeface, while University of KwaZulu-Natal had more than six colours in their logo.

It is also essential to recognise that universities in Africa tend to represent their country in their brand visual identity. This in particular with the use of the country's flag colour. The red diagonal band radiating diagonally from the lower hoist-side corner of the Namibian flag was replicated in the Namibia University of Science and Technology logo. Likewise, the red colour is shown on the University of Namibia's logo as a red book. The green and white colours of the Nigerian flag is well represented on the University of Nigeria's logo, albeit horizontally. The University of Port Harcourt also has the Nigerian flag colour on its logo. Usmanu Danfodio University, Federal University of Agriculture, Abeokuta, and Federal University Oye-Ekiti also adopted the Green colour of their Nation – Nigeria. Nelson Mandela University, University of KwaZulu-Natal, and Tshwane University of Technology also have used a shade of their national colour.

Universities with the inter-governmental agreement were also noted to be strategic with the choice of their brand visual identity colours. The German University in Cairo – which is an independent, non-profit oriented, Egyptian, the private institution managed by a consortium of Germans and Egyptians – had the black, red, and gold colours of German flags on their logo. Likewise, The British University in Egypt has both the flag of Britain and Egypt on its logo. Despite its link with the United States of America, The United States International University Africa, however, did not adopt the colours of USA. Instead, they went for blue and yellow.

Typeface

The typeface, as a logo element, represents the creative decision with regards to how the font is being presented to create a message. Some fonts are selected to make a bold statement, while some are presented to make a real statement. The font size and boldness are also creative decisions to make a statement and a form of identification. In the analysis of typeface used as logo elements in African's higher education, the study focused on the characteristics and not a response (e.g. innovativeness).

SERIFS AND SANS SERIF

Serif typeface contains a little decorative stroke at the end of the characters, while sans serif does not contain such decorative strokes. University logos were predominantly presented in the sans serif typeface, which is known to be modern, contemporary, and simple. Nine per cent of the sampled logo (n=18) were found to have used the serif typeface. Prominent amongst which are University of the Witwatersrand, Rhodes University, and Landmark University. Sans serif is considered modern, and it is not surprising to see that some of the newer universities are adopting such typeface on their logo. Examples include University of the Free State, Nelson Mandela University, and University of Johannesburg – all in South Africa. There are other instances where both typeface characters are combined. University of Namibia used the serif for the acronym (UNAM) and sans serif for the full brand name (University of Namibia). Modern Sciences and Arts University also adopted this approach. The United States International University Africa, however, had a different approach, as their wordmark was reshaped to have both serifs and sans serif.

LETTER CASES

Letter case is the written distinction between letters in upper and lowercase (Xu, Chen, & Liu, 2017). The letter case of the typefaces used in the logo was also analysed as an indication of the university's brand visual identity. Though consumers have been found to feel closer to lowercase wordmarks, which increase perceptions of brand friendliness, compared with the uppercase wordmarks (Xu, Chen, & Liu, 2017), majority of African universities are still adopting all uppercase wordmarks in their logo. As presented in the table below, a typology of five different letter cases strategies was adopted by the African universities. Fifty-one per cent of the sampled logo (n=102) used all uppercase in same font size for the logo wordmarks. This was followed by an uppercase first letter which was used by 15.5 per cent (n=31) of the universities. There were instances whereby both upper and lower cases where combined. For example, Strathmore University where the word 'Strathmore' was in uppercased first letter, while the word 'University' was in all uppercases while using the same font size. Sohrag University was the only university which has all lowercase for their logo wordmark\

Table 11.4 Typology of logo letter cases and examples of universities using them

s/N	—	Illustration	Example
1	All uppercase, same font size	UNIVERSITY OF UNIVERSITY	University of Pretoria, Kenyatta University, Landmark University
2	All uppercase, different font size	UNIVERSITY OF UNIVERSITY	Rhodes University, Sudan University of Science and Technology, Université Ziane Achour de Djelfa, Michael Okpara University of Agriculture
3	Uppercase first letter	University of University	Tshwane University of Technology, Ahmadu Bello University, University of Fort Hare
4	All lower cases	university of university	Sohrag University
5	Mixed cases	UNIVERSITY of UNIVERSITY	University of the Western Cape, Universidade Jean Piaget de Angola, Strathmore University

LETTER BOLDNESS

The boldness of the typeface as an indication of emphasis was also analysed. The brand identity of the University of Cape Town was boldly written in English, while the translation in two other languages had a smaller font and placed under the English translation. This was, however not the case with the University of the Free State, which made the 'Free State' bold in all the three languages used on the wordmarks. Likewise for the University of KwaZulu-Natal where 'KwaZulu-Natal' was made bolder and more prominent compared to other typefaces in all the two languages that were used. In the University of the Witwatersrand's wordmarks, 'Witwatersrand' was made bolder and more prominent than Johannesburg. Perhaps the emphasis was more on Witwatersrand and not on Johannesburg. Nelson Mandela University, Strathmore University, and Babcock University, all made their brand identity bolder by placing more emphasis on the brand and not the word 'University', which is used by every other brand in the market. Durban University of Technology and Alexandria University are examples of universities that placed more emphasis on brand location and not on the word 'University'. Namibia University of Science and Technology placed more emphasis on 'Namibia University' while the British University in Egypt placed more emphasis on their initials. This highlights how individual universities are making creative decision with regards to brand identifies.

LANGUAGES

The analysis of the typeface recognises the different languages used in the word marks. This use of different languages appears to be relatively unique for

African brands, especially universities in the south and north of the continent. In North Africa, where English is not the official language, universities such as Damietta University and Université Hassan placed more emphasis on the Arabic language on top of the wordmarks, while the English language was below. The German University in Cairo, the British University in Egypt, Future University in Egypt and Nahda University had the English language and then followed by the Arabic language, on their logo. This indicates that the universities considered the English language as their primary language, which is not necessarily the official language in the country. UniversitéAbderrahmane Mira de Béjaia, UniversitéDjillaliLiabès de Sidi-Bel-Abbès, and Université Larbi Ben Mhidi de Oum El Bouaghi had three different languages on their logo, but do not have an English translation.

In South Africa, especially where the constitution recognises 11 official languages, universities reflect this diversity in their brand identities. While some universities like the University of the Witwatersrand, University of Johannesburg, and Nelson Mandela University did not include any other languages apart from English, there are universities that included one or two additional languages. The prominence of English, however, varied. The University of Pretoria had three languages. All were in the same typeface, but Dutch language was used first; followed by the English language. The University of Cape Town had three languages but in different typeface. The primary language was English with larger fonts, followed by Xhosa, and Dutch language was used last. Universiteit Stellenbosch also had three languages with same typeface, but English language was used last. University of KwaZulu-Natal, however, had two languages in same typeface, but English was used first and followed by Zulu Language.

Selected top 20 HEI logos in Africa

The designers were asked to rate the design and select their top 20 logos from the pool of 200 logos and give justifications for their choices. The five designers initially selected 36 logos as their top logo. However, there were deliberations and discussion to witter the list to 20 (10% of the sample). In the end, Table 11.5 presents the selected 20 logos across different countries, with their justification for inclusion.

Discussion and conclusion

The study sought to understand the creative elements adopted in creating visual brand identities for African universities. While there are many forms of visual brand identities, this chapter focuses, especially on logos. Overall, there appears to be a lack of understanding with regards to the creative design of brand identities by African universities. The thought process behind the brand identities is questionable. The analysis raises question about the person/team responsible for designing Africa university logos. Could it be a staff within the

Table 11.5 Selected top 20 logos and their justification for inclusion

Rank	University	Country	Comments
1.	University of the Witwatersrand	South Africa	The choice of font The layout All in uppercase Emphasis more on Witwatersrand by increasing the font size and less on Johannesburg. The icon could have been made bigger to align with Johannesburg.
2.	University of Johannesburg	South Africa	Choice of colour Negative space (between birds)to form a book All in uppercase Emphasis more on Johannesburg by increasing the font size and less on university Structurally fit. Centrally aligned and balanced
3.	University of KwaZulu-Natal	South Africa	The choice of colour, closely related to multiple colours of the South African flag Balance and simple use of colour. Sunshine has more than one colour Same font and size for the wordmark Structurally balanced, icon aligns with the wordmark Emphasis more on Kwazulu-Natal by increasing the font size and boldness; and less on University
4.	Universiteit van die Vrystaat	South Africa	The line design is abstract but still relevant and relatable Initials on one side and full meaning on the other side. Three different languages, but well balanced and arranged. Emphasis more on Free State in all languages by increasing the font boldness, and less on University
5.	Nelson Mandela University	South Africa	All solid and flat Colour sparingly used but focused. The circle and triangle bring attention. Background colour contrasts as well Emphasis more on the name – bolder and bigger and less on University

(Continued)

Table 11.5 (Cont.)

Rank	University	Country	Comments
6.	Durban University of Technology	South Africa	Beautiful use of colours in the icon Initials used, but also full meaning is presented. Structurally balanced with key features Typography looks good with focus on Durban, making it bold and more significant. DUT is still prominent with a colourful balance on the left.
7.	The German University in Cairo	Egypt	The use of colour to represent Germany The shape of the icon –an arrangement from the initials Initials provided (could have been bolder and more imposing) Structural balance with other language going across the full length. Perhaps an indication of emphasis on the other language
8.	Namibia University of Science and Technology	Namibia	The choice of colour The red bar (from the flag of Namibia) is well integrated. Unique font. The 'N' is different, similar to the N in the logo. Emphasis on University and less on Science and Technology
9.	University of Namibia	Namibia	The choice of colour The icon is simple, relatable, and unique; moving from the usual nook and sunshine logo. The icon can stands well on its own without the wordmark (however, the word mark should have been made bigger to align with the icon) Initials were boldly presented and full meaning provided
10.	The British University in Egypt	Egypt	The choice of colour. Sticking a balance between both the British and Egyptian shield. Having both countries flag equally placed. Structurally balanced and aligned. Like the concept of GUC (no. 7), the initial is provided and also the initials. However, both languages were aligned under the initials. It appeared more structurally balanced.

(Continued)

Table 11.5 (Cont.)

Rank	University	Country	Comments
11.	Strathmore University	Kenya	The choice of font. Solid enough to convey strength. Imposing and cannot be missed. It was not used in upper case to avoid too much noise, but instead, the word university appeared relaxed and subtle, even though it's all in uppercase. The emphasis still on Strathmore and less on University The icon could be made to refreshing like the words Words could also be made more colourful, but still looks good in black.
12.	United States International University Africa	Kenya	Very unconventional. Looks modern, simple, and refreshed. Moves away from the use of the country's colour. America was not well represented with its stripe and stars, more so there is no yellow colour in then Kenya flag. The font is also unique and appears bespoke as it has been customised. It contains both serifs and sans serif features. Initials provided, and likewise the full meaning.
13.	Université Hassiba Ben Bouali de Chlef	Algeria	One of the best logo in circle. Key features are all contained – the name of the university is included in both halves in different languages. The colour is simple enough – green and orange with white The best thing is the use of negative space to contain all the elements – the face, the bird with leaves, the bridge, the year, and lettering.
14.	Babcock University	Nigeria	The shape looks solid and imposing. It contains the icon. There is much emphasis on Babcock; which is bolder, and less on the word 'University', and more so less on location. The location was allowed to be out of line with the icon as it appeared aligned with word 'University' The word on the logo. However, it appeared to compete with the wordmark.

(Continued)

Table 11.5 (Cont.)

Rank	University	Country	Comments
15.	American University of Nigeria	Algeria	The choice of colour – the Green of Nigeria and Blue of America, unlike BUE (No 10) where both country's flag was equally placed. Nigeria was given more priority here. The arrangement of the initials also looks unique, which raises questions with regards to emphasis. Perhaps the A is the red of America flag colour and N is the white of Nigeria flag colour.
16.	Future University in Egypt	Egypt	Both icon and wordmark are aligned Emphasis on 'future' by making it upper case (but it could have been bolder) 'University in Egypt' was also well placed (it could have been made bigger) More emphasis on English as the official language of the university. Hence, the other language was made smaller under the logo Structurally balanced, but size needs to be increased. Simple colour as well
17.	Nahda University	Egypt	The panel considered this as one of the best logos from an Egyptian university. The icon moved from just having a pyramid, graphically illustrating it in a simple, related, and unique style. The focus is on the initials. Unlike DUT (Number 6), less emphasis on the full meaning, even less emphasis on the university and location. More emphasis on English as the official language of the university, as the other language was made smaller under the logo Choice of colour – background colour contrasting the text and icon very well.
18.	BA ISAGO University	Botswana	The shape is unique and straightforward. It looks like a flame with colourful light, flying like a flag. The choice of multiple colours makes it stand out. Emphasis on 'Ba Isago' made bolder and more prominent, and less on the 'University'. The question is, could 'University' be well spaced out to be aligned under the 'Ba Isago'? The logo looks well aligned, as well.

Table 11.5 (cont.)

Rank	University	Country	Comments
19.	Nile University	Egypt	Another beautiful logo from Egypt. The focus is on 'N' and 'U' which has been reshaped to offer a unique and intriguing perspective. Though it looks imbalance, it is simple, unique, and structurally fit. The wordmark was well placed as well. Both words have equal emphasis, same font, boldness, and size. The font looks solid enough to complement the shaped icon. The choice of colour – fresh and appealing. No emphasis on another language.
20.	Université Hassan II de Casablanca	Morroco	The typeface is aligned with an emphasis on the first language (different colour shade) which indicates the priority The icon is also creatively arranged under the wordmark. The U is placed on top of the H with different shades and Roman figure II cutting across. The choice of colour – using different shade makes it unique as well.

university adopting a template or a brand agency was commissioned to develop the identity? There appears to be confusion between logo and coat of arms. African universities tend to have logos with features of coat of arms as different elements, and perhaps inherent meanings were included in their logo. This makes the logos very congested, making it more confusing, busy, and challenging to integrate. Though with some exceptions as illustrated in the top 20 logos selected, there is a considerable need to recognise the importance of brand identities and making an effort to rejuvenate and rebrand the institutions.

On a more positive note, these cultural elements incorporated into the African universities makes it unique and offers a different perspective to brand identity and design. Perhaps this can be better integrated to develop a coat of arms that wholeheartedly celebrate and encapsulate the diverse cultural heritage on the continent, as seen with the logo of Obafemi Awolowo University, which had the face of Oduduwa – who was the first ruler of Ile Ife. The University was founded in 1961 as University of Ife as a federal government-owned and operated Nigerian university. The university is in the ancient city of Ile-Ife, Osun State, Nigeria, which suggests the reasons for having Oduduwa on the logo. However, it was renamed Obafemi Awolowo University in 1987 in honour of Chief Obafemi Awolowo (1909–1987), first premier of the Western Region of Nigeria, but the logo was never changed (at the time of writing this chapter) to the face of the founder. This highlights respect for the cultural heritage of the university.

African universities tend to adopt the heraldic devices, which can be considered a coat of arms. However, these are not done correctly and well-executed. It appeared the universities and designers have seen it on other universities and older institutions, like churches and the military, and though such ideas could be adopted in their case, Machado et al. (2015) noted that heraldic devices elicit a sense of familiarity as the association of heraldry with older institutions provides some indication of what may be considered a 'meaningful' name/logo. Simply because numerous established universities have long associated themselves with them, it is not surprising that some African universities adopted it. However, as Mogaji (2019b) noted, coat of arm is different from a logo. Coat of arm is often used for ceremonial act and generally used as the university's identity. It will be necessary for African universities to align with the principles of the coat of arm by redesigning it and restrict its usage to very formal or legal communications as well as for prestigious occasions, such as graduations, and have a logo that is more public-facing and regularly used.

We believe this article contributes to expanding our understanding of the logo literature, especially from an African perspective, and this allows for some essential managerial considerations. Universities can benefit from having a strong brand image and identity within the competitive market (Ali-Choudhury et al., 2009); it is, however, crucial that the university recognises the need and urge to develop and reposition their brand. This might take a new Vice-Chancellor to recognise this and provide a new strategic direction. As African universities seek to position themselves in the market place, they also need to update their image (Peterson, AlShebil, & Bishop, 2015) and stand out from other players in the market place. The University must decide on their distinct positioning as they engage with stakeholders – what it is and what it stands for (Khanna, Jacob, & Yadav, 2014). Recognising the fact that the university identity is not useful, current, and no longer relevant, taking effort to work on it is crucial. A survey or opinion poll on the university's brand identity might justify this need. It is also essential to look at how other universities around the world are designing their identity for motivation.

Theoretically, this chapter presents a conceptual framework which highlights the three key features of a logo design. The framework recognises the relationship between the shape of the logo which serves as the container for other creative elements, the choice of colour and the typeface for the wordmark. As illustrated in Figure 11.2, the design process of a logo involves a creative decision around these three elements. A detailed explanation about these elements are presented in Table 11.6. This offers theoretical underpinning for future improvement of brand identity. Not only for African HEI's brand identity but for other brands as well.

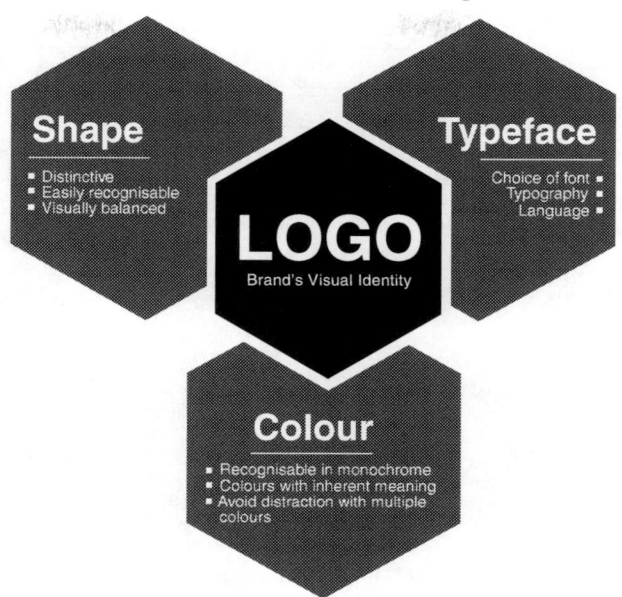

Figure 11.2 The conceptual framework which highlights the three key features of a logo design

While it is recommended that African universities need to consider updating their CVI, Airey (2009) noted that there are two types of logo redesign – i.e. evolutionary logo redesign and revolutionary logo redesign. Some universities, perhaps the more established universities, may decide to carry out an evolutionary logo redesign as this involves a small change in logo design, while others may go for a revolutionary redesign which involves a substantial change.

In making these changes, universities must recognise that stakeholders, especially students and staff, will have some reservations about the logo redesign. Brand identity is dynamic and can be very subjective, so, therefore, stakeholders must be carried along through the process. The brand (or marketing managers) of the university is not the sole creator of brand identity. As Foroudi et al. (2017) suggested, the logo needs to be managed through a multidisciplinary approach, perhaps not just an individual from the communications team developing the logo, but carrying everyone along. Students, staff, and alumni should be asked what the university means for them. Students can be encouraged to come up with new logos, organise a competition to pick the best five logos and then they can work with brand agencies to develop the best identity. This is about co-creating identities that reflect the values of the university and its identities.

The idea of using more than one language is recognised and respected. However, effort should be made towards better integration. This includes aligning it properly and giving preferences or making all the languages the

Table 11.6 Description of the three key features of a logo design

LOGO DESIGN		
Shape	*Colour*	*Typeface*
Distinctive, unique, simple, easily recognisable, and memorable enough for people to easily recreate by hand, off memory.	The logo should be recognisable in mono-chrome. Start design in black and white before adding further colours as Colours are very subjective and emotional.	Consider the use of font – Bespoke, commercial, or system fonts.
Avoid irregularly shaped logo, and it should be scalable and be able to be used on different media and platform appropriate for the intended audience.	Using colours with inherent meaning and associations with other brands (like colours of the country) is encouraged.	The text should always be readable on all platform. Consider font type, size, spacing, boldness, and letter case.
Visual balance of all elements (including internal components of shape). Wordmark and shape should be aligned and sized up.	Explore two or three colours. Avoid distraction with multiple colours.	Making a font bold is seen as making an emphasis, uppercase typeface can indicate a strong sense of authority, while the use of lowercase exudes a more approachable, casual vibe.
Make it versatile, structurally sound, and fit.	Background colour should give enough contrast with the text.	Typography, the style, and appearance of wordmark can also present a different meaning. Is an emphasis on the city or the word 'University'.
Icons and conceptual ideas can be explored.	Colour of shape and typeface should be considered.	
Internal components should be timely and relevant to the target audience. There is more to university than book and microscopes.		The emphasis on language is essential. How many languages? Which is the most important or all are essential?
		Taglines are not needed. Year pf establishment may be included.

same. Most of the South African universities have done it very well. However, the North African universities have not all done this well, with some few exceptions. Besides, the use of initials is not discouraged, but it should be thought out properly. If those initials are adopted as the name, then it should be consistent with websites and other profiles. Both the University of South Africa (UNISA) and Durban University of Technology (DUT) had initials on their logo, and this was reflected in their website addresses.

While recognising that icons (of African universities) are known to have an imbedded meaning, not everything can be used, and that is where the creativity comes in. The University of Johannesburg had an image of two hoopoo birds, and the negative space had the outline of a book. Another good example was the logo of Université Hassiba Ben Bouali de Chlef in Algeria, which has a different element that was creatively integrated within the circle. It has a bridge with a year (1983), a dove carrying leaves and a negative space that forms the face of a woman.

It is considered worthwhile that the swirls should be removed on all the logo. It is an element of the coat of arm, and therefore it should be appropriately designed and used. Irregularly shaped icons should be changed, as this makes it difficult for brand consistency and integration. Colours are essential brand elements, and they are highly communicative. They play an essential role in reinforcing the universities' brand identity programme and the consistent use of these colours is encouraged by universities, as it will contribute to the cohesive and harmonious look of identity across all relevant media (Mogaji, 2018). Even though there is evidence of universities adopting the colours of their countries, they need to choose colours that are consistent with their images to avoid sending conflicting messages (Hynes, 2009).

The typeface is essential elements of brand identities and universities are encouraged to be unique in their selection. Mogaji (2018) recognised a typology of typeface which is 1) bespoke font which are customised fonts for the university – it provides a distinctive look; 2) commercial font which is bought by the university – quite expensive, but unique even though still available for any brand who wants to buy it; and 3) system fonts which are freely available on most of all word processing software and are free to use, thus, do not require a font licence. As a brand, universities are better off using the bespoke font or the commercial fonts as that makes them unique and stands out.

While designing with the fonts, emphasis should be placed on critical features of the universities – the university of the location. This could also be achieved with the capitalisation (upper/lower cases) and the font size or boldness of the names. For example, University of South Africa placed more attention on their abbreviation 'UNISA' by making it bigger and all in upper cases, while the full meaning was in lower cases, unlike the Durban University of Technology with the full meaning in all uppercase. Tshwane University of Technology's name on their logo was not presented in all uppercases, unlike the University of the Witwatersrand, Johannesburg, while the University of the Western Cape had all its name in upper case apart from 'of the'. Also, the University of the Witwatersrand gave less attention (in terms of size) to 'Johannesburg' regarding their logo, unlike the University of Johannesburg where 'Johannesburg' had a much bigger size. These highlight creative design decisions to place emphasis and hierarchy with the brand identity.

With various elements coming together to form the University brand identity, it is essential to communicate these elements in a clear, consistent manner across different touchpoints as this is necessary to build an efficient and powerful brand (Mogaji, 2019a). To achieve this, a brand guideline is essential. The brand guideline is considered one of the rebranding deliverables that is prepared for the brand by the brand agency. The brand guideline should contain information about the font, the shades of colour, and how to use the university logo. Both internal and external users should be made aware of the brand guidelines and encouraged to use it to ensure consistent use of the brand identities. This document should be made available online on the company's website or a downloadable PDF version.

There are various ways of presenting the logo in several consumer touchpoints (e.g. packaging, website, mobile/mobile application, logo placement, etc.), animated logos, and sonic logos (Kim & Lim, 2019). This implies that stakeholders will be exposed to the university's logo multiple times in different circumstances. The adoption and integration of the new logo are essential. This integration is not just about changing the logo that no one wants to use; universities must make an effort to integrate the new brand across these different touchpoints properly. To create more awareness and also to be consistent, create more familiarity and recognition.

Creating a logo or rebranding incurs a considerable expense, and it is crucial to get it right (Mogaji, 2019a). This suggests the need for managers to make an effort in creating an identity, that corporate identity of the university in a reliable manner (Van den Bosch et al., 2006), reflect its values, mission statement, strategy, and characteristics, and the logo design (Hynes, 2009) and stakeholders will find it appealing and relevant (Mogaji, 2019c). Effective positioning of the university brand should focus on what the stakeholders perceive is essential and not necessarily what university administrators believe is significant (Khanna et al., 2014). The emotional aspect of the corporate logo is recognised as a critical element of corporate identity (Foroudi & Nguyen, 2019). Rather than merely focusing on what is fashionable and modern, efforts should be made by the designers and managers to recognise this possibility and arouse emotions through the logo, perhaps through the use of colours and images (Mogaji, 2018).

The finding of the current research has vital implications for university decision-makers, brand agencies, and graphic designers who wish to understand the African universities' CVI and identify how to improve their brands. This clear understating of the dimensions of the relevant concepts of African universities' CVI can assist managers and designers in understanding the principles of designing, selecting, and modifying a university logo, which will create a strong marketing communication, brand image, and reputation.

This chapter provided some suggestions to extend the current body of knowledge in the literature on the corporate logo and corporate visual identity, especially with a focus on HEI branding in the African context. This study employed exploratory research. A replicated study is needed to explore whether the relationships found in this study hold in other countries and continents, and also in order to gain greater generalisability and validity for the typology and the theoretical framework of universities' brand identities.

Limitations and directions for future research

The limits of the study should receive consideration before generalising any findings. One limitation of this study is the selection of the logos which may not give a holistic approach about logo designs of Africa universities. While efforts were made to use logs from the top 200 Universities which are considered the best, there are many other hundreds of logos that were not included. Besides, only universities from 24 countries (of 54) in Africa were included in the analysis. As creativity (in brand identity design) can be very subjective and relative to different individuals, organisation, and culture, it should be noted that the critical appraisal of the logos was based on the professional opinion of selected brand designers which may not necessarily be generalisable. In like manner, there could be some inherent cultural meanings which were not discovered during the analysis. It should be noted as well that some universities may have changed their logo and rebranded since these samples were collected. Hence, readers' discretion is requested when referring to this chapter.

Having acknowledged that there is a shortage of theoretical understanding of the CVIs of African universities, future research is needed to have a better understanding of these brands' element. Future study should examine the effect of logo design on affective response towards the brand. Perhaps exploring how stakeholders are engaging with the logos, to have a better understanding of their perception and response to logo design, and in particular, the influence of the different types of designs as this may lead to co-creation of better brand identities. With universities aiming to differentiate themselves in the market and provide an element of brand distinctiveness, it is suggested that there be future research to examine the perceived brand personality of the institution by students, staff, and other stakeholders (Watkins & Gonzenbach, 2013).

Further research can explore wordmark design characteristics (Xu et al., 2017). This includes the letter case and boldness, and how they affect consumers' perceptions of the brands. Besides, future research should acknowledge the unique contextual situation of African universities to understand better the various factors that build a higher education brand. This can be approached from an individual country approach or a regional approach (like West Africa). As a university's brand becomes an aid to efficient recruitment of staff and students, future research can explore the congruency in values between the individual and the organisation. University brand managers could benefit from developing a better understanding of how the prospective staff and students interact with their brand in order to develop more effective recruiting material, advertisements, and other marketing efforts.

References

Airey, D. (2009). *Logo design love: A guide to creating iconic brand identities*. Berkeley, CA: New Riders.

Alessandri, S. W. (2007). Retaining a legacy while avoiding trademark infringement: A case study of one university's attempt to develop a consistent athletic brand identity. *Journal of Marketing for Higher Education*, 17(1), 147–167.

Ali-Choudhury, R., Bennett, R., & Savani, S. (2009). University marketing directors' views on the components of a university brand. *International Review on Public and Nonprofit Marketing*, 6(1), 11. https://doi.org/10.1007/s12208-008-0021-6.

Balmer, J. M. T. (1995). Corporate branding and connoisseurship. *Journal of General Management*, 21(1), 24–46.

Balmer, J. M. (2001). Corporate identity, corporate branding and corporate marketing: Seeing through the fog. *European Journal of Marketing, 35*(3/4), 248–291.

Balmer, J. M., Gray, J. M., & Balmer, E. R. (2000). Corporate identity and corporate communications: creating a competitive advantage. *Industrial and Commercial Training*, 32(7), 256–261.

Bunzel, D. J. (2007). Universities sell their brands. *Journal of Product & Brand Management*, 16(2), 152–153.

Chapleo, C. (2010). What defines 'successful' university brands?. *International Journal of Public Sector Management*, 23(2), 169–183. doi:10.1108/09513551011022519.

Childers, T. L., & Jass, J. (2002). All dressed up with something to say: Effects of type-face semantic associations on brand perceptions and consumer memory. *Journal of Consumer Psychology*, 12(2), 93–106.

Farinloye, T., Mogaji, E., Aririguzoh, S., & Kieu, T. A. (2019). Qualitatively exploring the effect of change in the residential environment on travel behaviour. *Travel Behaviour and Society*, 17, 26–35.

Foroudi, P., & Nguyen, B. (2019). Corporate design: What makes a favourable university logo? In B. Nguyen, T. C. Melewar, & J. Hemsley-Brown (Eds.), *Strategic brand management in higher education*. London: Routledge.

Foroudi, P., Melewar, T. C., & Gupta, S. (2017). Corporate logo: History, definition, and components. *International Studies of Management & Organization*, 47(2), 176–196.

Furey, S., Springer, P., & Parsons, C. (2014). Positioning university as a brand: Distinctions between the brand promise of Russell Group, 1994 Group, University Alliance, and Million+ universities. *Journal of Marketing for Higher Education*, 24(1), 99–121.

Gumede, M. (2017). Nelson Mandela Metropolitan University to rebrand itself. Retrieved from   https://www.businesslive.co.za/bd/national/education/2017-07-10-nelson-mandela-metropolitan-university-to-rebrand-itself/l.

Henderson, P. W., & Cote, J. A. (1998). Guidelines for selecting or modifying logos. *Journal of Marketing*, 62(2), 14–30.

Henderson, P. W., Giese, J. L., & Cote, J. A. (2004). Impression management using typeface design. *Journal of Marketing*, 68(4), 60–72.

Hynes, N. (2009). Colour and meaning in corporate logos: An empirical study. *Journal of Brand Management*, 16(8), 545–555.

Jiang, Y., Gorn, G. J., Galli, M., & Chattopadhyay, A. (2015). Does your company have the right logo? How and why circular-and angular-logo shapes influence brand attribute judgments. *Journal of Consumer Research*, 42(5), 709–726.

Kapferer, J. N. (1994). *Strategic brand management: New approaches to creating and evaluating brand equity*. New York: Simon & Schuster.

Khanna, M., Jacob, I., & Yadav, N. (2014). Identifying and analyzing touchpoints for building a higher education brand. *Journal of Marketing for Higher Education*, 24(1), 122–143.

Kim, M. J., & Lim, J. H. (2019). A comprehensive review of logo literature: Research topics, findings, and future directions. *Journal of Marketing Management*, 1–75.

Krishnan, V., Kellaris, J. J., & Aurand, T. W. (2012). Sonic logos: Can sound influence willingness to pay? *Journal of Product & Brand Management*, 21(4), 275–284.

Lieven, T., Grohmann, B., Herrmann, A., Landwehr, J. R., & Van Tilburg, M. (2015). The effect of brand design on brand gender perceptions and brand preference. *European Journal of Marketing*, 49(1/2), 146–169.

Lomer, S., Papatsiba, V., & Naidoo, R. (2018). Constructing a national higher educa-tion brand for the UK: Positional competition and promised capitals. *Studies in Higher Education*, 43(1), 134–153.

Luffarelli, J., Stamatogiannakis, A., & Yang, H. (2019). The visual asymmetry effect: An interplay of logo design and brand personality on brand equity. *Journal of Marketing Research*, 56(1), 89–103.

Machado, J. C., de Carvalho, L. V., Torres, A., & Costa, P. (2015). Brand logo design: Examining consumer response to naturalness. *Journal of Product & Brand Management*, 24(1), 78–87.

Marsden, J. (2019). Visualising corporate brands: Towards a framework of brandmark expression. *Journal of Brand Strategy*, 7(4), 377–388.

Mollerup, P. (1999). *Marks of excellence*. London: Phaidon.

Mogaji, E. (2018). UK universities, corporate visual identities. Academy of Marketing Annual Conference, University of Stirling, Stirling, 3–5 July 2018. Stirling: Academy of Marketing.

Mogaji, E. (2019a). Brand Guideline. Research Agenda, 1–9. doi:10.2139/ssrn.3316485.

Mogaji, E. (2019b). Top 200 African universities' logo. ResearchGate. doi:10.13140/RG.2.2.33969.94562.

Mogaji, E. (2019c). Branding private Universities in Africa: An unexplored territory. Research Agenda Working Papers, 2019(9), pp. 120–148. http://dx.doi.org/10.2139/ssrn.3457571.

Ndofirepi, E., Farinloye, T. & Mogaji, E. (2020). Marketing mix in a heterogenous higher education market: A case of Africa. In E. Mogaji, F. Maringe & R. E. Hinson (Eds.), *Understanding the higher education market in Africa*. London: Routledge.

Olaleye, S., Ukpabi, D. & Mogaji, E. (2020). Public vs private universities in Nigeria: Market dynamics perspective. In E. Mogaji, F. Maringe & R. E. Hinson (Eds.), *Understanding the higher education market in Africa*. London: Routledge.

Peterson, M., AlShebil, S., & Bishop, M. (2015).Cognitive and emotional processing of brand logo changes. *Journal of Product & Brand Management*, 24(7), 745–757.

Pratt, M. G., & Rafaeli, A. (1997). Organisational dress as a symbol of multilayered social identities. *Academy of Management Journal*, 40(4), 862–898.

Robson, J., Roy, S. K., Chapleo, C., & Yang, H. P. (2019). Co-creating brand identity. In B. Nguyen, T. C. Melewar, & J. Hemsley-Brown (Eds.), *Strategic brand management in higher education*. London: Routledge.

Singh, S. (2006). Impact of color on marketing. *Management Decision*, 44(6), 783–789.

Solomon, M. (1986). *The art of typography: An introduction to typo-icon-ography*. New York: Watson-Guptill.

UniRank. (2019). Top 200 Universities in Africa. Retrieved from https://www.4icu.org/top-universities-africa/.

Van den Bosch, A. L. M., Elving, W. J. L., and De Jong, M. D. T. (2006). The impact of organizational characteristics on corporate visual identity. *European Journal of Marketing*, 40(7/8), 870–885.

Van Grinsven, B., & Das, E. (2016). Logo design in marketing communications: Brand logo complexity moderates exposure effects on brand recognition and brand attitude. *Journal of Marketing Communications*, 22(3), 256–270.

Walsh, M. F., Page Winterich, K., & Mittal, V. (2010). Do logo redesigns help or hurt your brand? The role of brand commitment. *Journal of Product & Brand Management*, 19(2), 76–84.

Watkins, B. A., & Gonzenbach, W. J. (2013). Assessing university brand personality through logos: An analysis of the use of academics and athletics in university branding. *Journal of Marketing for Higher Education*, 23(1), 15–33.

Williams, Jr, R. L., & Omar, M. (2014). Applying brand management to higher education through the use of the Brand Flux Model™–the case of Arcadia University. *Journal of Marketing for Higher Education*, 24(2), 222–242.

Xu, X., Chen, R., & Liu, M. W. (2017). The effects of uppercase and lowercase wordmarks on brand perceptions. *Marketing Letters*, 28(3), 449–460.

12 Leveraging universities' value through branding

Babatunde Abina, Oluseyi Ajayi, and Azeez Lawal

Introduction

A university represents both a higher learning institution and a community of scholars or persons engaged in research and study to bring men and women to a high level of intellectual development in various disciplines (Alemu, 2018). They are institutions vested with the authority to award degrees and are preeminent in the field of research (Allen, 1988). Universities are tertiary educational institutions established for purposes of advancing human knowledge and improving the lot of society at large. Due to the insatiable need for knowledge such as obtainable in universities, every country of the world has universities as citadels of learning from which knowledge to advance their environment can be obtained from. This is predicated on the belief that university education is a powerful and proven vehicle for sustainable development to make the world a better place.

This has, however, led to a proliferation of universities to cater for the growing demand of university education which is due partly to the exponential growth in human population and the sophistication of human lives. The proliferation of universities has demanded a concerted effort from the management of universities at ensuring that they gain visibility in the market so that they can attract a large pool of diverse student population and, in turn, shore up their revenue (Mogaji, 2016). Those universities that are successful at this have been able to attract students from within and outside the shores of the country. Those at the forefront of these are universities in the advanced economies, with those in the emerging or developing economies of the world creating comparatively less costly alternatives for quality university education. This has led to a trend whereby there is a mass drift of prospective students seeking qualitative university education from less developed countries.

Universities, like every organisation, strive to deliver value to their target markets and earn value in return. They aim to do this by offering services that satisfy consumers' needs and wants better than those of their competitors. In order to differentiate their services from their competitors', universities develop and adopt all possible strategies that will lead them to build a strong base of loyal customers. All strategies that may be adopted by any university will ultimately be based on building the strength of its 'brand'.

Current state of African universities: the Nigerian situation

University education in Africa, as is obtainable in other climes of the world, is either government-owned and financed or privately owned and financed. Great universities are dotting the African landscape. Examples of these great African universities include Al-Azhar University Cairo, Egypt; Makerere University Kampala (MUK), Uganda; Universite Cheikh Anta Diop, Senegal; Fort Hare University, South Africa; Fourah Bay College (University of Sierra Leone); University of Cape Town; Cairo university Egypt; University of Ghana; University of Zimbabwe and University of Ibadan. These universities have earned their reputation through their history, research output, and alumni as they have served the continent as centres for literary activity and culture that formed a nationalistic identity.

The Nigerian university market is a rapidly expanding one with different types of ownership. On the one part, universities (public) in the Nigerian environment are established, owned, and funded by the government (federal and state governments), while on the other hand, universities (private) are non-government founded and owned (in this case it is either owned by private individuals or by faith-based organisations). However, both forms of universities are regulated by an organ of government; The National Universities Commission (NUC). With the establishment of the first university in Nigeria (The University of Ibadan, formerly University College Ibadan) in 1948, there has been an upward trend in the number of universities in the country, particularly with the licensing of private universities. The figure currently stands at 174 universities: 91 public universities (43 federal universities and 52 state universities) and 79 private universities (NUC, 2019; Mogaji, 2019a), all competing for the same target market (secondary school leavers who have undertaken the Unified Tertiary Matriculation Examination (UTME)) yearly. In all, there is little or no difference at all in all the offerings of these universities. Hence, differentiating them on the bases of educational services offered is a herculean task.

Presently, there is a considerable loss of patronage for the majority of the universities existing within the Nigerian environment as a significant number of prospective students are seen enrolling in universities outside the shores of Nigeria as prospective students are seen registering for university education in other African countries as well as those in European, North American and Middle and South-Eastern Asian countries. This trend in itself defeats the purpose of the Nigerian government in granting licensing for universities to cater for a large number of university admission seekers. Thus, there a lot of universities within Nigeria with spaces for prospective students but with limited enrolment. A significant factor that could be adduced for this is the lack of proper brand management. Besides the name of the various Nigerian universities and their location, little, if any, is done about the university's brand.

Few amongst the 174 universities have an easy recall motto, pay-off, or slogan. Others merely exist on paper or the nameplate of the university. In addition to these, a small number of Nigerian universities (especially private universities) conduct promotional campaigns to create awareness about their existence, their location, and the accredited courses offered by them. This does amount to very little in terms of the potential proper deployment of branding strategies can provide to the schools. The publicly owned universities hardly engage in any branding and promotional activities. The paucity of funds is the number one attributable factor, followed by their perception of being a scarce commodity to multitudes of students who continuously patronise them for the limited spaces for the programmes they offer. These practices are self-destructive to Nigerian universities collectively; it weakens the Nigerian university brands and makes them mostly unsuccessful. To overcome this conundrum, universities need to develop the right image and identity. This can help them gain competitive edge over other universities in an upwardly saturated market.

For Nigerian universities to be successful, each of them must have a clear brand identity. This is achievable through the adoption and deployment of pervasive strategies that can aid in the achievement of strong brand identity. First amongst these is the precise definition of the tertiary education market, and university education market in particular. According to Kotler and Trias de Bes (2003) defining a market is the basis of segmentation, targeting, and positioning strategies and ultimately the definition of the marketing mix to be deployed. Extant literature has documented the propensity of universities to eschew segmentation as a strategy to be deployed in building the university brand (Bock, Poole, & Joseph, 2013). However, a recent trend in the Nigerian university market has shown heavy utilisation of segmentation strategy; majorly on the bases of private/public, federal/state, or faith-based/private individual owned. In terms of targeting, they collectively aim for a share of the pool of UTME candidates using the NUC benchmark as the criteria for qualification. The third aspect of defining the market, positioning, as espoused by Kotler and Trias de Bes (2003) has been handled feebly by Nigerian universities where it has been attempted. Effective positioning demands that the issue of branding needs to be taken with utmost seriousness as it is expedient to have a proper brand in place before positioning can be effectively done. Moreover, as advanced by Lindstrom (2005) 'building brands requires building perception'; thus, it is when the brand has been appropriately built that positioning for perception by consumers can properly take place.

Importance of branding for universities

Issues of branding are commonly associated with consumer goods. However, the service industry has also exploited the benefits of branding to build strong brand equity for its service offerings. This has also been extended to the educational services by way of moving beyond their corporate name to developing their institutions into powerful brands with a strong base of consumers who are strongly associated with the institution, who perceive the institution as offering high quality educational services, and have become loyal to the institution amongst other similar educational services offering institutions. Universities within Africa and those in Nigeria, in particular, need to strengthen their brands by adopting and deploying corporate branding to improve many their institutions and earn high brand equity in the ranking of global institutions.

Literature

According to the American Marketing Association (AMA, 2010), a brand is a 'name, term, symbol, or design, or a combination of them, intended to identify the goods and services of one seller or group of sellers and to differentiate them from those of competition'. Shimp (2007) advanced that a brand is more than just a name, term, symbol, and so on. It is everything that one company's particular offering stands for in comparison to other brands in a category of competitive products. It represents a set of values that officials of organisations consistently embrace and communicate for an extended period.

Brands identify the source or maker of a product and allow consumers to assign responsibility to a particular manufacturer or distributor; hence, it takes on special meaning to consumers (Keller, 2008). In doing this, branding helps in signifying the origin of a product and also assists and simplifies choice for consumers by reducing the processing of information needed to make a product decision as branding aids consumers' product recognition and instils some knowledge about the product (Sherrington, 2001). Brands help to create unique meaning, thus, help in changing perception and experiences with a product (Keller, 2008).

The signalling theory of branding explains the interactions between brands and target consumers. Signalling theory is compatible with the idea that brand meaning is co-created between firm and customer (von Wallpach, Voyer, Kastanakis, & Muhlbacher, 2017). Signalling theory suggests that brands are an essential medium of quality assessment between consumers of brands and the firms manufacturing the brands as it emphasises that companies learn from how customers react and which signals they should deploy in their marketing (Davies, Rojas-Mendez, Whelan, Mete, & Loo, 2017; Grigoriou, Davcik & Sharma, 2016). The purpose of brands as signals is to convey some important information about the firm and its brands to other stakeholders, particularly the target market (Gabbert, 2015).

Branding for consumers represents the mark of a given level of quality and value that helps them choose between one product and another (Sherrington, 2001). Therefore, the fundamental driving force behind brands is that they have utility for consumers. Products within the market space which are unbranded are referred to as commodities. These types of products cannot be physically differentiated in the minds of consumers. The image of a brand and the emotional perceptions consumers attach to specific brands is a crucial determinant of long-term business-consumer relationships (Dobni & Zinkhan, 1990; Fournier, 1998). The adoption of logos and seals by universities helps establish easy recognition for consumers. University seals serve as an artefact that helps to capture, as well as used to signal, organisational identity and ultimately contributes to its image (Drori, Delmestri & Oberg, 2013).

Brand image influences consumers' perception of a brand and, consequently, the association that comes to the consumers' mind when contemplating a particular brand (Gbadeyan, Abina, & Sowole, 2016). It results from the consumers' interpretation of all the signs which are emitted by the brand (Louis & Lombart, 2010). In general, brand image influences consumers decision and also aids the decision making process (Gbadeyan, Abina, & Sowole, 2016). This influence is pervasive and is also obtainable in the institutional context. Brand image can influence decision making of potential students for choosing a university and also influence public attitudes towards universities (Wang, Chen & Chen, 2012). In Nigeria presently, universities are patronised mainly based on their image of having a non-truncated calendar as disruption of academic calendar is an endemic issue in the Nigerian higher institution environment.

This is due to the incessant strikes embarked upon by the Academic Staff Union of Universities (ASUU) in their bid to demand and force the government (federal and state) to fund education and ensure the reversal of the fall in standard of education. This has led to academic programmes and courses being extended far beyond the stipulated period. Smart universities have built their image around this. Private universities in Nigeria benefit from the incessant strikes as prospects seek institutions that promise no break in academic calendar. Some government-owned universities have excelled by turning this to an advantage. For example, universities in Kwara State, Nigeria (University of Ilorin and Kwara State University) do not embark on the national strike called by ASUU, and, thereby, have been able to maintain an uninterrupted calendar which has led to a sharp increase in the number of prospective students seeking admission into these institutions.

Despite this opportunity, a large number of private universities are still left with the unfilled quota for the programmes and courses they offer. This is because many prospects are not inclined to paying the kind of fees being demanded in the private universities as similar programmes are obtainable in the public universities at little or no cost (Otabor, 2018). Also, the over-supply of private universities in some geographical locations in Nigeria could be advanced as a reason for low students' enrolment in a significant number of private universities (Adamolekun, 2019). The resultant low student enrolment in many private universities in Nigeria is posing a severe threat to the survival of the universities (Otabor, 2018). A factor that may be adduced for this is their lack of adequate understanding and exploration of the opportunities that branding promises. Marketers and indeed universities can benefit from branding whenever consumers are in a choice situation as the vital advantage branding offers is that consumers perceive differences amongst brands in a product category because a brand is an entity rooted in reality; it is something that resides in the minds of consumers. Thus, when thoroughly explored, it provides essential benefits to both consumers and organisations (Keller, 2008). Similarly, branding can also create utilities for universities as consumers' loyalty to a university will be based on their experience of the university and this has potential of giving the university protection against rival universities. It also allows the university to target different groups of prospects or segments of the market, with different branded offerings (Sherrington, 2001).

Three key points that must be taken cognisance of in the process of building a strong brand for a university include the following.

1. Understanding the essence of branding

This implies that any university to build a valuable brand must understand the core characteristics which determine essence of a brand:

i.   a promise of desired benefit-giving properties and a quality level to consumers;
ii. a guarantee of the quality of customers' satisfaction;
iii. a tool of quick and confident consumer choice and purchasing decision making;
iv. the most crucial factor of firm's competitive advantages and incomes, a base for a higher price.

The brand is one of the essential integrated factors contributing to university competitiveness growth (Valitov, 2014). Brand essence is the heart and soul of a brand; it is the fundamental nature or quality of the brand.

2. Understanding factors that can make a university brand strong

Keller (2008) iterated some activities that must be performed in order to create a strong brand. These activities must be performed by any university that is desirous of creating a strong brand and aim to maximise brand equity. They include:

i.   Understand the brand meaning and appropriately market the products and services. Understanding the meaning of the brand demands that the university clarifies who their institution is for, what the university stands for, the purpose of the university brand, and what universities is their brand to compete with. Programmes and courses offered by the university should be in tandem with the underlying philosophy of the institution, as well as its mission and vision. The programmes should suit the needs of the environment and should be delivered in a manner that ensures maximum satisfaction to consumers.
ii. Properly position the brand. A university with a strong position strategy will attain a robust emotional selling proposition (ESP). An example of this was evident during the attempted name change from University of Lagos (UNILAG) to Moshood Abiola University Lagos (MAULAG). Because of the strong emotional connection to the university brand, all stakeholders of the university vehemently rose against the attempt, and the Nigerian government shelved the planned attempt.
iii. Provide superior delivery of desired benefits. A superior benefit will be educational services that are satisfactory to all stakeholders; students,

internal employees, parents/guardians, as well as the broader community the output of the university will be of immense benefit too. Universities with technology-enabled learning, promising state of the art infrastructure, well-qualified faculty, maximum courses under one roof, / fellowships offered to students / faculty and research and innovation are on the right path to building a strong brand.

iv. Employ a full range of complementary brand elements, supporting marketing activities, and secondary associations. Universities that are desirous of building a strong brand can leverage brand value from secondary sources. The brand equity of a university can be enhanced through several approaches. These, according to Shimp (2007), include speak-for-itself approach, message-driven approach, leveraging approach. Universities in Nigeria have been found to adopt and deploy the first two approaches while the inherent benefits of the third approach have been largely ignored. Brand associations can be shaped and equity enhanced by leveraging positive associations already contained in the world of other brands, people, places, and things that are available to consumers. This is because a brand leverages positive associations when it is identified with other entities that have an image that the brand itself would like to be known for (Shimp, 2007). Universities can partner with leading organisations, professional associations, and other institutions in a manner that can complement their brand value. Examples of this as highlighted by Bansal (2014) include proper accreditation and affiliation, proper industry linkages, student and faculty exchange programmes, career counselling, and placement services.

v. Embrace integrated marketing communications (IMC) and communicate with a consistent voice. Employing advertising only to create awareness about the existence of an institution; its location and programmes are not enough to gain the desired response in a hyper-segmented market with high media fragmentation. The way to circumvent this will be to employ and deploy all the touchpoints (advertising, public relations, publicity, personal selling, sales promotion, direct marketing, viral marketing, and forms of social media marketing) available to communicate with potential and actual consumers consistently.

vi. Measure consumer perceptions of value and develop a pricing strategy accordingly. This is an essential part of a brand audit. Findings from this exercise will be used to determine the appropriate pricing strategy for the institution's programmes.

vii. Establish credibility and appropriate brand personality and imagery. The university should avoid issues that have the potential to tarnish the institution's image. Any unplanned event that comes up should be addressed frontally, and the institution's side of the story should be handled by a public relations expert. The personality of a brand reflects its values. The more distinct the values, the better the opportunity the brand has to create a distinct sensory appeal (Lindstrom, 2005).

However, for effective branding activity to take place in a university, such need to have a clear definition of its brand image.

viii. Maintain innovation and relevance for the brand. A university to build strong brand image for its institution must be innovative in its approach. Such a university should adopt a lateral approach to the development of its curriculum and teaching pedagogy. Innovation, as advanced by Kotler and Trias de Bes (2003), is the key and basis of competitive strategies today.

ix. Strategically design and implement a brand hierarchy and brand portfolio. Universities should strategically define the branding strategy that guides brand elements to apply. An institution that wants to build a strong brand should have a dashboard of all programmes and courses, including other products that carry the university's name. This, according to Keller (2008) will enable the university to capture the potential branding relationship amongst the different offerings of the university.

x. Implement a brand equity management system to ensure that marketing actions accurately reflect the brand equity concept. Any university that intends to achieve high brand value must ensure that all actions towards this must be those that add to the value accruable to the university's value; they must be actions that are capable of making the target markets and partners of the university to associate with them continuously.

3. Understanding the role of services in branding university education

Universities are services providers, and they must conduct all their brand building activities considering the characteristics of services production and the delivery process which can ensure production and delivery of quality services. These brand building activities as advanced by Gummesson (2001) are:

i. Interaction between the service provider's contact person and the customer (lecturers, administrative staff, student, guardians/parents) the shared experience can cement or prevent long-lasting relationships. The university responsiveness and willingness to help customers and deliver prompt service and the manner of interaction between universities and all stakeholders will determine the success or failure of the brand building process.

ii. The interactions among customers which can be partly produced if there is an avenue for customers to meet and interact. Universities should adopt the use of technology to augment inter-personal face-to-face communication. Websites of institutions should serve as a real-time functional website that receive, respond, and communicate with the visitors to the site. There should be trained personnel who will handle the website. Universities should also participate in social media so that they get involved in customers' interaction.

iii. Interaction between the customer and the provider's physical environment, equipment, and products. An essential part of this is that the tangibles in the universities' environment; equipment, people (personal appearance and clothes are essential aspects of the perception of quality).

iv. The interaction between the customer and the provider's system. The interaction must be reliability and customers assured credible service. The interaction must be filled with individualised attention in a manner of 'Me Selling Proposition' (MSP) which makes consumers take ownership of their brands.

Findings

Findings from the review of extant literature and the current situation of the Nigerian university system reveal that majority of Nigerian universities have not taken cognisance of the imperativeness of the three critical points towards leveraging the value of their brands. Standard features in the operations of these universities concerning branding are:

1. Majority of the universities (private) do not understand the essence of a brand

Within the Nigerian environment, many of the management members' perception of a university is that it exists to provide access to tertiary education for prospects. This perception is based on the belief that a lot of qualified university education prospects who are not able to secure admission in the limited spaces available in the public universities would form a fulcrum of students to patronise their brands, and one from which their investments can be recouped. Therefore, all their plans are geared towards having a name with which they can distinguish their university from those of other institutions and having enough buildings to have academic and non-academic offices and lectures rooms for students. Essentially, they overlook the essence of branding as a promise of desired benefit-giving properties which guarantees the quality of customers' educational satisfaction. This aligns with findings from Mogaji (2019b)'s analysis of brand integration on social media by African universities. Without adequately taking care to put the essence of brands at the fore in building the image of universities, the substantial drift in the number of prospective students to foreign universities will be a continuous experience.

2. Majority of the universities do not perform activities that enable them to build a strong brand and aim to maximise brand equity

Many universities do not have an understanding of the meaning of the brand. Hence, they are unable to clarify who their institution is for, what the university stands for, the purpose of the university brand, and what universities their brand competes with. The absence of this understanding has hindered their development of programmes and courses that with be closely tied with the underlying philosophy of the institution. Inability to understand the meaning of the university brand has resulted in lack of proper positioning of majority of Nigerian universities. In this situation, a large number of Nigerian universities have failed to provide superior delivery of educational services that are satisfactory to all stakeholders. In addition, many of the universities have failed to, or are unable to attract partners in the form of accreditation and affiliation, industry linkages, exchange programmes, career counselling and placement services, thus, there is a wide gap between the knowledge needs of the labour market and those of the graduates being produced for the market.

Another gap evident in the practice of Nigerian universities is their inability to embrace integrated marketing communications (IMC) in communicating with potential and actual consumers consistently. All they (private universities) do is advertising. Even this is done majorly during the beginning of new sessions when adverts are done for placements into programmes run by the school. It is hard to see these universities sponsor or support laudable programmes or causes in society. Without being innovative in their approaches, their brands will remain highly uncompetitive.

3. Improper understanding of services role in branding university education

Services are central to the function of universities. To fulfil their mandates, universities must provide educational services to their numerous customers. For many Nigerian universities, this is their weak point. Educational services are rendered to the customers in a manner depicting favour to those who patronise them. It is commonplace to experience harsh responses and unwillingness to help during interaction between staff of universities and customers/prospects. This is so because a majority of the staff believe they are doing the customers and prospects favour. Hence, their enquiries should be responded to at their leisure and by their measure.

Also, the majority of Nigerian universities that have tried to improve their services by adopting the use of Internet technology in their interaction with their customers and prospects have been found wanting concerning they are operating without a functional website that receive, respond, and communicate with the visitors to the site in real-time. This is because many of these universities do not have trained personnel who will handle the website or do not participate in social media which provides them the opportunity to get involved in customers' interaction on issues concerning them.

Furthermore, many of the universities do not consider the importance of the universities' environment as an integral part of service branding. The ambience of many universities in existence in Nigeria is not attractive. For many, what they consider as important in the running of the university are the buildings, staff, and the number of courses on offer.

Discussion

This study is an attempt to stir the consciousness of university management to the importance of branding towards building a valuable university brand. Branding has always been about establishing emotional ties between the brand and the consumer. Expectations vary depending on what a brand communicates to its audience and their perception of that message. As in any relationship, emotions are based on information gathered from our senses (Lindstrom, 2005). Factors such as academic staff quality, non-academic staff efficiency, physical facilities and equipment, library services, working hours, as well as educational materials are essentials in the internal branding of universities (Abina & Uthman, 2018).

Universities that practise branding holistically have the potential to provide its target markets with a reliable decision making as it signals that the university has designed a particular service offering that is special and deserving of its name (Keller, 2008). Thus, the performance of branding activities must be done with expediency by any university that is desirous of creating a strong brand and aim to maximise brand equity in a highly competitive environment. Also, it is pertinent to note that branding activities cannot be wholly achieved by a university doing and executing it by themselves only; there must be a productive interaction between parties involved with the brand. It is the interaction between universities and their stakeholders that determines the success of the brand exercise. A university with the intent to improve its long-term reputation must first evaluate its current image, goals, and how these elements relate to branding efforts (Hanover Research, 2015).

Conclusion

This study provides a logical extension of the signalling theory of branding by extenuating how branding can be used to signal quality attributes of a university to prospects and customers, and, by extension, build a valuable brand as the increasing competition for student enrolment in Nigeria has demanded that universities need to differentiate their brands from others consistently. Universities have a broad group of target audiences with different levels of brand commitment, knowledge, experience, and motivators. Hence, they must have strategies to recruit, engage, and retain faculty and donors.

The implications of understanding and practising branding are numerous. First, it is imperative for universities that want to earn high value for its brands to emphasise its purpose, history/reputation, location, student niche, public ethos, and the fame it has earned over time. An example of this is that of Universiti Sains Malaysia (USM) that emphasises its consistent upward position in the ranking of global universities as it attains the golden age of 50 and is currently ranked as the 49th positioned university in world ranking of universities by Times Higher Education World University Rankings 2019. This can indicate to consumers that the university, as it is with wines, can only get better with age. Similarly, the University of Ibadan prides itself as the Number 1 University in

West Africa in the Times Higher Education World University Rankings 2019 global ranking. Universities should leverage on their rankings to attract prospects to the institutions (Kiraka, Maringe, Kanyutu, & Mogaji, 2020)

Second, a university's image can also attract significant funding for it if adequately harnessed. Having a robust strategic agenda or a clear vision is crucial to a successful university brand. Nigeria's Afe Babalola University's ability to clearly articulate its purpose earned it the African Development Bank's (AfDB) grant. Universities that can build a good and strong brand image can overcome the issue of funding. This strong brand can be attained where there is massive support from the leadership of the university. The resources available for branding activities need to support the university's brand image building activity. As encapsulated by Chapelo (2010), this includes the size of marketing function, growth and structure, internal support, and brand experience.

Third, location is also an essential part of many 'successful' brands. This can be used in building the brand image of a university, particularly in the area of international branding. Universities need to emphasise their historical antecedents and the reputation and fame they have been able to achieve during their years of existence (Wayne et al., 2020). Closely related to this is the placement of emphasis on student niche and the principles or values they have achieved with these.

In summary, the need to understand the branding of services as a competitive weapon for universities is essential. As summed up by Keller (2008) brands help:

- make the abstract nature of services more concrete;
- identify and create meaning for the different services provided by a firm;
- organise and label new offerings in a manner that consumers can understand;
- signal to consumers that the organisation has designed a particular service offering that is special and deserving of its name.

Delivering on the promise of the university is the most critical aspect of branding a university (Black, 2008). It is the 'expression' of what stakeholders can expect from their interactions with the institution over time. If a university's brand contains a promise, it must never be broken. It is an essential part of building stability (Lindstrom, 2005). Universities with the intent of building a sharp brand image must deliver on brand promise; it is the actualisation of the brand message communicated to stakeholders of an institution, including students, employees, alumni, and funding agencies.

Despite the contribution of this study to articles on branding and higher education marketing, there are also several limitations associated with it. First, the article drew examples from the Nigerian environment only. Perhaps further studies can be extended to other parts of Africa.

Second, the article is empirical, thus, future studies can be conducted using data collected from prospects and customers to have firsthand information relating to their perception of different universities in the Nigerian environment. Such as the potential to create additional insights that will make an incremental contribution to the subject area and help in providing feedback on the branding strategies employed by universities.

Finally, future studies could examine the branding strategies adopted by Nigerian universities and compare with those of universities in developed nations to understand the marketing environment and factors that inform strategic branding approach that can work best under different situations.

References

Abina, M. B., & Uthman, A. B. (2018). Internal brand equity of universities and students' academic performance: An empirical survey of accounting students. *Sona Global Management Review*, 12(1), 1–20.

Adamolekun, L. (2019, 6 March). When private universities fail. *Vanguard News*. Retrieved from www.vanguardngr.com.

Alemu, S. K. (2018). The meaning, idea and history of university/higher education in Africa: A brief literature review. *Forum for International Research in Education (FIRE)*, 4 (3), 210–227.

Allen, M. (1988). *The goals of universities*. Maidenhead: Open University Press.

American Marketing Association (AMA). (2010). Brand. Retrieved from http://marketingpower.com.

Bansal, S. K. (2014). Branding an academic institute: The strategic issues. *Journal of International Academic Research for Multidisciplinary*, 2(4), 370–376.

Black, J. (2008). The branding of higher education. SEM works. Retrieved from www.semworks.net/papers/wp_TheBranding-of-Higher-Education.pdf.

Bock, D. E., Poole, S. M., & Joseph, M. (2013). Branding in higher education: A strategic perspective. *Annals of the Society for Marketing Advances*, 2,183–184.

Chapelo, C. (2010). What defines 'successful' university brands? *International Journal of Public Sector Management*. doi:10.1108/09513551011022519.

Davies, G., Rojas-Mendez, J. I., Whelan, S., Mete, M., & Loo, T. (2017). Brand personality: Theory and dimensionality. *Journal of Product and Brand Management*, 27(2), 115–127. doi:10.1108/JPBM-06-2017-1499.

Dobni, D., & Zinkhan, G. M. (1990). In search of brand image: A foundation analysis. In M. E. Goldberg, G. Gorn, & R. W. Pollay (Eds.), *Advances in consumer research*, Volume 17, (pp. 110–119). Provo, UT: Association for Consumer Research.

Drori, G. S., Delmestri, G., & Oberg, A. (2013). *Branding the university: Relational strategy of identity construction in a competitive field*. London: Portland Press.

Fournier, S. (1998). Consumers and their brands: Developing relationship theory in consumer research. *Journal of Consumer Research*, 24, 343–373.

Gabbert, E. (2015, 3 April). The signalling theory of marketing: What your actions say about your business. Retrieved from www.wordstream.com.

Gbadeyan, R. A., Abina, M. B., & Sowole, M. O. (2016). A quantitative study of the effects of brand image on students' attachment and commitment. *Al-Hikmah Management Review*, 1(1), 20–38.

Grigoriou, N., Davcik, N., & Sharma, P. (2016). Exploring the influence of brand innovation on marketing performance using a signaling framework and resource-based theory approach. In M. W. Obal et al. (Eds.), *Let's get engaged! Crossing the threshold of marketing's engagement era* (pp. 813–822). doi:10.1007/978-3-319-11815-4_238.

Gummesson, E. (2001). Marketing of services. In M. J. Baker (Ed.), *Encyclopedia of marketing* (pp. 604–612). London: Thomson Learning.

Hanover Research. (2015). Best practices in improving reputation and brand recognition in higher education. Academy Administration practice, 1–21. Retrieved from www.hanoverresearch.com/evaluation/index.php.

Keller, K. L. (2008). *Strategic brand management* (3rd ed.). New Delhi: Dorling Kindersley.

Kiraka, R., Maringe, F., Kanyutu, W., & Mogaji, E. (2020). University league tables and ranking systems in Africa: Emerging prospects, challenges and opportunities. In E. Mogaji, F. Maringe, & R. E. Hinson (Eds.), *Understanding the higher education market in Africa*. London: Routledge.

Kotler, P., & Trias de Bes, F. (2003). *Lateral marketing*. Hoboken, NJ: John Wiley & Sons.

Lindstrom, M. (2005). *Brand sense*. London: Kogan Page.

Louis, D., & Lombart, C. (2010). Impact of brand personality on three significant relational consequences (trust, attachment, and commitment to the brand). *Journal of Product & Brand Management*, 19(2), 114–130.

Mogaji, E. (2016). Marketing strategies of United Kingdom universities during clearing and adjustment. *International Journal of Educational Management*, 30(4), 493–504.

Mogaji, E. (2019a). Types and location of Nigerian universities. Research Agenda Working Papers, 2019(7), 92–103.

Mogaji, E. (2019b). Branding private universities in Africa: An unexplored territory. Research Agenda Working Papers, 2019(9), 120–148.

National Universities Commission. (2019). Nigerian universities. Retrieved from nuc.edu.ng.

Otabor, O. (2018, 6 July). Why private universities have low students enrollment – NUC. *The Nation Newspaper*. Retrieved from https://thenationonlineng.net.

Sherrington, M. (2001). Branding and brand management. In M. J. Baker (Ed.), *Encyclopedia of marketing* (pp. 376–389). London: Thomson Learning.

Shimp, T. A. (2007). *Integrated marketing communications in advertising and promotion* (7th ed.). Mason, OH: Thomson Higher Education.

Valitov, S. M. (2014). University brand as a modern way of winning competitive advantage. *Social and Behavioral Sciences*, 152, 295–299.

von Wallpach, S., Voyer, B., Kastanakis, M., & Muhlbacher, H. (2017). Co-creating stakeholder and brand identities: Introduction to the special issues. *Journal of Business Research*, 70, 395–398.

Wang C., Chen, C., & Chen, C. (2012). Investigation on the influence of the brand image of higher educational institutions on satisfaction and customer lifetime value. *Educational Studies*, 38(5), 593–608.

Wayne, T., Farinloye, F., & Mogaji, E. (2020). Analysis of African universities' corporate visual identities. In E. Mogaji, F. Maringe, & R. E. Hinson (Eds.), *Strategic marketing of higher education in Africa*. London: Routledge.

Part IV

Moving from research to practice

13 Marketing higher education in Africa

Moving from research to practice

Tai Kieu, Emmanuel Mogaji, Christine Mwebesa, Samer Sarofim, Taiwo Soetan, and S Pee Vululleh[1]

Introduction

The provision of higher education is becoming more competitive as the skill needs of increasingly knowledge-based and innovation-driven economies have spurred demand for tertiary education worldwide. Coupled with a growing middle class, the globalisation of education has stimulated the quest for quality education, often in the developed countries' wave of students studying abroad (OECD, 2018). There are many universities around the world aiming to attract prospective students, develop their network, increase their reputation and revenues, and promote cross-faculty fertilisation (Hénard et al., 2012).

Marketing of higher education is necessitated based on the need to deliver another service to the market – to those who can afford it (Mogaji & Yoon, 2019). In other words, education provides people with choices. Students can decide to leave their home countries and travel to another country because they have found the education worthwhile, based on the way it has been marketed. While effort has been made in understanding the motivation of students and the marketing strategies of universities around the world, studies on marketing higher education in Africa is scarce (Mogaji et al., 2017). Despite the enormous potentials of students and the increasing number of private universities, and more institutions creating off-shore satellite campuses, it is worthwhile to consider how higher education is being marketed in Africa.

It is essential to highlight that this chapter is not presenting empirical research findings, but explicitly focusing on managerial implications of marketing higher education in Africa. They are presenting relatable action plans for university managers and proprietors on how to navigate and stand out in the competitive higher education market. This chapter presents consolidated yet multiple perspectives on practical implications for marketing managers of higher institutions in Africa. The focus of this chapter is to address marketing challenges for marketing managers. Firstly, managers who are trying to redevelop their university brand and reposition themselves for global domination; and secondly, managers and proprietors of new universities that are just starting up and looking to compete in the higher education market.

The African context is acknowledged here, as it comes with its challenges. Africa is a big continent with diverse cultures and forms of education. A significant challenge that colleges and universities in Africa face, apart from the state and standards of the campuses, is that they are not deemed to be competitive enough for consumers to perceive them as offering better products and services than their competitors. In addition, there are challenges which include the state of the external environment where these colleges and universities are located; that is the safety, security, and opportunities, and the macroeconomic stability of the external environment (country), in terms of living standards (Gross Domestic Product (GDP), GDP per capita, inflation, and unemployment rates) of the countries these colleges and universities are located.

Students are trooping to Western countries like Canada, the United States of America, the United Kingdom, Australia, etc., not only from Africa but from other developing countries of the world. This is because they consider these countries to be both safe and secure and have many opportunities for them to benefit from. This is in addition to the fact that the colleges and universities in these countries boast of superior products and services compared to their African counterparts. Regardless of the standard of the colleges and universities in the developed countries, if these countries are not considered to be safe and secure with lots of opportunities, consumers (students) are not likely to patronise the products and services that are offered by those colleges and universities.

While recognising that these challenges are multifaceted, this chapter aims to address one of the many sectors involved in developing the capacity of universities in Africa. The chapter focuses on the marketing strategies for building, integrating, and developing higher education brands to appeal to prospective students and stakeholders. Researchers with an interest in marketing communication and also possess knowledge about the different Africa education systems, present this consolidated action plan to offer managerial recommendations and extend knowledge on marketing higher education in Africa. The style of writing is specifically unique, as the chapter is speaking directly to the managers, and presenting actionable plans and ideas.

The chapter proceeds with the discussion about a marketing task checklist for managers responsible for marketing higher education and understating their challenges and expectations. This is followed by the action plans which are developed to cover the needs of the managers. Recommended action plans are covered in three sections. The first section discusses strategic aspects to be considered to build the brand, including repositioning and aligning it with the core values and objectives, new identities and philosophy. The second section presents ideas for integrating the new brand – making all the stakeholders aware of the brands' offering. At the core of this section is the integration of marketing communication strategies for reaching out to prospective students. The third section presents ideas for managing and developing the brand. This section also discusses building global reputation, enhancing student experiences and learning facilities. The chapter then ends with a concluding section.

The marketing orientation mind-set checklist

While it may be the case that public universities seldom have a marketing manager as they receive governments' funds, and administrative bureaucracy in implementing these strategies is recognised, countries are opening up to the world and the governments are cutting subsidies for or deregulating the higher education sector; for example, in Australia or South Africa (de Jager & Gbadamosi, 2013) or in Vietnam where the government is cutting subsidies, and public universities have to compete with private universities. Therefore, not only do existing private universities in Africa now need to be 'marketing-oriented', but also public universities need to also consider that as a possibility (Beneke, 2011).

Marketing managers of higher education institutions need to acknowledge the trends that have changed the landscape for higher education marketing (Maringe & Gibbs, 2008; Mogaji, 2019). Students are more empowered as they are more informed and even may voice their discontent (whether right or wrong) on online platforms. Nowadays, students have more alternative and more affordable ways to earn qualifications. Secondly, the internationalisation of the sector around the world has led to even more intensified competition as domestic universities right now compete with international institutions vying for local students, for off-shore and onshore programmes. Several institutions from the developed world have established campuses in developing countries (e.g. European universities in Africa such as Lancaster University in Ghana, Henley Business School in South Africa, and Technische Universität Berlin in Egypt), competing for students who cannot afford to go to overseas and yet get the international certification and quality of teaching (Ndofirepi et al., 2020).

Indeed, African higher education is one of the most internationalised (Jowi, 2012). In the face of increasing competition, perhaps the biggest challenge for marketers of higher education in Africa is to implement a marketing-oriented approach to higher education, as previous research in South Africa shows institutions' hesitation to embrace relationship marketing (Beneke, 2011). Higher education institutions must be marketing-oriented, student-focused, and entrepreneurial. Particularly, marketing managers of higher education need to ask themselves how well they have performed on the following aspects.

Well though-out marketing strategy and organisation

First and foremost, marketing managers of higher education institutions need to have well thought-out, relationship-oriented marketing strategy that aims not only to attract and recruit students but also to retain current students as well as to build strong relationships with them during and after their time with the institution. There is a widely accepted view that students are consumers in higher education (Reddy, 2012; Mogaji, 2016). Theories of consumer relationships in the marketing literature suggest aspects that managers will need to attempt to build: customer trust, customer commitment, customer satisfaction, love of and identification with the institution, brand communities (Fournier et al., 2012). Higher education institutions need to win and retain students through engagement supported by content development, co-creation, and crowdsourcing (Kotler et al., 2010).

Bringing together the magic of marketing and the science of technology

Perhaps nothing other than technology has profoundly changed marketing around the world. Technology causes market disruptions across industries. In higher education, technology transforms the higher education marketing practices from the introduction of online or personalised courses to authentic approach underpinned by real-time conversations, taking students from awareness to advocacy (Mogaji, 2018; & Ajjan Hartshorne, 2008). The last step of advocacy in the consumer (student) journey is of relative importance in higher education because the opinions of our family, friends, and word of mouth have enormous impact on buying decisions. The modern marketing department needs to blend the creative and often intuitive marketing process – understanding consumer motivations and using these insights to create compelling integrated marketing – with the technology to gain data-driven insights, creating real-time conversations with students, and engaging with them at every touchpoint – prior, during, and post-experience with the institutions.

Researching and finding opportunities

Many higher education institutions invest in academic research to build up their profile, but they need to also think of marketing research to understand the needs and wants of their 'special customers' and the influencing roles of parents. There are certain segments of prospective students with distinctive expectations at different ends of the market. Besides traditional research approaches, marketing managers can also use modern research techniques, such as marketing analytics and netnography, to research prospective students' expectations. Marketing managers need to research the reference or influence of others, such as family, friends, and acquaintances; e.g. students in some countries make decisions in conjunction with their parents (Garwe, 2016)

Innovating successfully

Upon selecting the target segment and identifying opportunities, managers have to ask themselves how they would innovate their products. While marketing managers of higher education institutions are typically involved in recruitment and communication efforts, they need to be get involved in the design of 'products' – courses and experiences offered to students. Just like a consumer product and service company may have different products meeting their customers, higher education institutions can design different courses to target different market segments. Examples of such could be Finance for Non-Finance Managers and Corporate Communications for Small and Medium Enterprises. Universities may consider courses as products, and as such marketers need to think of all product decisions – from positioning the product, giving it a brand name, to determining support services. Within an institution, the leaders may consider building their own 'international environment' (such as English-based environment of International School of Business at Woosong University, South Korea) as a star brand and also to attract the segment aspiring to international certification. Higher education institutions need to consider dual transformation design strategy to address different ends of the market (Gilbert et al., 2018): (1) optimise current operations and improve capacities to respond to market challenges, such as lowering cost or even exiting offerings that are not sufficiently differentiated; and (2) carefully design a capacity to take advantage of market opportunities (new models and separate student segments), e.g. online learning, distance education, MOOCs (massive open online courses) and so on. Accreditation is essential and universities should make effort to get accreditations from regulatory bodies if needed.

Delivering services and managing student experiences with the right team

Like any service, marketing managers need to pay attention to extended marketing mix elements affecting student experience (Booms & Bitner, 1981), including people (academic and non-academic staff), process (course and support services delivery), and physical environment (brands and facilities). This is crucial to not only student recruitment, but also student retention. An established marketing team is also essential to achieve this objective. Trained and qualified human resources, who possess the sophisticated know-how that will determine where resources should be deployed immediately in the universities' marketing plans, are needed within the team. Because of the crucial nature of making such a decision, hiring professionals in the department should not be based on 'who knows you'(i.e. favouritism), but by considering the extent of compelling performances of staff who are able to deliver on the set objective of the department. Besides, a comprehensive higher education marketing policy with their mandatory implementation strategies or techniques put in place that will modify and bring more significant change into the current operations, might not be working as expected to be on par with other successful higher education institutions around the world.

Communicating and running recruitment team effectively

Marketing managers of higher education institutions (HEIs) may learn different communication practices ranging from traditional advertising and outdoor sponsorship to open-day events to in-school presentations, or career orientation to recruitment via alumni to database marketing (Beneke, 2011). Prior research has shown that promotional information and marketing are important factors affecting students' choice of private higher education institutions (Garwe, 2016). New media have to be blended with traditional media, in a mutually reinforcing way, to recruit and retain students. Managers need to have a well thought-out digital communication strategy to engage with and build relationships amongst students and alumni, and ultimately encourage student and alumni engagement in forms of co-creation, referral, and positive word of mouth. An important task for managers is to develop a 'selling', rather than 'information provider' mind-set for their recruitment force. Recruitment staff need to be trained with consultative selling skills to unravel the needs of the students and close the 'deal' (Farinloye et al., 2020).

Facilitating societal changes with insights from student (market) evaluation

Similarly, conducting regular surveys at the close of every fiscal period, to evaluate the system is an essential aspect of running HEIs in Africa. Data from these surveys and their professional interpretations might assist authorities to make informed decisions as to which aspects of the marketing policies and implementation are working for the betterment of the higher education sector. Perhaps artificial intelligence and learning analytics can play a prominent role in this data aggregation and processing for better understanding of the students' needs (Dwivedi et al., 2019).

Building the brand

Branding of an African university is still an evolving area of literature. Wayne et al. (2020) analysed brand identities of the top 200 universities in Africa and concluded that there is still a lack of understanding with regards to the creative design of brand identities by African universities, suggesting that the thought process behind the brand identities are questionable. Likewise, Farinloye et al. (2020) presented a typology of Africa universities, providing a strategic marketing and brand implication on brand identities of universities. Vasudeva and Mogaji (2020) also analysed the mission and vision statement of top African universities, highlighting how African universities are making efforts towards world domination. These studies recognise the need for universities to take ownership of the brands. With the marketing team in place, it is essential to make effort in building the brands.

The task of building brand applies to both established universities which need to build their existing brands, and also new universities with new brands that need to be developed. Building brand is always mistaken with having a fancy logo. It is not the logo that makes a brand, but the other way round. Once the offerings satisfy the needs of the consumers, they will seek it out in order to be sure that they are purchasing the same good and services, and they will look out for any clue like a symbol (in this case the logo) that differentiates it from the others. So, before investing heavily in the design of a logo, one needs to ask questions: what am I offering? What attributes does my product have that are different from the rest in the industry? How can I make these attributes known to my target audience? How can all these be displayed (or captured) in my logo? Hence, strong brands are identified by their logos because of the offerings the brands make. While a new university needs to establish its presence in the industry, having a logo that displays its uniqueness is paramount. Whereas it is also true that new institutions or products need beautiful colours, catchy words, and promises to attract prospective and curious customers. The success of this depends on keeping up to the promise explicitly or implicitly communicated through the logo.

The brand name

This is very important, especially for a new university. What should be the name of the university? The university needs to select the right name that will appeal to their market bases and all stakeholders. The availability of the name as a website domain name and social media profile names should also be considered.

The brand philosophy

This is crucial in developing the university's brand. The study by Vasudeva and Mogaji (2019) presents an analysis of the mission and vision statement of top African universities. It was suggested that the university must have a mission and vision, made publicly available for all stakeholders to know what the university is set to achieve. The frequency at which it is changed and modified is also essential; perhaps every five to ten years, provided the objectives are being achieved. This must align with the strategic direction of the university. This is considered a significant purpose of marketing, which has been shown as the critical success factor for winning companies (Kotler, 2015). For example, IBM's higher purpose is to 'build smarter planet'. Like winning companies, universities need to build their core values so that they can occupy the minds, hearts, and spirits (Kotler et al., 2010) of their students; and purpose marketing is probably concerned with the broadest boundary set in the vision and mission in the organisational strategy. That boundary is the limits within which marketing managers can take actions. Thus, university leaders need to embrace sustainability and corporate social responsibility as their guiding principles in order to build reputation for the institution.

The brand identity

The brand identity, which includes the logo and graphic elements of the university must be well thought of. The logo is considered a signpost or global positioning system (GPS) metaphor. Efforts should be made towards having a professional touch and conveying values of the university. The integration of the logo across different touchpoints should also be considered. A logo is not just an emblem to be associated with an institution or product. It is more than that. That is why we use the metaphor 'signpost versus GPS' to show the importance of creating a successful logo. A logo remains only a 'signpost' until the product's attributes transform it into GPS. A signpost will appeal to only those trying to locate where it is pointing them to or passing by that way. A signpost is, therefore, limited geographically.

On the other hand, GPS will locate whatever position as long as you give it the right coordinates (quality attributes), and hence it has unlimited potential, in terms of space and time. Therefore, the big question for any university trying to create its unique brand should be: how can we ensure that our logo is immutable and interminable? Answering that question requires considering three key elements: a) a logo should be able to transcend boundaries of time and space, b) a logo should be able to exhibit specificity of the brand's uniqueness at the same time capturing diverse demographics of the target audience, and c) a logo should be able to display hope by pointing to the future. We will discuss the three elements below.

Transcending time and space

Building a strong brand requires utilising all the available and relevant tools to harness both space and time. The best vehicle to achieving that is investing in technology. Therefore, a successful logo that defies geographical or time zone barriers must be created and conserved through technology. Also, it should be easily accessed by whomever, from wherever, and at whatever time it is sought after. The technology used to design and display the logo should be sophisticated enough to appeal to the young generation, at the same time user-friendly (accessibility, affordability and usability) to all that would desire to identify with it. Finally, a good logo needs to position its brand in such a way that it gains global recognition without losing its local relevance, mission, and vision.

Specificity and diversity

A logo should be able to exhibit distinctive qualities of the brand's uniqueness at the same time capturing varied demographics of the target audience. For example, a university logo ought to create an impression in the customer's mind of specific attributes like success, excellence, mastery, and knowledge, amongst others. It should be appealing to all categories of the populace – rich and poor, young and old, local and international. All the different stakeholders should be taken into consideration while design-ing a logo. The motto should also be in agreement with the emblem. Take for example an East African private university whose emblem is a giraffe reaching out to the skies. Even in silence, the motto screams out – *the sky is the limit*. Thus, the only space that specificity communicates with diversity in harmony is the logo.

The future in perspective

Building a recognisable brand takes a lot of effort and time. It is therefore imperative that a logo not only takes into consideration the complexities of building a great brand, but also one that will live on through generations. For example, referring to the previous example of the East African private university whose emblem is a giraffe, the logo shows a *greater goal and farther vision*. A good logo should be able to attract customers today because of displaying the best that lies ahead. No one wants to associate with a brand whose future is not clear.

Strategic co-branding

African universities would benefit tremendously from strategical co-branding with academic and non-academic institutions. The co-branding must be done strategically and carefully to ensure the brand image transferability between the African university and the co-branding entity. Both brands' core values, though not necessarily to be similar, need to complement each other to ensure a synergetic effect that leverages the unique proposition of each of the two brands. In other words, the co-branded African university needs to be able to achieve specific goals related to its unique positioning, while it also provides the co-branded entity with beneficial associations, transformations, reach, etc. The co-branding efforts should not be limited to academic endeavours, such as offering educational opportunities (e.g. workshops, trainings, seminars, degrees), rather African universities' co-branding activities should extended to shared sponsorships for community and sport events, fundraising events, supporting arts and music, and other opportunities that deem in line with the university brand proposition. Co-branding initiatives should also be diversified to include local and global, academic and non-academic institutions, and emerge with sustainable and impactful support to the national identity of the university hosting country, and the leading global issues related to the welfare of the people and the protection of the environment.

Integrating the brand

African universities must make an effort to integrate their marketing communications to reach prospective students and other stakeholders. There should be a narrative that appeals to everyone involved in the university. It is one thing to create a strong brand and another thing to make your brand known. Developing a communication system that drives the brand is multidimensional: 1) the leader must involve all the stakeholders in understanding and believing in the vision, 2) the internal customer (employees) must be given priority before emphasising the external customer, 3) channels of communication must be horizontal regardless of the hierarchical structure, 4) and one should be able to identify your particular niche and plugin. The last dimension is very critical because, in this technology-driven age, it is easy to copy and paste without much thinking and creativity. While technology has fuelled less creativity than we are made to believe, it has also enabled information access. As customers get informed, their demands become more sophisticated, which calls for more creativity and innovation. It even gets more complicated when it concerns universities where the functions are meant to be similar (research, teach, and community). So, how does a university stand out amidst the sameness?

We use another East African private university which gave a pseudonym – Pathfinder University, which decided to identify its niche in sports and games. Its name became synonymous with university games long before its graduates could be celebrated in the workplace. Consequently, the nation went on to win sports' medals on the international scene because of the products of this university. Pathfinder University, however, started with one strategy of attracting bright sports students with studentships (attracting bright student was deliberate), so that not only would they excel in sports but also their academics. Another deliberate effort was maintaining discipline of both academic staff and students and standard of scholarship.

Consequently, the university became a household name – attracting students, guardians, sports' fans, and industry. When other private universities were beginning to integrate sports into their programmes, Pathfinder had already spread its wings into another sport from Asia. Not only did it engage seriously with the game, but was also given the franchise of manufacturing the tools for this game, and the African president for the game is an employee of Pathfinder University. Therefore, it is essential that universities identify or create particular areas that are uniquely their own, and through a well-developed marketing system that showcases that uniqueness.

The core messages should be amplified

Based on the comprehensive higher education marketing policies developed by these universities, the key message of the universities should be identified and effectively broadcasted. What are those things that make the university unique? A social media strategy should also be a part of the marketing strategy that is being developed. What is the goal and objective of the social media strategy? To engage with students and share updates about the university? How many social media profiles is the university going to manage? What are the achievable goals that have been set? The number of followers or engagement rate? Who are those responsible for updating and managing social media? What is the content creating strategies in place?

Marketing communication strategies

As a means of integrating the brands, the website design and layout are also outstanding. Managers should be aware that different stakeholders (staff, students, parents, prospective staff, and funders) are accessing the website for information, and relevant information should be made available (Mogaji, 2016b; Olaleye et al., 2018). The layout and user interface should be appealing and inviting. Often the university's ICT team might be responsible for the website. If needs be, professional website developers can be employed to develop a website that can be managed by the university's marketing team. This could be building on a content management system that allows flexibility in updating the websites.

While printed prospectuses may be going out of fashion, universities can provide an online prospectus for prospective students. This can be made available as PDF on the university's website. This allows the university to tell their story in their way and engage with prospective students. Prospectus can be used to share insight into the university, share testimonies from current students and alumni, and also provide detailed information about the courses, to complement information on the website. Students can download this prospectus and engage with it in their own time. It should be noted that the prospectus should be colourful, with images and emotionally appealing messages.

Open Days as well could be used as an opportunity to explore the university, especially for those who have never visited the university before, they can be invited to have a tour of the university and see the facilities. It is important to note that the best foot should be put forward. Those who have the facilities, especially private universities, are encouraged to have open days and invite prospective students and parents. Tasters' Days as well can be organised to give students experience of what teaching is like in a university. This further primes the name of the university to the attention of prospective students and their parents.

For those who may not have been able to come in contact with the university brand, getting involved with school outer to feeder colleges can be an essential way to integrate the university's brand. This involves visiting secondary schools within the area, especially private universities (as the public universities are oversubscribed already). Universities should go into these schools, give lectures, present what the university is like, and create a form of association and integrate the brand. The perception of students about the university is essential as choice decision linked to perceptions which are formed at a young age (Foskett et al., 2008). It is all about catching them young and making them stay with the university.

Focus on brand outreach

The visibility of the university brand among the regional and international community of scholars, potential students, and other stakeholders (businesses,

NGOs, governmental institutions, etc.) is key to the global recognition of the university's brand. African universities should dedicate budgetary amounts and effort to conduct effective and strategic outreach that supports and enhances their brand propositions. The university's outreach should focus on the core brand values and the unique proposition of the specific university brand. For instance, student projects with local institutions, faculty consulting services, and university-offered workshops and training to the public, along with other outreach initiatives, need to strategically integrate the university's unique brand proposition, rather than only focusing on the recipient need. Brand outreach should also be conducted in ways that transform the perceptions about the university's brand, and portray the brand as an integral part of both the local and global community.

Additionally, the outreach should include all identified stakeholders in a meaningful way to increase engagement and ultimately build a brand community that serves the university brand in its future endeavours. Brand outreach should aim at achieving a high level of engagement with all stakeholders. This way, the outreach could create brand ambassadors that reciprocally advocate and benefit the university's brand in their circles of influence.

Build the brand around a unique concept

In many cases, African universities focus on what they lack instead of what makes them unique. For instance, due to the geographic location and its accompanying challenges (e.g. political systems, lack of economic recourses, etc.), the international academic community may perceive African universities as less developed. To cope with negative perceptions, the university's brand may revolve around the concept of how this admittedly challenging conditions create a set unique opportunity for students to learn and succeed in such a challenging environment, a skill that is transferable, and shall increase students' opportunities of success in a variety of working conditions in Africa and beyond. In other words, rather than focusing on arguing against the negative stigmas, university brands can use the stigmas to their advantage and flip the coin to show the advantageous side of what is perceived as a disadvantage.

Create consistent brand synergies

Once the brand proposition is set, administrators at African universities would need to ensure consistency amongst the various offerings to support a unified brand image. Faculty research, curricula, public events, community engagements, and other strategic initiatives and activities, need to resonate with the brand proposition and ensure the creation of a synergetic effect that further supports the brand development. For instance, if a university found its competitive advantage in operating under tight economic conditions, then dealing with poverty should be an integrated element in faculty research, curricula of all programmes, community outreach initiatives, etc. This way, the brand will avoid possible dilution, and the odds of global recognition will be enhanced.

Developing the brand

Developing the university's brand requires building and communicating a unique proposition that ensures the sustainability of the brand identity and its implication of targeted outcomes (e.g. increasing enrolment, attracting high quality and diverse students, securing funds, etc.). African universities face some unique challenges related to building global recognition, meeting international accreditation standards, widening the students' experiences, and attracting grants. Many of these challenges are related to the unfavourable stigma that is associated with Africa and the preconceived notion that African universities lack a competitive proposition when compared with non-African universities.

Global recognition through research

No doubt, African universities are struggling to compete with universities across the world (Kiraka et al., 2020). According to the 2019 QS World University Rankings, there were only 17 universities from 4 African countries (out of 54) presented on the list. These are South Africa (9), Egypt (6), Kenya (1), and Morocco (1). Even Nigeria, which is the largest by population and education system, was not represented. The best university in Africa, according to the 2019 QS World University Rankings, is the University of Cape Town. Though with a very high research output, the university's QS Global World Ranking is at Number 198. While recognising the challenges of African universities, it is essential to make an effort towards building more global recognition. Not just universities from South Africa or Egypt doing great things, but other universities from other parts of the continent. It is crucial to have more representatives on the global scene (Kiraka et al., 2020). In that regard, it is essential to recognise the leap progress made by Covenant University, a private Pentecostal Christian university, which has been operating with official status since 2002 in Ota, Nigeria. The Nigerian Universities Commission named it the best private university in Nigeria in its 2018 rankings, and it is ranked 601–800th in the Time Higher Education (THE) 2019 World University Rankings. The university has made progress in ranking based on the research activities, even though it was founded in 2002.

Global recognition through investment in resources

This highlight challenges for university managers to invest more resources in building the global recognition of an African university, primarily through a research grant, scholarship and support for publications. Efforts should be made in improving facilities and engage student experiences as an initiative to build the university brands and compete on a global scale. Traditional classrooms need to be replaced by integrated learning and web-enhanced hybrid classrooms. Higher education institutions need to invest in technology to ultimately maximise student educational and student life experience. African universities may partner with international institutions for franchising courses/programmes. The institutions may also partner with the industry to conduct field trips/field study as well as develop real-world assessments.

Higher education institutions need to monitor student satisfaction constantly, and perceptions of quality of teaching and learning, bridging the gap between students' perceived importance and experience, and ensure overt use of students' feedback (de Jager & Gbadamosi, 2013). While it is not possible to address all sentiments, the brand must meet international standards – in terms of general environment (safe and secure), facilities (use of up-to-date technology), skilled workforce who wholly embrace the institution's vision, active collaboration (network) profile, good governance, and community relationships (CSR).

African programs and initiatives

Also, African universities can better market themselves to promote African programmes/initiatives/activities globally in order to attract an international audience and competition. Why would an English/American student come to Africa to study English language, for example? However, these students can come to Africa to study Tropical Medicine, Yoruba language or Swahili, or any dominant African language that has been promoted globally, given the continent's population of about 1.2 billion, according to the United Nations (n.d.). Indeed, students come to a Nigerian university at Ibadan from the US to study Yoruba language as exchange students (Clement, 2013). African universities need to better develop their institutes of African Studies, History, Business, and probably Science, and Medical School, to develop workable African solutions to the challenges facing the continent, which the solutions proffered by the World Bank/IMF and other global bodies have not been able to address in order to compete globally with their counterparts from the developed world.

International partnership

The best of Africa's universities, probably those in the top 500 in the world, can also form a consortium to develop campuses in other emerging markets of the world, such as China and India in Asia, Mexico in North America, Turkey in Europe, and Brazil in South America. This is a first step of registering their international presence with off-shore campuses. In addition to attracting international students from these countries, some developed countries, and several developing countries to learn about demonstrated and workable homegrown solutions from Africa to the global challenges confronting humankind today.

Conclusion

While recognising the multifaceted challenges of higher education in Africa, this chapter has focused on its marketing communication and branding strategies for higher education. The study brings together the collective insights from academic researchers and practitioners of marketing higher education across the continents, to recommend evidence-based and practically proven practices for African universities' marketing managers and leaders. At the core of marketing, African higher education institutions have to ensure a marketing orientation encapsulating their business strategies and implementation. This section highlights the role and expectations for marketing managers of African higher education institutions. Particularly, marketing managers of African universities have to ask themselves how well they are (1) on having market-based, relationship-oriented strategy and well-organised marketing structure; (2) on keeping with and utilising technological changes effectively; (3) on using market research to understand students' motivations and their contemporary 'consumer' journey; (4) on innovating their offerings successfully; (5) on delivering services – not just teaching, and managing student learning experiences through multiple and omnichannel; (6) on managing mass communications and personal selling efforts effectively; and (7) on monitoring student evaluation and facilitating changes for higher purpose marketing.

The rest of the chapter delves into actionable ideas for higher education branding for African universities. The section 'building the brand' sets out the need to understand what a higher education brand is – not just a name or logo as they are part of the brand identity, then moves further to discuss considerations for setting brand spirit (brand philosophy), and brand tangibles (brand identity), as well as brand connections (brand co-branding). The section 'integrating the brand' presents practical thoughts on critical aspects of marketing communications for higher education. Rather than discussing every element like in any marketing communications textbook, the section focuses on the essential tips for managers – amplification of core messages, implementation of integrated marketing communications campaign around a unique concept, and ensuring brand outreach and synergies of marketing efforts. The last set of recommendations is concerned with managing and developing the higher education brand. This focuses on establishing a global stance, including building global recognition and international partnerships. These actions may help African universities not only to enhance their reputation through leveraging the secondary sources of brand equity, but also allow them to transform their offerings and marketing communications, and ultimately improve their competitive advantages in the global higher education market

In the era of globalisation, African universities need to take responsibility for their brand as they compete for prospective students. It must be acknowledged that these recommendations are based on empirical findings in the extant higher education marketing literature and observations of current practices in the industry. The chapter also recognises that there will be variations across different universities and different countries.

Notwithstanding, it offers insights that can be applied as deemed fit. The action plans may not necessarily be transferable and generalised across universities in Africa. The chapter is aimed at providing a toolkit for African higher education marketing managers. Just as marketing is creative and intuitive, managers have the discretion to the tool provided as deemed fit to their markets and circumstances.

Note

1 Author names are listed alphabetically. All the authors contributed equally to the chapter.

References

Ajjan, H., & Hartshorne, R. (2008). Investigating faculty decisions to adopt Web 2.0 technologies: Theory and empirical tests. *The Internet and Higher Education*, 11(2), 71–80.

Beneke, J. (2011). Student recruitment and relationship marketing-convergence or contortion? *South African Journal of Higher Education*, 25(3), 412–424.

Booms, B. H., & Bitner, M. J. (1981). Marketing strategies and organisation structures for service firms. In J. Donnelly & W. R. George (Eds.), *Marketing of services*. Chicago, IL: American Marketing Association.

Clement, O. O. (2013). Learning Yoruba at the University of Ibadan. Retrieved from www.ias.columbia.edu/blog/learning-yoruba-university-ibadan.

de Jager, J., & Gbadamosi, G. (2013). Predicting students' satisfaction through service quality in higher education. *The International Journal of Management Education*, 11(3), 107–118.

Dwivedi, Y. K. et al. (2019). Artificial intelligence (AI): Multidisciplinary perspectives on emerging challenges, opportunities, and agenda for research, practice and policy. *International Journal of Information Management*.

Farinloye, T., Mogaji, E., & Kuika Watat, J. (2020). Social media for universities' strategic communication. In E. Mogaji, F. Maringe, & R. E. Hinson (Eds.), *Strategic Marketing of Higher Education in Africa*. London: Routledge.

Foskett, N., Dyke, M., & Maringe, F. (2008). The influence of the school in the decision to participate in learning post-16. *British Educational Research Journal*, 34(1), 37–61.

Fournier, S., Breazeale, M., & Fetscherin, M. (2012). *Consumer-brand relationships: Theory and practice*. London: Routledge.

Garwe, E. C. (2016). Increase in the demand for private higher education: Unmasking the 'paradox'. *International Journal of Educational Management*, 30(2), 232–251.

Gilbert, C. G., Crow, M. M., & Anderson, D. (2018). Design thinking for higher education. *Stanford Social Innovation Review*, 36–41.

Hénard, F., Diamond, L., & Roseveare, D. (2012). *Approaches to internationalisation and their implications for strategic management and institutional practice*. Paris: OECD/Institutional Management in Higher Education.

Jowi, J. (2012). African universities in the global knowledge economy: The good and ugly of internationalization. *Journal of Marketing for Higher Education*, 22(1), 153–165.

Kiraka, R., Maringe, F., Kanyutu, W., & Mogaji, E. (2020). University league tables and ranking systems in Africa: Emerging prospects, challenges and opportunities. In E. Mogaji, F. Maringe, & R. E. Hinson (Eds.), *Understanding the higher education market in Africa*. London: Routledge.

Kotler, P. (2015). *Confronting capitalism: Real solutions for a troubled economic system.* Saranac Lake, NY: Amacom.

Kotler, P., Kartajaya, H., & Setiawan, I. (2010). *Marketing 3.0: From products to customers to the human spirit.* Hoboken, NJ: John Wiley & Sons.

Maringe, F., & Gibbs, P. (2008). *Marketing higher education: Theory and practice.* London: McGraw-Hill Education.

Mogaji, E. (2016b). University website design in international student recruitment: Some reflections. In T. Wu & V. Naidoo (Eds.), *International marketing of higher education* (pp. 99–117). New York: Palgrave Macmillan.

Mogaji, E. (2016). Marketing strategies of United Kingdom universities during clearing and adjustment. *International Journal of Educational Management, 30*(4), 493–504.

Mogaji, E. (2018). With the integration of learning apps, what are Moodle's prospects? *Compass: Journal of Learning and Teaching, 11*(2).

Mogaji, E. (2019). Branding private universities in Africa: An unexplored territory. Research Agenda Working Papers, 2019(9), 120–148.

Mogaji, E., & Yoon, C. (2019). Thematic analysis of marketing messages in UK universities' prospectuses. *International Journal of Educational Management, 33*(7), 1561–1581.

Mogaji, E., Farinloye, T., & Aririguzoh, S. A. (2017). *Marketing higher education in Africa: A research agenda.* Academy of Marketing (AM) Marketing of Higher Education Special Interest Group (SIG) Conference, Kingston University London, 16 April 2017. Kingston: Academy of Marketing.

Ndofirepi, E., Farinloye, T., & Mogaji, E. (2020). Marketing mix in a heterogenous higher education market: A case of africa. In E. Mogaji, F. Maringe, & R. E. Hinson (Eds.), *Understanding the higher education market in Africa.* London: Routledge.

OECD. (2018). *Education at a glance (2018): OECD indicators.* Paris: OECD Publishing.

Olaleye, S. A., Sanusi, I. T., Ukpabi, D. C., & Okunoye, A. (2018). Evaluation of Nigeria universities websites quality: A comparative analysis. *Library Philosophy and Practice (e-journal),* 1717.

Reddy, K. (2012). Students as consumers: The implications of the Consumer Protection Act for higher education institutions in South Africa. *South African Journal of Higher Education, 26*(3), 586–605.

Vasudeva, S., & Mogaji, E. (2020). Paving the way for world domination: Analysis of African universities' mission statement. In E. Mogaji, F. Maringe & R. Hidson (Eds.), *Understanding the higher education market.* London: Routledge.

Wayne, T., Farinloye, F., & Mogaji, E. (2020). Analysis of African universities' corporate visual identities. In E. Mogaji, F. Maringe & R. E. Hinson (Eds.), *Strategic marketing of higher education in Africa.* London: Routledge.

14 Conclusion

Emerging challenges, opportunities, and agenda for research, practice, and policy on marketing and brand communications of higher education institutions in Africa

Emmanuel Mogaji, Felix Maringe, and Robert Ebo Hinson

Introduction

The higher education landscape is changing. The global competition for students' enrolments has increased around the world. Universities are competing with each other within their home market as well as in the international market. As government funding for public universities is reducing (Olaleye et al., 2020), there is pressure on universities to seek additional income by increasing their student enrolment. Attracting and enrolling students has become increasingly more challenging, as student behaviour is changing. Students, as customers, and their desires and expectations are changing; their choice-making process and information request process are changing. These students are savvier and more opened to processing many options before making a choice. All these challenges present the need for higher education institutions to be more strategic in their approach to reaching out to prospective students.

This book has presented critical insights into strategic marketing and brand communications of higher education institutions in Africa. These issues were covered over four themes. The first theme identifies the marketisation strategies of African universities as the chapters present an integrative model for marketing higher education in Africa and exploration of tools for promoting higher education in an African context. Part II delves into digital marketing for the universities, with chapters exploring how universities have used social media, specifically Facebook for communicating with stakeholders and a chapter that provides a conceptual insight into using various social media for stakeholder communications. Brand and reputation management was the focus of Part III of the book. Chapters explored the brand identities of top universities in Africa, their reputation management system, and most importantly, how universities can leverage their position through branding. The last theme offers a managerial implication for managers and practitioners with interest in marketing higher education. The chapter moves away from research to provide practical implications.

In concluding this book, this chapter has three objectives. First, to summarise the key findings presented in the book in developing a theoretical framework for strategic marketing communications between university stakeholders. Second, to provide a concise marketing strategy with the understanding of the different university systems. Thirdly, to highlight research agendas for a better understanding of marketing higher education in Africa, making both theoretical contributions and managerial implications for scholars, students, managers, practitioners, and policymakers in the field of higher education marketing.

Strategic marketing and brand communications between university stakeholders

Strategic marketing has emerged as the key strategy used in educational institutions to strengthen their competitiveness and profitability in the competitive higher education market (Maringe, 2006). Strategic marketing communications for a university recognises the need to understand the stakeholders and how best to engage with them in an effective manner (Mogaji, 2019). This form of marketing provides information that is relevant and upon which stakeholders can make an informed decision, either to apply as a prospective student or as a member of staff or make donations to the university.

Recognising the wide variety of stakeholders engaging with a university and numerous brand marketing communication strategies to engage them, a theoretical framework is presented which recognises the university's need to communicate with stakeholders. As illustrated in Figure 14.1, the theoretical framework identifies the relationship between the university and the stakeholders, and the business decisions being made to strategically communicate with an end goal of enrolling students and increasing the financial support based on positive brand image of the university.

Importantly, the country context of the university is recognised. Even though this chapter explores the marketing of higher education in Africa, it is essential to know that the market is heterogeneous – there are many countries on the continent with various systems of higher education and marketing needs and challenges (Ndofirepi, Farinloye, & Mogaji, 2020), therefore one size may not fit all. Understanding the variations in admissions requirements is needed in developing marketing communications, targeting prospective students, and providing relevant information. Likewise, the number of universities and the population of the country may influence the marketing strategies. Perhaps if the supply of universities (number of universities in a country) is meeting the demands for tertiary education (number of prospective students), there may not be much competition as compared to when the market dynamics are different because the need for tertiary education is higher than the supply (Olaleye, Ukpabi, & Mogaji, 2020).

Private universities are gaining ground, meeting the needs for tertiary education because the public universities are underfunded. While some public

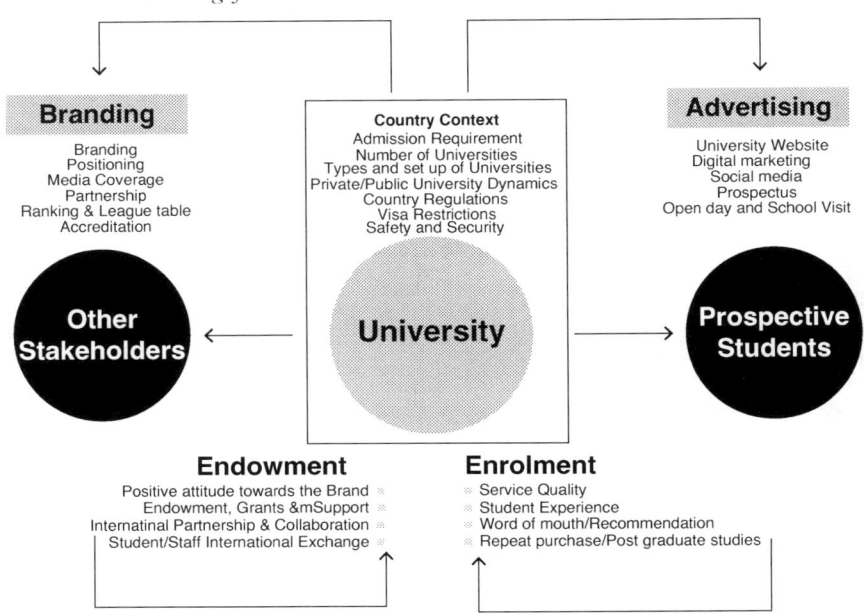

Figure 14.1 Theoretical framework for strategic marketing communications between university stakeholders

universities are solely funded by the government, private universities rely mostly on the students' tuition fees. However, there is evidence of *cost-sharing,* which is a form of private revenue supplementation for public universities for the support of their expanding higher educational needs. Also, there are the *dual-track tuition fees* which are common in the East African countries. Under this system, selected students of merit have free or very low cost higher education, with other applicants admitted on a higher fee-paying basis (Marcucci, Johnstone, & Ngolovoi, 2008). This fee structure can also influence marketing strategies as universities aim to get a significant share of the high fee-paying students. Marcucci et al. (2008) reported the influence of the dual-track tuition policies on Makerere University which have greatly expanded capacity as illustrated by the dramatic increase in enrolment between 1992 and 2002 that grew from 5,000 to over 30,000.   ·

An alternative to choosing between a public or private education within their home country, students may also decide to pursue their education internationally. This option, however, has some limitations such as visa restrictions and frequent changes in regulations, fear of not being able to find suitable part-time work, failure to meet course targets, fear of failure, and negative aspects of environmental influences can affect the students' choice of their prospective university (Ahmad & Hussain, 2017; Camilleri, 2020). These are part of the political, socio-cultural, and legal factors affecting students' choice and this also the marketing strategies of universities. The security and safety in these host countries can also influence the strategic marketing communication.

With the understanding of these country contexts, universities have the responsibility to engage with their stakeholders, especially prospective students who are key stakeholders. Maintaining an adequate rate of student enrolment is essential for universities to remain commercially viable. Thus, the university must use multiple marketing strategies including their website to provide information for prospective students on their student-centred teaching culture, employability, and career support, investment in facilities, and resources to enhance student experience in order to attract and recruit new students (Mogaji, 2016). Universities can also adopt digital marketing even beyond social media as a content creation strategy is essential to engage with and inform the students. Traditional media like newspapers, billboards, and prospectus cannot be ignored as well. The choice of media will depend on the prospective students being targeted, the effectiveness of the media, and marketing communications budget (Camilleri, 2020). Inviting the students (and their parents) to attend open days and taster sessions to see the facilities is also beneficial as the student can experience the university before enrolling also allows the university to create an impression which enhances their brand image. Country specific promotional strategies, recognising the local language, cultures, and values should be adopted for promotional content to different markets (Camilleri, 2020).

The primary strategy should be towards making the university appealing, standing out from other institutions. Importantly, the outcome of all these marketing strategies is for the students to enrol and make a financial commitment to the university. At this stage, the service quality becomes essential; students must see value in what they are being offered. Their experience as students is also essential, recognising the role of academic support, extra curriculum activities, facilities, and tutors to support them. With a positive experience, there is a high probability that current and former students will recommend the university to their siblings and friends as a form of word of mouth marketing and students may even progress to do their post-graduate degree in the university.

For other stakeholders, the brand position is essential. Universities are expected to be strategic in the way they present themselves to the community, alumni, funders' government and its policymakers, as well as with business and industry. The strategic marketing communication should recognise the need for a unique brand identity based on values and philosophy of the university. Media coverage of activities, events, and achievements of the university are essential in creating a positive brand image. Partnership and collaboration with an international organisation are also important, and it highlights a reputation which other organisations may want to be associated with as well. Research output and it impacts and contribution to the field, as well as position on the league table and rankings, can also be used to position the university and enhance its brand image.

While the primary outcome for the students is the enrolment, the primary result for the engagement with other stakeholder is endowment. This outcome is not just limited to the financial endowment, but positive brand images and perception, which will increase the brand equity of universities. If the university is seen in a good light and seen to be making advancements in society, other stakeholders will be more inclined to partner with the university. This will aid in forging collaborative relationships with other universities and organisations which will enhance the quality and stature of the university (Camilleri, 2020). Universities need to develop their brands to position themselves in the marketplace (Marginson & van der Wende, 2007). A positive brand image, among many possibilities, built through the influence of the private tertiary institutions proprietors' reputation opens funding opportunities for the universities (Ademola et al., 2014), as Afe Babalola University (ABUAD), a private university in Nigeria got a US $40-million corporate loan from the African Development Bank (AfDB) (AfDB, 2017). This endowment concept also recognises the opportunities to attract talented individuals to the university, not just through enrolment, but also student exchange, staff exchange, and partnerships and collaborations in research and teaching.

Practical implications of marketing higher education in Africa

It is essential to recognise the heterogeneous nature of the higher education market as this will influence the strategic marketing communications that are applicable. This section highlights a typology of universities in Africa, their marketing challenges, and the impact on marketing communications.

The public universities

Public universities are created and funded by the government and often are some of the first higher education intuitions established in a country. Due to their heritage and often lower tuition fees, public universities are appealing to prospective students, and often become overpopulated because the demand for a place is higher than supply. This suggests that these universities may not be interested in marketing and advertising, because they do not need more students; this, however, poses a different marketing challenge for these universities. It is, however, paramount for managers and administrators of public universities to note that if they are not advertising to recruit students, they should attempt towards repositioning their brands through various brand management strategies. This is important for building a positive attitude towards the brand, developing international collaborations and partnerships, and getting philanthropic donations and grants. These efforts should make them more appealing to prospective partners and other stakeholders. This involves having an updated and user-friendly website with relevant and accurate information, as well as content creation for social media marketing to engage with stakeholders and update them with the activities of the university.

The private universities

Private universities are non-public or independent universities that are owned, financed, and managed by private individuals, with denominational or secular boards and are often operated for profit (Mogaji, 2019). The numbers of private universities in Africa are increasing as public universities alone cannot meet the demands of prospective students seeking higher education. Also, the demographics of students are changing and likewise their expectations of a university such as the need for excellent facilities and an uninterrupted academic calendar. The growing number of universities is also creating competition in the sector. Private universities are not only competing with public universities; they are also competing with other private universities within the country and other universities outside the country. This, therefore, presents a different marketing challenge. Unlike public universities, private universities recognise the need to stay viable and competitive within the sector (Mustafa, Sellami, Elmaghraby, & Al-Qassass, 2018). They not only have a user-friendly website for information and brand position but also recruitment, making sure the information is available and prospective students can engage with it. Their marketing strategies need to also involve open days and taster sessions, inviting students on campus to come and experience the facilities and engage with lectures. As there are many factors known to influence students' choice, private universities need to be mindful of these factors and develop their marketing campaign to engage with the stakeholders. This could be around their facilities, uninterrupted academic calendar, or their connection with the industry which can enhance job prospects of their graduates.

The dual-track tuition universities

Some universities receive additional funding from the government, regardless of if they are private or public universities. These universities adopt a *dual-track tuition fee structure* (Marcucci et al., 2008). In the case of public universities, the government sponsors students who have been selected on merit, while the university charges other students who have not been sponsored by the government. This structure is widespread in East African countries. Makerere University in Uganda admits a fixed quota of government-sponsored students and then also admits 'private' fee-paying students, especially in the lucrative areas of medicine, law, and engineering. Likewise, in some countries, the government sponsors selected students to attend private universities because there are limited spaces in public universities. In Botswana, the government supports students to attend private institutions by providing them with tuition fees and living expenses. As these private universities are also benefiting indirectly from the public funding, there are marketing priorities to attract these students that get funded by the government. Just as seem in England where the international students pay much more than the local students, this difference in fee scheme influences universities to deploy marketing strategies to attract prospective international students as means of making significant financial gains from through their higher student tuition fees (Findlay, McCollum, & Packwood, 2017).

International branch campus

As an effort towards globalised higher education, there has been a surge of international branch campuses and partnerships with local universities around the world. These international branch campuses are an entity that is owned, at least in part, by a foreign higher education provider, operated in the name of the overseas education provider, and provide an entire academic programme, substantially on-site, leading to a degree awarded by the international education provider (Ndofirepi et al., 2020; Cbert, 2019). There are some in Malaysia, China, Cyprus, and many African countries. For example, Webster University, an American University based in St. Louis, Missouri, has international campuses in Ghana, while Middlesex University in the United Kingdom opened a second overseas campus in Mauritius. These universities takes pride in the brand reputation of their home university as they engage with prospective students in the host country. These universities have a different marketing challenge as they are torn between two campaigns – following the home campaign or localising their campaign. These campuses have often been viewed differently as it is not always a guaranteed success for the universities (Iqbal, 2019) as many universities have closed their campus less than five years after opening. The University of Wolverhampton closed its Mauritius campus less than four years after it opened in March 2012 (Morgan, 2015). Maintaining enrolment is essential to justify the enormous investment of international campuses, highlight the unique marketing challenge of these universities. While students may feel the need to be associated with these universities to get the international degree, their student experiences may not be as great as studying in the campus of a public or private university in their home country. Since the structure of the university offers a different marketing challenge for these universities, reaching out to prospective students with the right marketing messages, making them see benefits of holding an international degree and the experiences they will have on campus will be crucial.

Dual-curriculum universities

These universities are partnerships between two countries, establishing a university on two different educational curriculums. It is a hybrid between the private universities and the international branch campuses. The American University in Cairo was founded in 1919 by Americans devoted to education and service in the Middle East. Other examples around Africa are the American University of Nigeria and the German University in Cairo and the British University in Egypt. These universities are created based on cooperation between the home country (e.g. USA, Germany, or the UK) and the host

(Egypt or Nigeria) country. The key idea of these types of universities is to provide a home-country style of education to meet the host country's needs for practical applications and professional specialisations. The degrees from these universities are validated by both home and host country. Importantly, these universities have campuses, and they are not just a branch campus of international universities. It is more like a permanent version of international branch campuses and with their own identity, not just a replicated identity of the university in the home country. These are advantages for the universities to market themselves as they can boast oh having a dual-curriculum, the vibrant student experiences on campus, and being supported by international faculties. The marketing strategy should be about making students see value in what is being offered; instead of travelling abroad (which is more expensive), they can still experience a high-level international education in their home country. Content creation strategies, especially on social media to showcase what life is like on campus, will be valuable in attracting prospective students.

Agenda for future research on strategic marketing of higher education in Africa

It is essential to acknowledge that this book covered only a limited scope of strategic marketing of higher education in Africa. While attempts have been made in providing theoretical insight through the chapters in this book, there are opportunities to extend knowledge about this subject area as findings will be relevant for:

- Students studying and researching higher education marketing, branding, and education management;
- Scholars and academic researchers in higher education marketing, providing a theoretical underpinning for their research and theory development;
- Universities' managers and administrators considering enhancing the marketing communications of their universities;
- Practitioners – marketing, advertising, and brand agencies with interest in marketing higher education in Africa; and
- Policymakers who are responsible for the quality and quantity of higher education in Africa.

This section highlights five broad areas for future research to shape knowledge about the educational sector in Africa.

Understanding the higher education market in Africa

While there is growing research to better understand this vast market, more research is still expected to uncover its unique feature and characteristics. Africa is vast, dynamic, and heterogeneous. There are different higher education systems in different countries, and this needs to be theoretically examined. It is essential to understand the market to know the type of marketing strategy that may work. One approach of marketing strategy will not fit all universities in Africa. Farinloye et al. (2020) developed a typology of Nigerian higher education, understanding the different structures of higher education in the country. Replicating this research in other countries will open more understanding of the intricate nature of higher education in Africa. Universities need to be aware of their market which includes their competitors (other universities within the country and outside the country) and their customers (home and international) and external stakeholders like (parents and government) who can influence the universities' operation. Marketing models developed in the context of higher education can be used to understand the market.

Understanding student decision-making processes

To develop an effective campaign to recruit students, it is essential to have a better understanding of the choice-making process of the students. This understanding is becoming critical as 'the policy context for higher education moves towards market-based systems in many countries' (McManus, Haddock-Frase, & Rands, 2017, p. 2). Though several empirical works have been done on this topic, describing it as 'a complex process that involves different perspectives and a myriad of factors' (Mustafa et al., 2018, p. 2), this is however not enough in the African context. Future research needs to recognise the unique features of the African university settings and culture which inform decision-making.

Further research can explore why students are choosing to study in religious affiliated private universities instead of mainstream private universities. Perhaps this could be influenced by the strength of students' religious belief, or it is the parents' decision. Also, more research could discover why students are choosing to study in an international branch campus or dual-curriculum university; perhaps the fact that they will get two degrees was appealing to them. A better understating of these factors influencing choice is needed in developing an effective marketing campaign.

Understanding students' information sources

While most studies and universities may be focusing on digital marketing and social media campaigns for attracting prospective students, is this working for African students? Adefulu et al. (2020) recognised that Nigerian parents as a source of information were an influence for their children, as participants noted that they rarely disregard the significance and opinions of their parent in their choice-making process. This aligns with findings of Le et al. (2019), which suggests that the students in a collectivistic society like Nigeria recognise the influence of the parents. Understanding the information sources unique to students in Africa is also essential in developing strategic marketing communications. Are African students engaging with their universities on social media or do they still prefer the traditional media? With the known challenges of access to the Internet in Africa, how are students using social media in their information search and decision-making process? Perhaps they are relying on word of mouth from teachers, friends, and families? Are they visiting the campus or better still, are they requesting prospectus forms from the universities? Having this understanding will be necessary for managers as they prioritise marketing strategies that are essential for a successful marketing mix in higher education (Maringe, 2005).

Understanding the existing marketing communications strategies

Research is needed to evaluate the existing marketing communications strategies being adopted by universities in Africa. There is evidence of using social media for recruitment (Olaleye et al., 2020), but how effective are these media in reaching out to the prospective students? Future research should endeavour to uncover the effectiveness of these strategies. These findings will inform managers and practitioners about how to improve and plan their campaign for effective engagement.

Understanding the perception about university brands

There is a perception about Africa, more so there is a perception of university brands in Africa. Research is needed to understand these perceptions and how it shapes stakeholder's engagement. Previous studies have examined stakeholders in university settings and identified staff, students, alumni, and government bodies as some of the key players (Mainardes, Alves, & Raposo, 2013; Mogaji, 2019). While most of these studies have focused on universities in the developed world, it is essential to understand how African university staff, students, and even the society perceive universities. This strand of research can build up on Maringe's 2006 study, which evaluated how vice-chancellors and internal marketers in Zimbabwe recognised the marketing concept and its organisation within the universities. This understanding of the university brand is essential in managing the reputation of the university which is extremely important for universities seeking both local and global recognition (Kiraka, 2020) These findings will be relevant for university managers who need to understand what their university stands for and build long-term brands beyond mere survival (Mwebesa & Maringe, 2020). Having a robust strategic brand agenda reflected in brand identity design, brand culture, and values is crucial to a successful university brand (Mogaji, 2019).

Conclusion

Strategic marketing communications is essential for universities as the higher education landscape is changing due to various documented reasons. The expectations of students are changing and importantly communicating with them is evolving. Irrespective of the type of university, there are marketing challenges that need to be addressed for the university to remain viable and attract partnership and global recognition.

Empirical insights have been provided through various chapters of this book, and this chapter attempts to offer key summaries and present a theoretical framework for strategic marketing communications between university stakeholders. Universities need to recognise the need for a strong brand position and effective marketing communications.

There are limitations with regards to this book which should be considered. Not all the countries and education systems in the continent have been covered, and some areas still need further research to extend our understanding of marketing higher education in Africa. The preceding section presents five areas for future research. It has been a great pleasure to contribute to knowledge on higher education marketing, and it is anticipated that this will shape further discussion and theoretical advancement which will be relevant for scholars, students, managers, practitioners, and policymakers in the field of higher education marketing.

References

Adefulu, A., Farinloye, T., & Mogaji, E. (2020). Factors influencing post graduate students' university choice in Nigeria. In E. Mogaji, F. Maringe, & R. E. Hinson (Eds.), *Higher education marketing in Africa: Explorations on student choice*. Cham, Switzerland: Springer.

Ademola, E. O., Ogundipe, A. T., & Babatunde, W. T. (2014). Students' enrolment into tertiary institutions in Nigeria: The influence of the founder's reputation – A case study. *Computing, Information Systems, Development Informatics & Allied*, 5(3), 55–82.

AfDB. (2017). African development bank supports Afe Babalola University expansion with a US$40 million loan. Retrieved from https://www.afdb.org/en/news-and-events/african-development-bank-supports-afe-babalola-university-expansion-with-a-us-40-million-loan-17108.

Ahmad, S. Z., & Hussain, M. (2017). An investigation of the factors determining student destination choice for higher education in the United Arab Emirates. *Studies in Higher Education*, 42(7), 1324–1343.

Camilleri, M. A. (2020). Higher education marketing communications in the digital era. In E. Mogaji, F. Maringe, & R. E. Hinson (Eds.), *Strategic marketing of higher education in Africa*. London: Routledge.

Cbert. (2019). Branch campuses. Retrieved from http://cbert.org/resources-data/branch-campus/.

Chapleo, C., & Simms, C. (2010). Stakeholder analysis in higher education: A case study of the University of Portsmouth. *Perspectives: Policy and Practice in Higher Education*, 14(1).

Farinloye, T., Adeola, O., & Mogaji, E. (2020). Typology of Nigeria universities: A strategic marketing and branding implication. In E. Mogaji, F. Maringe, & R. E. Hinson (Eds.), *Understanding the higher education market in Africa*. London: Routledge.

Findlay, A. M., McCollum, D., & Packwood, H. (2017). Marketization, marketing and the production of international student migration. *International Migration*, 55(3), 139–155.

Iqbal, M. (2019). *Africa's higher education landscape*. Retrieved from https://www.qs.com/africas-higher-education-landscape/.

Kiraka, R. (2020). University reputation management. In E. Mogaji, F. Maringe, & R. E. Hinson (Eds.), *Strategic marketing of higher education in Africa*. London: Routledge.

Le, T. D., Robinson, L. J., & Dobele, A. R. (2019). Understanding high school students use of choice factors and word-of-mouth information sources in university selection. *Studies in Higher Education*, 1–11. doi:10.1080/03075079.2018.1564259.

McManus, R., Haddock-Fraser, J., & Rands, P. (2017). A methodology to understand student choice of higher education institutions: the case of the United Kingdom. *Journal of Higher Education Policy and Management*, 39(4), 390–405.

Mainardes, E., Alves, H., & Raposo, M. (2013). Identifying stakeholders in a Portuguese university: A case study La identificación de los stakeholders en una universidad portuguesa. *Revista de Educación*, 362, 429–457.

Marcucci, P., Johnstone, D. B., & Ngolovoi, M. (2008). Higher educational cost-sharing, dual-track tuition fees, and higher educational access: The East African experience. *Peabody Journal of Education*, 83(1), 101–116.

Marginson, S., & van der Wende, M. (2007). *Globalisation and higher education*. Paris: OECD Education Working Papers.

Maringe, F. (2005). Interrogating the crisis in higher education marketing: The CORD model. *International Journal of Educational Management*, 19(7), 564–578.

Maringe, F. (2006). University marketing: Perceptions, practices and prospects in the less developed world. *Journal of Marketing for Higher Education*, 15(2), 129–153.

Mogaji, E. (2016). University website design in international student recruitment: Some reflections. In T. Wu & V. Naidoo (Eds.), *International marketing of higher education* (pp. 99–117). New York: Palgrave Macmillan.

Mogaji, E. (2019). Strategic stakeholder communications on Twitter by UK universities. Research Agenda Working Papers, 2019(8), 104–119.

Mogaji, E., & Yoon, C. (2019). Thematic analysis of marketing messages in UK universities' prospectuses. *International Journal of Educational Management*, 33(7).

Mogaji, E., Farinloye, T., & Aririguzoh, S. A. (2017). *Marketing higher education in Africa: A research agenda*. Academy of Marketing (AM) Marketing of Higher Education Special Interest Group (SIG) Conference, Kingston University London, 16 April 2017. Kingston: Academy of Marketing.

Morgan, J. (2015). Wolverhampton to shut down Mauritius campus. Retrieved from https://www.timeshighereducation.com/news/wolverhampton-shut-down-mauritius-campus#survey-answer.

Mustafa, S. A., Sellami, A. L., Elmaghraby, E., & Al-Qassass, H. B. (2018). Determinants of college and university choice for high-school students in Qatar. *International Journal of Higher Education*, 7(3), 3–15.

Mwebesa, C. C., & Maringe, F. (2020). An integrative model for marketing higher education in Africa: Branding beyond survival for posterity. In E. Mogaji, F. Maringe, & R. E. Hinson (Eds.), *Strategic marketing of higher education in Africa*. London: Routledge.

Ndofirepi, E., Farinloye, T., & Mogaji, E. (2020). Marketing mix in a heterogenous higher education market: A case of Africa. In E. Mogaji, F. Maringe, & R. E. Hinson (Eds.), *Understanding the higher education market in Africa*. London: Routledge.

Olaleye, S., Ukpabi, D., & Mogaji, E. (2020). Public vs private universities in Nigeria: Market dynamics perspective. In E. Mogaji, F. Maringe, & R. E. Hinson (Eds.), *Understanding the higher education market in Africa*. London: Routledge.

Index

Page numbers in **bold** refer to figures, page numbers in *italic* refer to tables.

Printed in the United States
By Bookmasters